Grasping HEAVEN

TAMI L. FISK
a young doctor's journey to China and beyond

ANNELIES AND EINAR WILDER-SMITH

Deep River BOOKS

3-5-2011

Ms Melvin,
Thank you for your referral to be able to
get Tami's biography in Ires Ryleds
hands. In appreciation, we present This Copy
to you, Lord Bless, Ron & Ann

Published by
Deep River Books
Sisters, Oregon
http://www.deepriverbooks.com

ISBN 13: 978-1-935265-34-4
ISBN 10: 1-935265-34-2

Library of Congress Control Number: 2010928689

Printed in the USA

Cover design by Robin Black, www.blackbirdcreative.biz

TABLE OF CONTENTS

TAMI'S POEM

As Tami slipped into a coma, her parents and her brother Tim took turns staying with her. They held her hand, spoke gently to her, and prayed quietly until late at night. In the early morning hours, Tami passed away peacefully. She was thirty-nine years old.

The pain of the loss was overwhelming. Grieving, Tami's parents and brother returned home. Tim sat down in the living room and turned on Tami's laptop. She had so often worked on this computer over the past months. He found the folder with the title "Last Things." She had asked them to open this folder upon her death.

"Mom! Dad!" Tim shouted. "Come and see what I've found. Tami left a message for us!"

Together they read Tami's poem.

Today I am healed.
Perhaps not the way you had hoped for,
*   Prayed for, waited for*
But I'm in a glorious new body,
*   Free of pain, full of new strength*
Free to run and dance in a place
*   Where God Himself wipes my tears away*
Immersed in a love, joy and peace
*   That we have a mere taste of*
*   During our time on earth*
In the presence of my God and Savior, Jesus Christ,
*   Who loves me more than His own life*
Know that today I am healed.

PART
one

PREPARATION FOR THE JOURNEY

Chapter 1

LOVE NEVER FAILS

She hardly dared breathe for fear of being discovered. Her heart, bursting with anticipation, was furiously pounding in her tiny little chest. Would Dad find her before the air ran out in the small stuffy closet where she was hiding? Surely he could follow the instructions she had left for him in the Christmas package! *C'mon, Dad!* she silently urged. *You can do it! Just follow the instructions.* The map she had drawn for him showed the route to his two Christmas presents. Outside, the footsteps were coming closer. At last! He was fumbling at the closet door. The door began to open.

She burst onto her open-mouthed father's arms and recited, "If I speak in the tongues of men and of angels, but have not love, I am only a resounding gong or a clanging cymbal. If I have the gift of prophecy and can fathom all mysteries and all knowledge, and if I have faith that can move mountains, but have not love, I am nothing."

She went on to recite the rest of 1 Corinthians 13 from the Bible, basking in the joy and delight of her dad.

"There's one more gift for you." As she took his hand to tug him along, she asked loudly, "I wonder where Tim is?"

And it was Tim's turn to startle their dad by leaping from the linen closet, also reciting Bible verses.

It was Christmas 1974. Tami was nine; Tim, seven. They had spent endless hours pacing the basement trying to memorize the verses under the encouragement of their mother. Tami loved Christmas. She especially loved to carefully choose just the right Christmas gifts for her family—and this one, memorizing Bible verses, was a hit!

"Tami and Tim, this is my best Christmas gift ever!" Dad exclaimed, beaming with joy and pride.

The Fisk family lived in a large home in Denver, with majestic views of the snow-peaked mountains of Colorado. In the middle of their living room, the Christmas tree shone brightly. The smell of freshly baked cakes, mixed with the scent of cinnamon and almonds, permeated the house. Tami's favorite was the braided bread filled with almond paste and raspberry jam.

"Let's go and visit Grandma and Grandpa Fisk in Colorado Springs," Dad said.

"Yeah!" Tami and Tim shouted. They adored their grandparents and thoroughly enjoyed the many memorable visits with them. Grandpa would often surprise them with a special toy. And there was the little blue woolen coat that Grandma had made for Tami some time ago. Tami kept it like a treasure.

The car engine was already spluttering away, the heater trying to warm up the freezing morning air.

"What are we going to do at Grandma's house?" Tami questioned as she jumped in the car.

"Why not do something really special for her?" Dad suggested. "Grandma is very ill. She has cancer. How about sharing the gift you gave me earlier?"

Tami and Tim did not need much prompting. "Sure, let's do that!"

Grandma's face lit up with a broad smile when the two grandchildren recited the scriptures they had so carefully memorized. They all sat around Grandma's bed, savoring the delicious home-baked goodies that Mom had brought along.

"Tami, how is school these days?" Grandma asked.

"Good," Tami, never a person of many words, answered.

Her mom filled in the details. "Tami is bringing home excellent grades. Her teachers speak very highly of her. They have discussed moving her up one grade because she is doing so well and learning so fast. But then her teacher decided she is too young to skip grades and suggested keeping her in the same class, but challenging her a bit more by giving her extra assignments. As soon as Tami finishes her schoolwork, she's allowed to wander off to the library to read on her own. The teacher is currently challenging Tami to read and write some special poetry."

Grandma looked pleased. "Well done, Tami!" And then she asked, "Have you thought about what you want to be when you grow up?"

"I want to become a doctor, Grandma. I want to be a missionary doctor," Tami answered, determination written all over her face.

Grandma looked questioningly at Tami, then at her parents.

"That sounds like a great plan, Tami," she said. "But it may change when you get older, don't you think so?"

"No, Grandma," Tami answered solemnly. "God wants me to do this. He told me so at missions evening at church. During the missions movie. And I will do it."

It was said with such great resolve that it did not allow for any objections.

Dad laughed. "That is our Tami, always determined. You should have seen her in church the other day. I will never forget the sight. Tami was performing in church with her blonde little pigtail bouncing up and down with the rhythm, singing at the top of her voice: 'This little light of mine, I'm going to make it shine, this little light of mine, I'm going to make it shine.' She almost burst her little lungs with the refrain: 'Hide it under a bushel? No! Hide it under a bushel? NO!' She mustered each 'No' with all of her energy. I'm sure you can picture her bright blue eyes full of determination."

They all laughed. Grandma gave Tami a big hug.

"I'm so proud of you," she said with a smile.

"Grandma is tired," Mom observed. "I think we should go home soon."

Home again, the whole family settled down for their Christmas routine. They made themselves comfortable in front of the large open fireplace, and Dad opened the mystery jigsaw puzzle.

"Let's see if we can complete this before tomorrow."

"Last year we kept on going till midnight," Tami said.

Tim was chosen to read the mystery story, and the challenge of unraveling the mystery began. They had to assemble the puzzle using visual and literal clues.

"This year's is really difficult! The puzzle is made up of one thousand pieces!" Mom exclaimed while searching for the right pieces.

Soon the first rudiments of a recognizable picture could be seen. By late evening, there was only one unfinished section. They arranged and rearranged the pieces, squeezing them in. But it was to no avail. Midnight was approaching. The full day and the warmth of the fire had made the whole family tired.

"This one is too difficult. I think I've had enough. Let's go to bed," Dad announced.

"We can't give up! How can we give up? We have come so far already," Tami protested.

Under Tami's encouragement, they persevered for another hour. Suddenly, shortly after midnight, Tami exclaimed, "I think I know what the problem is!" and with that she snapped in the last pieces of the puzzle.

⌇

The next day, the family set out early for the mountains to go skiing together. Copper Mountain was their destination. Tami and Tim enjoyed the difficult slopes there.

"Before we go," Dad said, interrupting the hurried last- minute packing of ski gear, "I want to show you something I made before Christmas."

It was a wooden scroll with saw-cut letters. He unrolled the large scroll in front of the family, and the words "Let us celebrate—Christ is born" appeared in bright red and yellow colors.

"Looks great! Where shall we hang it up, Dad?" Tami and Tim asked at the same time.

"It would be nice if people driving by would be able to see it too," Tami suggested.

So they attached the sign high on the entry column to their house, so that all those driving by could see it.

"Just the right place, Dad." Tami nodded in approval as she studied the words intently. "You know what? For Easter, we can just change *born* to *alive*. And then we can keep the sign out almost all year!"

And that was what they did. The sign hung in the same place for many years, leading friends and neighbors to refer to the Fisk's home as "the sign house."

The family home, on an acre of land adjacent to an irrigation ditch, was an ideal place for the children to play during the long warm summer days in Colorado. Tami and Tim feasted on the raspberries, gooseberries, and red currents growing in the large garden. They had their own cookouts, "rafted" in the irrigation ditch on inner tubes, played badminton, and bounced on the large trampoline. Stretching out on the green grass, they read books or simply sat there, enjoying the view of the mountains. The large backyard was ideal for inviting friends for sleepovers. When night fell, the children formed a circle with their sleeping bags, and the sounds of talking and laughter could be heard until late into the night. Evenings under the open skies, gazing at the stars, made Tami dream of countries far away.

ৼ

"Mom, I'm off to swim practice," eleven-year-old Tami shouted across the hallway.

Mom yawned her way out of bed. "Tami, it's only six a.m."

"This week we have extra practice for the swim competition. I really want to win."

"Sure, Tami. Go ahead!" Tami's mother stood at the door and looked out at her daughter, who was just pedaling out of the driveway. "Don't exhaust yourself!" she called. "We still have our outing in Estes Park next weekend!"

Tami laughed and waved good-bye. "I know!"

Tami and her mom spent the next weekend at Estes Park while Dad and Tim had their father-son outing. They hiked for hours, enjoying one another's company. Tired and hungry one afternoon, they sat down on a mountainside to savor the views. Before the hike, they had listened to Dr. James Dobson's tapes, and now they discussed some of the principles in the messages.

"Tami, I'm really delighted to see you grow in the Lord," Mom said. "Both Dad and I are also very proud of your achievements in school. And then your swimming awards!" Mom smiled. "But Tami, sometimes we think you are holding yourself and others at too high a standard. Always remember one thing: God loves us just as we are. He loves us unconditionally. There is nothing we need to achieve to make Him love us more."

Tami was pensive. They quietly took in the clear mountain views, savoring the blending bright green and brown colors of the mountains. Occasional bird song wafted on the refreshing breeze gently blowing across the valley.

"Tami, do you remember the words from 1 Corinthians 13 that you learned by heart two years ago?" Mom broke the silence.

"How can I have forgotten those words? I spent so much time memorizing them that I can still recite them!" Tami stretched out her long and slender frame and looked up to the sky.

"How about reading the passage again?"

They opened the Bible and read through the whole chapter.

"Love is the most important part of our lives," Mom said. "God's purpose for your life and mine is to love. Things may go wrong in our lives, but love will never fail."

Tami nodded. After some time for reflection, they prayed together.

"Tami, what would you think of hanging a poster by your bedroom door with 1 Corinthians 13 on it?"

"I'd love that! This chapter is my favorite in the Bible." Tami hugged her mom.

Mom put up a poster on Tami's bedroom door after they returned home:

"Love is patient, love is kind. It does not envy, it does not boast, it is not proud. It is not rude, it is not self-seeking, it is not easily angered, it keeps no record of wrongs. Love does not delight in evil but rejoices with the truth. It always protects, always trusts, always hopes, always perseveres." (1 Corinthians 13:4–7)

The words on her bedroom-door banner stopped fourteen-year-old Tami in her tracks. She was preparing for an exam, and her backpack, heavy with books, made her upper body lean forward. She took a few steps backward and silently mouthed the words. Even after three years, they would still catch her eye, even during the rush of her busy lifestyle. She had made it a habit to read the words when passing by, although she had memorized them a long time ago. She wanted those words to change and mold her.

If everything fails, love never does, she thought.

Chapter 2

GLIMPSES OF HEAVEN

" I had a simple but sufficient understanding. I pictured God's love as similar to, yet greater than, my parents' love for me. When I was seven, I believed in God, but I had never asked Jesus to forgive my sins and come into my life. I knew that I needed God's forgiveness for the things I had done wrong. So I prayed for His forgiveness and for Him to come into my heart so I could be changed and become clean."

Tami was sharing her faith with a group of young girls at Camp Cherith, run by the Pioneer Girls of Colorado. At seventeen, she was tall and slender. The blonde hair of her early childhood had turned warm brown, worn at shoulder length. Her clear blue eyes had a riveting gaze and shone in her freckled face. She had participated in the Pioneer Girls' camp for many summers, and over the years, she had put together files of ideas for Bible studies, activities, and crafts for the girls. Now she was a counselor in Leadership Training.

"Struggles with insecurity in my teen years made me reevaluate what I said I believed. I was a late bloomer physically and was extremely clumsy. I learned to rely on God's peace and comfort through those awkward years. Through this, I was able to affirm that His love, forgiveness, and plans for the future are the realities in my life, not mere concepts passed on to me from my parents or church friends."

The girls followed closely as she continued to share stories about her faith.

"Do you still want to be a doctor?" one girl interrupted.

"Yes, I have always wanted to be a doctor since I was nine. There has never been any doubt."

Tami smiled as she looked at the girls. She took great effort in caring for each of them. Quite a few were from broken homes. *I'm so grateful,* she thought, *that in these times when broken families seem to be the norm, I grew up in such a loving and caring family.* Her parents had always lived out their faith in front of her. She thought of how Mom and Dad openly showed their affection and support for each other. Both had set an example by memorizing Bible verses and always seeking to put God's principles first in their lives.

"C'mon, girls" she continued. "Let's sit down in a circle for some Bible exploration. We'll continue with the book of Daniel. Who was Daniel? Why was he in a foreign land? Why did he end up in the lion's den? And remember, tonight is skit night. So, let's be creative and turn the story of Daniel into a skit."

When the girls started work on the evening skit, Tami returned to her tent to work on her own assignment. She had been preparing an essay for an advanced-placement high school class in literature. As C.S. Lewis was one of her favorite authors, she had chosen his Space Trilogy as her subject.

The three books about space fascinated her. Whenever she had a free minute in the camp, she jotted down notes as she read the books. The main character of the story was Ransom. From Planet Earth, he was traveling through space, visiting two planets—first Malacandra and then Perelandra. On Malacandra, he discovered the concept of real beauty and realized that his own planet—Earth—was in actual fact devoid of beauty and real joy. On Malacandra he found splendor and glory, harmony, and the "charm of speech and reason," as though Paradise had never been lost. On Earth, all creatures were full of fear. On Malacandra, there was no fear, only perfect love. Ransom delighted in floating on the oceans, being dazzled by Malacandra's colors, and discovering new pleasures in the taste of its exotic fruits. He enjoyed harmony with all the planet's creatures. He realized that all his desires were ultimately for Malacandra, which, as Tami was quickly discovering, was imagery for heaven.

The next day Tami asked the girls, "What will you be doing in heaven?"

One girl answered, "We will be sitting on clouds, plucking the strings of golden harps, resting while watching the angels pass by . . ."

Tami laughed out loud. "You must be kidding. Those are clichés—you really think of those as true? C'mon, the Bible gives us a much better picture, much greater and bigger things to expect! Heaven is far better than that!"

They picked up their Bibles and started examining a few passages while the girls gave her dubious looks. Their expressions quickly changed to those of interest and curiosity.

"From a biblical point of view, the highest and most joyous experiences of earth will be far exceeded by the realities of heaven," Tami continued. This set the ball rolling as they brainstormed what heaven would be like. Tami summarized their ideas on the white board: A *place of ultimate love, a place without pain or tears; a place where we will see Christ; a place where we will have royal tasks to do; a place of joy; a place of worship; a place of perfect harmony with others.*

"Any more descriptions, girls?" *A mansion with many rooms; a most glorious city; beautiful; the river of life; wonderful music . . .*

"All excellent thoughts! Indeed, heaven is not endless dull bliss, but a place where we will be challenged, a place where we will have plenty of congenial work to do. I'm particularly looking forward to being in the presence of God. And then—I'm also looking forward to seeing my grandma again."

Grandma Fisk had died ten days after that Christmas in 1978, and Tami missed her deeply. She had been a woman of God, and it gave Tami comfort to know that she was in heaven.

"What about food in heaven?" one small plump girl interrupted.

Tami chuckled. "Food? Yes, it's lunchtime. Let's all walk over."

Walking to the mess hall, Tami explained, "I'm not so sure about food in heaven. However, it seems to me to be quite conceivable that we will enjoy food there. After all, even Jesus continued to eat after His resurrection. And then the Bible also talks about the wedding supper, a banquet with the most delicious food. I'm personally pretty sure that the food there will taste even better than ours here."

After dinner, Tami worked late into the night on her essay. She wrote:

Lewis' novels as well as other Christian fantasies provide enjoyment through their imaginative settings and narratives. Their works reveal a variety of applicable principles and wisdom. Lewis changes the names of all spiritual beings, including God, whom he calls "Maleldil" ("mal" meaning "chief" in Hebrew). Maleldil is the "chief," creator and commander of the Eldils, the angels. Through the juxtaposition of the sinless worlds of Malacandra and

Perelandra, and fallen Earth, Lewis explains the results of rebellion against God and the rewards for obedience to Him. Accordingly, Eldila (= angels) protect the unfallen planets while Satan occupies Earth. The other planets will remain pure while sinful Earth faces endless misery. However, there is a story of redemption woven through the book.

Tami continued, absorbed in her work. "When Ransom despairs that his planet has no hope, he finds out that Maleldil has come to Earth to save it. He is told that 'In your world, Maleldil first took upon Himself the form of your race. Maleldil was the Savior to those who would accept him.' Ransom notices blood on his feet and is told that this is the substance wherewith Maleldil remade the worlds . . ."

〜

As soon as summer camp was over, the realities of her last year in high school struck. As she ran down the stairs with a pile of books under her arm, her mom interrupted, "Tami, you need some new clothes to update your wardrobe."

Breathlessly Tami answered, "Sorry, Mom. I have no time just now. I have to run to the library to work on my assignments."

"But Tami, you need to be dressed nicely. You really need to take some time off to go shopping with me," her mom insisted.

"Fine. Tomorrow afternoon then. But when we go, it has to be fast, really fast. Not more than an hour. I am more concerned about my school projects than about new clothes."

Tami picked up her bassoon from her bedroom and swung the books and bassoon into the car. She spent several hours in the library studying German and science. After that, she rushed to the high school orchestra to practice her bassoon piece.

Driving home in the evening, she thought about the clothes issue. *Maybe Mom was right*, she thought. *Maybe I should pay more attention to my clothes. All the other girls in my class do.* Perhaps it was true that she did not fit into the crowd.

Once she had overheard a teacher in the schoolyard say, "She is too serious."

"No, she is not serious," another teacher, her own, had defended her. "In fact, she has the most amazing sense of humor. It's just that she's much more mature than the other students. She is a cut above the rest, not a typical adolescent."

A cut above the rest? She didn't want to be different. The girls in her class were more interested in boys than in books. There had been one boy she was quite interested in. But after she got to know him better, she felt that they had few common interests. She wanted to talk about the future, about other countries, about God, about deeper spiritual issues—and then there was her goal to study medicine and go to foreign countries to help the poor. She really had no time to waste.

Once home, although exhausted, she dragged herself to her desk to work on her essay on the Space Trilogy. A few exams were scheduled in the next week, so there wasn't time to waste. She had entitled it "Analysis of the Christian Principles in C.S. Lewis's Space Trilogy." Opening the book on C. S. Lewis that she had borrowed from the library, her eyes fell on this sentence: "If we could even effect in one percent of our readers a change-over from the conception of Space to the conception of Heaven, we should have made a beginning." She looked up. Indeed, she aimed at understanding the concept of heaven.

The story had captured her imagination, and she continued with her writing.

On the unfallen worlds of Malacandra and Perelandra, life centers around communion with Maleldil. As a result of their constant obedience, the creatures on these planets enjoy freedoms unknown to mankind. The imagery of the Great Dance further emphasizes this joy. For example, fear of death, though chronic on this planet, does not cripple the unfallen Hnau, but, as Nardo reiterates, the Hrossa see death as "the final glorious moment which completes life."

Tami paused and thought about death and heaven. The quote still danced in her mind. She really wanted to grasp heaven. She elaborated further: "The people on Malacandra do not fear death, and they explain to Ransom that our bodies will be changed. Instead of imagining death as an end, they view it as 'the beginning of all things.'"

Chapter 3

HIGH ROAD PRAYER

Tami achieved an A for her essay. She went on to become a National Merit Finalist, selected from students all over the U.S. based on her national test scores. She now had to choose where to study. For a long time she had looked forward to this stage in life. Often, she had discussed the options with her parents. Tami brought the subject up again at the dinner table one evening.

"I think Wheaton College will be the ideal place," she said.

Her parents looked at one another in surprise.

"But Tami," her father said, "Carlton in Minnesota and others have offered you full tuition because you're a National Merit Finalist."

"But you told me the friends made at college are forever. Wheaton College has the kind of people I think I'd like to have as forever friends," she argued. "Besides, there are other things to consider. Wheaton offers better preparation for overseas work. Most of the professors have overseas experience or are involved in projects in other countries. And most importantly, they offer a summer mission project overseas which would be ideal for my future plans."

After another glance between her parents, her dad replied, "My business is actually not doing so well at the moment, and we would find it a struggle to support you financially at Wheaton." He paused. "However, we understand your reasoning. We will trust the Lord to lead us together in this." After some further discussion, the whole family prayed about the decision.

❧

It wasn't long before God opened the doors to Wheaton College. The Fisks were able to negotiate a three-year course instead of a four-year program for Tami. Three years served two purposes: first, it was less expensive, and second, it meant Tami could enter medical school one year earlier. She rejoiced.

For incoming freshmen, Wheaton offered something called "the Wilderness Experience." Carrying on Wheaton's rich history and the tradition of what was once called "High Road," the two-week wilderness track was a physical and spiritual challenge that set the foundation for the college experience. The track took place in the beautiful Wisconsin north woods.

As she heaved the heavy pack containing all the things she needed for the next two weeks onto her back, she began to prepare herself mentally. *I do so many endurance sports, I'm sure I'll be able to face this challenge without too much trouble.* Memories flooded back of the fourteen-day Navigator Eagle Lake Wilderness Camp the summer after her sophomore year. The twenty-five-mile hike, sleeping in tents, carrying her backpack—she was sure she could do it again for Wheaton.

A map in her hands showed her where she needed to go, and off she went. They were a team of nine girls, all freshmen, together with their leader. Tami enjoyed experiencing nature, praising God as she discovered beautiful new parts of the lakes and woods. Day by day the physical challenge increased. She soon realized that the physical challenge was greater than she had anticipated. Halfway through the experience, she was exhausted.

One day, as the group of freshmen struggled to push their canoes up a small winding creek swarming with mosquitoes, she fell into a bout of depression. Her tired, aching muscles, the dampness, and the prospect of enduring this for several more days weighed heavily on her.

This actually is a deep spiritual challenge, she explained to herself. *And a good chance for me to learn how God teaches discipline.*

Toward the end of the day, Tami gathered wood, placed it in a small stone enclosure, and lit a fire. No one had the energy to talk, but the sense of being together and going through the difficult challenge as a group gave them all strength and courage. The moment she lay down, she fell into a deep sleep.

The hard rocky ground woke her long before the sun reached the horizon. After a quick morning wash, her quiet time helped her gain perspective on the day ahead. Hebrews 12:11 said, "No discipline seems pleasant at the time, but painful." And she prayed after Hebrews 12:10: *Lord, I can trust that You discipline us for our good, that we might share in Your holiness. I ask You that You would provide the necessary strength for me to endure this discipline.*

After breakfast, she had to take down the tent, pack, and find her way to the next rendezvous station. She braced herself for the next part of the course, a thirteen-mile marathon. When she fell repeatedly on the rock climb and had to be pulled up, she found herself losing her temper repeatedly with members of her group. She just felt so miserable, and she soon regretted her outbursts.

"Oh Lord, help me. I have failed miserably, not only in Your eyes but also in the eyes of the group," she cried.

Her leader comforted her. "Tami, you must learn to accept failures constructively. We need to remind ourselves that although we want to be perfect, we often fail. We can trap ourselves by setting unrealistic expectations."

That night, she continued her journaling with the words, "Lord, thank You for this special group of girls. They have helped me learn to accept my failures because failures sometimes have a higher purpose."

The hike over the next days continued to be exhausting, but Tami's physical stamina proved to be better than some of the other girls'. Their feet and shoulders ached, and often they were on the brink of giving up.

"I'm sure God will provide the necessary strength for us to endure," she reminded herself and the others.

As she prepared to forge a wide, deep creek, despairing at the thought of getting soaked in cold water, she discovered a beaver dam that formed a perfect bridge. "Wow, Lord. Thanks for looking after us in this way. This incident shows me how You even care for the small things in our lives," she penned in her journal.

When the team returned to Wheaton, they were welcomed back by cheering crowds of fellow students.

"Tami, you look absolutely exhausted, but so happy! Tell me all that happened during the trip!" one of the students remarked.

Tami shared about the beautiful nature they had enjoyed, the hardships endured, and how she had experienced God's presence when she thought she had reached the end of her limits. "The hardships challenged me. But I felt God using them to mold me. I knew that God was teaching me some important lessons and truths for the future."

Every student had to write a report about the wilderness experience. So over the next days, Tami condensed her experiences onto paper. She described how, during some of the most difficult times on the journey, words from the Psalms had come to her mind: "Why, O Lord, do you hide yourself in times of trouble?" She distinctly remembered praying but not believing that God would be able to raise her spirits. But a curious thing happened in response. She wrote, "Then Your peace and joy began to overcome my depression, and I began praising You! This total change in my attitude was repeated a week later when I was bushwalking in the dark and falling constantly. Once again I could rejoice because You had given me the physical and emotional strength to thrive in difficult circumstances."

Tami closed her eyes. She wanted to remember the details accurately so that, should she encounter similarly difficult times later, she would be able to look back and remind herself of God's faithfulness. As Tami reflected, she wrote: "Help me, Lord, to learn to concentrate on You instead of on my problems. You will provide the necessary strength for me to endure. My love for others should be a response to Your infinite love for me. So many times on the trip, I concentrated only on my own aching feet and shoulders, and as a result, I was unable to reach out with love to the others in my group. Lord, I know that I cannot exhibit the sacrificial love of Your Son without Your help. Please let me give Your love to each person so that I can pass on to others what Your love has developed in my life."

She paused for a few minutes, and then scribbled: "I pray that You will enable me to 'come forth as gold' and to be 'mature and complete, not lacking anything.'"

Tami wrote several pages about her experience and titled the piece, "High Road Prayer."

College started. Tami shared her room with Kathy and Pam, and the three became close friends—the sort of "forever friends" Tami had dreamed of. Soon her life at Wheaton was happy and fulfilling. She thrived on the intellectual challenge of the college environment and the exchange with similar-minded students and teachers.

She joined the Wheaton College swim team, where she further gained many close friends, including the coach. She practiced faithfully and rigorously, as she felt she should be like the apostle Paul, "buffeting the body." To Tami, physical discipline was also a spiritual discipline. She swam the five hundred and fifteen hundred meters, one of the least desirable endurance races. When her teammates one day lined the side of the pool for her thirty laps, cheering her on in her matches, she envisioned "a great cloud of witnesses aligning her entrance into heaven."

To everyone, she became known as a hardworking student who was gracious and helpful to all those who needed help.

⌇

"Tami, what are you doing? Tomorrow is the exam—have you already finished your studying?"

Tami glanced up from her spot on the bed as her roommate, Kathy, entered. "I'm memorizing Bible verses, Kathy. I like to do this in the evenings before an exam."

"Memorizing verses?" Kathy was astonished.

"Yes, ever since I was nine, I've been memorizing Bible verses regularly. My parents must have read somewhere—was it Dobson? I can't remember—well, they read somewhere that memorizing is good for children." Tami's eyes sparkled. "At times I resisted, but as I grew older, I saw the benefits of memorizing whole parts of the Bible. This way, the text becomes part of my thinking. I have memorized the whole book of Philippians."

"The whole book of Philippians?" Kathy was impressed.

"Yes, it took me months. But now I really love this book."

"Tami, what about your exam preparations?"

"I finished studying last night."

"Do you mind explaining this part to me?" Kathy asked, opening up her science book.

"Yes, of course." And they spent the next hours reviewing science for the exam.

Another close friend was Suzie. Suzie had grown up in a missionary environment in South America, and Tami was thrilled to listen to her stories. They both relished talking about missions.

"Tutors are needed for Chicago's inner-city kids. That would be a way we could serve right now," Suzie mentioned during a time of sharing. "Okay, let's do it!" Tami immediately responded. So Tami and Suzie gave up their free time to serve the special needs of these children as tutors.

Mary Macaluso and her family moved to Wheaton around the same time as Tami did. The Macalusos had been close friends of the Fisk family even before Tami was born. Tami often spent her weekends with them, sharing what she had learned at Wheaton. And Mary often cheered her on during the swim competitions. The Macalusos became almost a second family to her.

Tami was popular among her fellow students and was also an attraction to the male students. One student was particularly interested in a friendship with her. He was a committed Christian. Handsome and intelligent, he shared her love for the outdoors. Her heart raced in anticipation whenever she met him. The idea of dating him excited her. But she had to sort out the most important question first: was he also interested in serving on the mission field?

Opportunity to answer the question came when they went hiking together. It didn't take too long for Tami to find out that while they appeared to be a perfect match in almost everything else, he did not share her passion for serving overseas. Tami did not delay her decision. It was painful, but she was sure that it was the right thing to do. They stopped dating.

⌇

The greatest highlights for Tami were the regular mission evenings at Wheaton, when missionaries from all over the world were invited to share their stories. The most memorable was an evening with Dr. Helen Rosevaere.

Helen Rosevaere was a medical doctor who had served the local tribes in Belgian Congo, Africa. She built a hospital of handcrafted bricks, stocked it with medicines, and for many years, treated malnourished patients, nursed lepers, delivered babies, and performed amputations.

All the things I'd like to do, Tami thought.

But it wasn't a story with a happy ending. Dr. Rosevaere's work ended tragically with the onset of a bloody revolution—five terrible months of savage brutality during which many missionaries were killed and nearly a quarter of a million innocent African civilians were butchered.

That evening, Helen Rosevaere shared her experiences. "There was an angry mob. Two men suddenly burst into my home, came after me, and struck me again and again. I lost my back teeth to the boot of a rebel soldier that night. They broke my glasses, and not being able to see, I felt utterly defenseless. I did not doubt God. I never doubted God. But I felt, for that moment, that He'd left me to handle the situation by myself."

Tami was on edge. How had this renowned missionary coped?

"For the next days, we were kept captive and then taken to a jury in front of the rebel soldiers. It had been preplanned. We knew they intended to kill us."

The unfairness of it struck Tami hard. Why should a missionary who had laid out her life to serve God be rewarded with cruelty and suffering? She listened intensely.

"I knew with every fiber of my being that God, the almighty Creator, was there," Dr. Rosevaere continued. "It was like God was asking me, 'Can you trust me in this difficult situation, even if I never tell you why?'"

She paused. "You know, that was a shattering new insight. It took me a while, but then I prayed, 'Yes, God. If somehow, somewhere this fits Your purpose, then yes, I trust You in this, even if I don't understand why.' God did not take away the wickedness, the cruelty, or the pain. It was still there. But He turned my fear into peace."

Dr. Rosevaere recounted how God used her to turn racial conflict into harmony. Instead of killing her, the eight hundred rebel soldiers ended up asking for forgiveness and seeking reconciliation. Dr. Rosevaere pronounced with quiet certainty that God never gives evil, but takes what is intended for evil and makes it good. "God used me as an instrument of peace and harmony in that country."

There was silence as the missionary doctor looked around the room into the intense expressions of her listeners, Tami included.

"Why does a God of love allow suffering?" she continued. "So many people ask me this. For me that question is, in itself, a contradiction. Love and suffering are inextricably linked." Her face shone. "God loves us so much that He gave His own Son to the cross. Because He loves, He suffered, giving us an example to follow in His steps."

Tami absorbed every word. She was more determined than ever to follow Christ with the same boldness and trust that Helen Rosevaere had shown. At the end of the talk, Tami walked down to meet Dr. Rosevaere.

"Hi, my name is Tami Fisk, and I'm preparing to become a medical missionary," she said. "I highly respect your sacrifices during your time in Congo. May I ask you a question?"

Dr. Rosevaere smiled and invited Tami to sit down in a private corner.

"I have a question about singleness for missionary doctors." Tami carefully formulated her question. "I know that you are single and have remained so until now. Why is that? Is that part of your sacrifice?"

Dr. Rosevaere paused to collect her thoughts before replying. "Tami, first of all, God does not want sacrifice. He wants our obedience. Some people know—yes, they just know—that God wants them to remain single throughout their lives. How is it with you: do you have that certainty?"

Tami thought for a while. "Hmm. I don't have a strong sense that I should remain single. In fact, I think I would like to get married. But to me, the most important thing in the world is to become a medical missionary and serve where God wants me to serve. That's definitely more important to me than marriage."

"Tami, singleness can be a practical consideration because of the places we go to. Are you prepared for that?"

"It will be hard, but I think I'm prepared for it," Tami answered.

"Being married can also be hard, Tami. Bringing up children, deciding on the best schooling, defining roles within a marriage on the mission field—these are all challenging issues."

Dr. Rosevaere looked into Tami's eyes and said, "The single most important thing is to be content with what you are now: single. If God wants you to marry, don't worry. He is in charge and will lead you to the right person." Tami nodded in agreement. "Tami, let's commit this to the Lord together."

They prayed together.

"One last thing, Tami," Dr. Rosevaere said as they parted. "Make sure you do not to give in to doubts and regret on this topic—whatever happens. Remember that God loves you and wants the best for you. He deserves to be trusted."

That evening, Tami called her parents. "Could you accept it if I were never to marry?"

"What brought this subject up?" her dad inquired.

"I just had an awesome evening with Dr. Rosevaere, the famous missionary from Congo. We talked about singleness, and I came to the conclusion that although I would not mind getting married, I may well remain single. I just wanted you to be prepared."

"If this is God's will for your life, we will accept it," was Dad's response.

The conversation with her parents over, she sat down to write more in her journal so as not to forget what she had learned. Would she ever be able to let God mold her as Dr. Rosevaere did? She skimmed through the ten pages of her "High Road Prayer." This time, instead of reading the words, she started praying through them.

I trust that You discipline us for our good, that we might share in Your holiness. I desire to discover more of You and Your Son Jesus, in whom are hidden all the treasures of wisdom and knowledge (Col 2.3). I want to "take down the shutters" so that I can see what You are truly like. Indeed, You say "Learn of Me." You have promised to strengthen me with power through Your spirit since You live in me. It is not my strength which will bring about these changes, but Your power that not only fills creation but also dwells inside me. I truly desire to let my "light shine before men, that they may see my good deeds and praise my Father in Heaven" (Matt 5:16). I know that You will continue to guide me with Your presence and give me sufficient strength to do Your will. Thank You for loving me unconditionally and helping me to love others in the same manner. Amen.

As she opened the Bible, a verse caught her eye. It was just the right verse to end her prayer. She smiled a little as she read it. "Being confident of this, that He who began a good work in you will carry it on to completion until the day of Christ Jesus" (Philippians 1:6).

Chapter 4

BECOMING A DOCTOR

"Tami, you're still determined to become a missionary doctor, aren't you?" Tim asked during Christmas at their Denver home. Tami was twenty-one, and he was nineteen. They were making Christmas goodies. He teased her, "All these years we've known your goal, but what none of us knows is _where_ you're going."

Tami sighed. "I don't know where God wants me to go. I wish I did; then I could prepare. But I do know He will show me one day, and that it will all be within His perfect timing."

As the whole family sat around the Christmas dinner table, Dad asked, "Tami, what project are you working on just now? Mary Macaluso told us that she met one of your professors, and he told her how impressed he was with your inquisitive research mind. We're curious too. Tell us a little more about your research at Wheaton."

Tami paused in the middle of lifting her fork. Her eyes sparkled. "For my degree in chemistry, I'm working on a project. The topic is enzyme kinetics as related to the treatment of cataracts by enzymatic digestion."

"Enzyme what?" her father asked.

Everyone laughed. Tami tried to explain the complicated chemistry in simple terms, but to no avail. None of her family was that well-versed in science.

During dessert, Tami's eyes sparkled again as she leaned back to make an announcement. "As you all know, Wheaton College offers an elective which can be done overseas. I have applied for it. And guess what? They have accepted me! I'm going to an African mission hospital called Mukinge Hospital—it's in Zambia." She glanced at Tim. "I'll go there to seek God's plan for me, whether God wants me to go to Africa."

That summer, Tami spent two months in a rural hospital in Africa. The minute she returned to Wheaton, she was greeted by eager friends.

"How was your time in Africa?" Suzie prodded when they were back at the college campus.

"I loved it!" Tami told her. "Zambia is a beautiful country, and the people are very special. The hospital chief and his wife were such wonderful people, and a great encouragement to me. We had such incredible conversations."

"What did you do there?"

"Well, that was exactly the problem. Because I'm only a college student, I couldn't contribute as much as I would have liked to. I did some clerical work, and later they asked me to help teach math to the nursing students. I even acted as librarian in the hospital library—a big one! But the highlight was when Dr. Wenninger, the hospital chief, invited me to observe, sometimes even in the operating theater." Tami grew quieter as she remembered. "There were so many pressing needs. Malaria is such a frequent problem there—I saw so many really sick patients. But often I felt so useless. It makes me want to study medicine even more. I can't wait to get to med school!"

Suzie smiled, sure of the answer even before she asked. "Have you been accepted?"

Tami smiled, and her excitement shone through her eyes. "Emory Medical Center in Atlanta has offered me a place—I just heard. I'm really thrilled, Suzie—Johns Hopkins has also accepted me."

"What are you going to do?" Suzie asked.

"I'm going to Emory. It's got a strong international health program and links with the Centers for Disease Control. I'm hoping to do an international elective when I'm there."

Suzie laughed, taking delight in her friend's delight. "Speaking of international, when in the world did your receive your MCAT exam scores?"

"Oh, I asked for them to be forwarded to Zambia." Tami paused. "I have to confide something. When I received the letter, I was so excited about the results. They were much better than I had expected."

Suzie laughed again, love for her friend in her eyes. "But we knew you'd have the best results! You always do."

Tami smiled, but she didn't chime in with Suzie's enthusiasm. "You know, I was jumping up and down for joy when they came. I thought nothing could equal that sense of achievement. But later that day, I joined the nurses' fellowship.

The Africans really know how to worship. Their beautiful voices, their rhythm, their intensity in worship; it was an amazing experience. That evening, I felt God's presence more than I had ever felt it before. A nurse preached, really anointed preaching. Three nursing students gave their lives to Jesus on that very night. My heart really rejoiced then—it was an intensity I can't describe. Like the kind of rejoicing that angels do when we turn to Christ."

Tami closed her eyes briefly. "The joy of seeing others come to Christ is the greatest joy in the world. Grades and achievements fade—they don't really matter at all in comparison."

Tami had in fact passed Wheaton College *summa cum laude*. Emory University offered her a scholarship, based—as they wrote in their letter to her—on "academic achievements and leadership potential."

Tami went through medical school at Emory with great discipline and commitment. She studied hard, very hard. In addition to her medical studies, she helped start a weekly Bible study and discussion group for medical students which continued throughout her years at Emory. With her interest in international students, she was surprised to find that the majority of international scholars were from China. Many of these Chinese scholars were working for the Centers for Disease Control, while others were doing undergraduate or postgraduate degrees. It was not long before Chinese students and scholars became her close friends.

Noticing that Tami always carried a Bible with her, one Chinese scholar asked, "Tami, you are a scientist. How can you believe in God?" He looked at her, puzzled and almost with contempt. In answer, Tami shared with him why intellectual integrity was not in conflict with a Creator God.

The Chinese scholar became more curious. "You see, in China, we say that religion is only for the uneducated, for the farmers, or for the tribal folks. As scientists, we cannot believe in anything that is not material."

"There is so much more to discover. Why don't you come with me to the International Fellowship on Sunday?" Tami asked.

That Sunday, a Chinese family was baptized in church. They were visiting scientists. The scholar was intrigued and astonished. "Even Chinese scientists believe in God?"

He was not the only one who went with Tami to the International Fellowship. Many other Chinese scholars and their friends were drawn to the church services. In time, Tami began asking whether God was drawing her toward work among them. "Lord, it is evident to me how clearly you are moving among the Chinese scholars. How do you want to use me in this?"

After her first year at medical school, Tami was involved in a summer project at the Malaria Branch of the Centers for Disease Control. As malaria was such a major problem in Africa, she had decided to spend her summer in malaria research rather than take a vacation. She assisted with the culturing of malaria parasites. The aim was to use these cultures to perform testing of chemotherapeutic compounds.

"I'm searching for parasite blobs in liver cells and attempting to dissect mosquitoes," she explained to her family over the phone.

As she worked alongside several Chinese scholars during the project, one particular doctor from China caught her attention. Increasingly, they spent time together, sharing information about their respective cultures, their families, and their traditions.

"Tami, you always pray before you eat. Why do you do such a superstitious thing?" her Chinese friend asked one day.

"Because God is real," she answered. "Praying to our infinite yet personal God is not superstition. If you like, you can come over for dinner at my place tonight, and I can share with you why I believe in God."

From this invitation, regular weekly meetings ensued. One day after a meeting, an idea suddenly shot into Tami's mind. "Would you agree to teach Chinese to me on a regular basis?"

"Of course. You teach me the Bible, and I teach you Chinese."

Tami worked for her summer research project right up until the day classes started. Quite unusually for a first-year medical student, the work she did on malaria that summer vacation, as well as in the following summer semester, resulted in two publications in international scientific journals.

But in Tami's mind, the second year at medical school was much better than the first. At last, students were allowed to see real patients and were given bedside teaching. In the letters she regularly wrote to her parents, she described her days:

Every Thursday afternoon, we go to a hospital, meet patients, take their history and do physical examinations. I have realized that if you wear a white coat and hang a stethoscope around your neck, people will tell you *anything*. It's great, although I'm also learning about the emotional burdens of dealing with hurting people. The first time I caught myself saying "my patient," I felt like jumping up and down! One guy even called me a DOCTOR!

In the same letter, she shared, "I'm so thankful for so many witnessing opportunities. One classmate in med school in particular has been asking lots of questions. Please pray for her. More importantly, pray that the Spirit would continue to work in her heart."

Other exciting things were happening at the International Fellowship. Two Chinese scholars publicly declared that they had become Christians. One of them was her friend.

Sharing with Suzie she said, "It is the joy I experienced in Zambia. There is no greater joy than seeing individuals come to Christ. It is so exciting to see more and more Chinese showing an interest in Christianity."

In Tami's third year in medical school, she was one of the few students selected to do an overseas project.

"Guess what?" she asked her parents on one of her regular phone up-dates. "Emory University has agreed to pay for my travel expenses to return to Mukinge Hospital in Zambia for a research project! It will be so exciting to be back, and this time as a doctor—well, almost a doctor." She chuckled. "I'll be doing a research project on malaria: an epidemiological study on the severity of anemia in children with malaria and other illnesses."

"Tami," her father chuckled, "we don't understand your medical jargon that well. But we are happy for you!" A pause. "Tami, do you think God is calling you to Africa?"

"Well, I'm not sure. In fact, I'm less and less sure. As time passes, my heart seems to be drawn to China. God has not told me firmly yet, but somehow . . ." She took a deep breath. "Somehow, I feel God is calling me to China. Please pray about it."

Tami's time in Zambia was fruitful, and she enjoyed every minute of it. In addition to her malaria research, she became the second physician to Dr. Wenninger, and she assisted during surgery. The evenings were filled with long conversations with Dr. Wenninger and his wife about missions in Africa and China. She listened intently to Mrs. Wenninger recounting how she had grown up in China. When Tami returned home, it was gratifying to see that her research work had resulted in yet another publication in a scientific journal. Yet despite all the positive experiences in Africa, in her heart she continued to wonder whether God was calling her there—or to China.

As she had done at Wheaton, so she did at Emory University: Tami graduated *summa cum laude*. Finally, Tami was a certified medical doctor.

She updated her friends in a letter:

Now that I have finished my medical degree at Emory, I plan to go to the University of Rochester. There, I will do my internship and residency, which will take a total of four years. I'll be doing a combined internal medicine and pediatrics program. After living in Atlanta for four years, I really miss snow and four distinct seasons, although I am sure that one winter in Rochester will cure me of that forever." She smiled to herself as she continued. "Two of my classmates will be doing their residencies in pediatrics up there too. I'm very excited—it's a great program, and lots of people up there are interested in Third World health. They also allow for a three–four month elective overseas. I think I will use this opportunity to go to China.

❧

Four busy years at the University of Rochester followed. Tami had chosen to do her residency in medicine and pediatrics, as this combination would offer the broadest range of clinical experience. She thrived under the challenge of the clinical responsibilities as a young doctor.

Tami particularly enjoyed cracking difficult cases. It almost had a Sherlockian feel to it. She examined the clues, weighed the different options, and then drew her conclusions. If she came to a diagnosis that nobody else had considered and it turned out to be the correct one, she felt like celebrating the outcome of her detective efforts.

As she spent so much time at the hospital, new friendships formed, in particular with three fellow residents: Ellen, Cathy, and Gary.

"When our program director told me who I would be working with, she said, 'And you wait until you meet Tami—she is extraordinary,'" Ellen recounted as they were sitting on the hospital cafeteria eating a belated lunch. "I must admit I felt intimidated. But then I got to know you and realized how much fun you are. Hardly intimidating at all."

Tami smiled. "I value our friendship so much. It helps me get through those long days in hospital."

"No kidding," Ellen laughed. "Speaking of which, thanks for going over those difficult cases with me last month. Without you I'd be a terrible slacker. Thanks for keeping me going."

"If I picture you in my mind, I see you striding down the hospital corridors with your notebook checking your to-do list," Gary commented with a laugh.

"Our program director was right. You are extraordinary, Tami. What I value most is your direction, your faith, and your clarity of thought," Cathy added.

Tami laughed. "C'mon guys, don't exaggerate. Anyway, enough about me. What I like most about our friendship is sharing our day-to-day things. Walking down the halls, writing up clinic charts, messaging each other, doing favors—the verdict's in. I think we're going to be friends forever!"

The weeks were often filled with more than eighty hours of work in the hospital. Tami knew that, although it was tough, the hours would help make her an experienced clinician so that she could better serve overseas. One day, a professor who had noticed Tami's achievements said, "Tami, I have so often heard that you want to go overseas to work as a doctor in a developing country. I honestly think that would be a waste of your talent and training! Bright young doctors like you should stay in the United States where you will have all the opportunities to develop a brilliant academic career!"

Tami thought for a long while before she responded. "Missions deserves only the very best. After all, God has given us His very best, His Son." She paused and then continued. "Last weekend I read the biography of Jim Elliott, a young missionary in Ecuador who was killed very early during his service in Ecuador. What struck me most about what he said was this quote: 'He is no fool who gives what he cannot keep to gain what he cannot lose.'"

Not long after she moved to Rochester, Tami found a good church where she was able to actively participate and serve. Not entirely to her surprise, a pattern similar to her time in Atlanta arose. She was being drawn more and more to the overseas Chinese—not only at church, but also during her hospital work. By the end of the third year of her residency, the certainty grew in her heart that God wanted her to serve the Chinese.

Chapter 5

CALLING TO SERVE IN CHINA

"There was no voice from God. It is just this definite knowledge that God wanted me to serve Him as a medical doctor."

Tami stood in front of her church in Atlanta—the Intown Community Fellowship—sharing her testimony with her church friends. She had only recently returned from her first trip to China.

"I can't even remember the details of that movie on medical missionaries I watched when I was nine years old. But the certainty of His calling while I was watching has never left me."

Tami paused—it seemed strange that there was nothing more spectacular or supernatural to add. But what really mattered was that there were no doubts in her mind. Through all these years, there had *never* been any doubts. Not once during her teenage years, not at Wheaton College, not at Emory University, not during her residency in Rochester. Never! This calling was so much a part of her that the opposite idea frightened her. She could not imagine herself without that calling, without this future. It had become part of her identity.

She smiled and went on to explain. "I had no idea God was leading me to China. At first, I thought Africa was the place where God wanted me. I went to Africa twice and did some medical work and malaria research in Zambia. It was a wonderful challenge for me both medically and spiritually, and I came back home thinking I could easily settle down and work there. But the Lord directed me differently. Emory University and now also my hospital in Rochester have many visiting physicians and students from all over the world, in particular China. I quickly got to know and befriend several medical doctors from China. Their culture and language fascinated me. I felt like this ancient rich culture had been hidden from me for years—I was stunned to learn about the huge upheaval that China went through.

"Looking back," Tami continued, "I can clearly see God's leading hand. As a result of those friendships and some university connections to China, the possibility of doing part of my residency training in China became real! This was unheard of at the time, and I quickly started learning Mandarin. Before I knew it, the door was open! Well, *after* completing the first part of internship, battling with seemingly endless mountains of paperwork, and studying Chinese at night."

As her audience chuckled, Tami went on with her story. She had left for China in August 1993. She worked for six weeks at the Beijing Children's Hospital, where she rotated through ten different wards. After that, she did a stint in the Public Health Department of Kunming Medical College in the southwest of China, in the province of Yunnan, which borders Thailand and Myanmar. She visited everything from tiny two-room village clinics, where the "doctor" might have had a year of post-high-school training, to a huge university hospital with cutting-edge technology like that in the U.S.

She rested for a while, with her eyes looking far into the horizon.

"When I arrived in China, I immediately fell in love with this vast country and culture. And here comes the most amazing part. Not long after I had stepped off the airplane in Beijing, a young Chinese woman—she was maybe in her early twenties—approached me. She spoke broken English, and I spoke even more broken Chinese! But soon she blurted, 'I have been waiting for a foreigner to explain me all about Christianity! I want to believe, but I know nothing.' At that moment, it became crystal-clear to me that God was calling me to serve in China. Many Chinese people are searching for deeper answers. This is where I see my role for the future. And this is the reason I'm standing here in front of you."

She looked around the audience, both at familiar faces and unfamiliar. So many times she had been the one hanging on a missionary's every word—and now her life had come full-circle. All were listening intently.

"In 1951, all missionaries had to leave. For several decades, China was closed to the outside world, and it only opened up in the '80s again. This took place just a little more than a decade ago. China now welcomes foreign experts. No one can imagine how rapidly China is developing, in particular the cities on the East Coast. However, the inland provinces of China remain very needy. Furthermore, there are more than fifty tribal groups or minorities, mainly in the interior and utmost western parts of China, most of them living in rural areas in abysmal poverty."

Tami took a deep breath.

"I believe God has called me to serve in China. I have a burden to go to China's inland provinces to serve the poor and sick. China is open to professionals. God has allowed me to train to become a physician. I'm not sure how long the doors will remain open for foreign experts. If the doors do stay open, I will return to China by mid-1995. In the meantime, I need to finish my residency, study for my board exams, and find a job for next year. I thank you for your prayers and support."

There was applause. Then the pastor prayed for Tami. Kneeling down on the church floor, Tami again committed the future to the Lord. Afterward, many of her church friends surrounded her.

"Tami, we will support you financially. Please send us your letters."

"Tami, that is so fascinating. I want to learn more about China, and I will commit to pray for this special country. Make sure you put me on the list for your newsletters."

Tami was touched and encouraged. As others dissipated, Paula Helms approached Tami. "Tami, as missions administrator of this church, I will support you in whatever you need in China. In fact, your testimony this evening was so inspiring to me! It made me start thinking about the possibility of going to China myself someday."

"Paula, that would be great. If God wants you to serve there, He will open the doors!"

Much still needed to be done. Tami returned to work and to planning. She passed her board exams with flying colors.

"Finally!" she told her friends and supporters. "I'm finally a specialist—a specialist in internal medicine and pediatrics!"

Over the last several years Tami had taken out some student loans, and she wanted to pay them off before she went to China. She chose to work a series of jobs so she could see more of the U.S. before heading off to China— what she called the "Loan-Repayment-Can-Be-Fun Plan." She first worked in Montana near Glacier National Park together with her fellow resident Cathy.

Then she went on to southwestern Michigan to work in a group practice. She was intrigued by the mission-plan concept of these doctors who covered several town clinics and rotated for three-month cycles to work in overseas locations. When Tami finished her rotation in Michigan, her coworkers assured her they would want to become her steady supporters.

At the end of this whirlwind of activity, covering four states in the U.S., she applied for a temporary job in Colorado. Excitedly, she called her parents.

"I found a job in Denver!"

"Great, Tami! We are looking forward to having you with us after all these years of college, medical school, and residency!"

"Thanks so much! I can't wait to see you. I hope to be in Colorado for most of the spring. I have to warn you, though: I will be busy working. I want to maximize my preparations for China, so I plan to do some extension courses with Wheaton College to learn more about the country. I also need to find a Chinese tutor, get plugged in to church life again, and ski—not necessarily in that order, of course!" She chuckled. "I'm planning to be back in China by August. At the moment, I'm in the process of applying to several organizations that place foreign experts in China. Please pray for the right organization for me."

In Denver, she connected with churches, friends, and prayer partners, building up a solid support group. It was important to her to be accountable to her supporters, so she started writing "accountability letters." In addition to all this, she pored over her Chinese language books.

"How is everything going, Tami?" Ellen asked over the phone one night.

"Well, the good news is that I've almost paid off all my loan debts."

"Have you found the right organization yet?" Her friends from Rochester were following Tami's journey closely.

"No, not yet. I've applied to various organizations, but so far I've not felt drawn to any of them. The whole issue is weighing heavily on me. Choosing the right organization is crucial. I have spent many months praying over this, even fasting. May God lead me to the organization He wants me to go with."

"I trust He will," her friend encouraged her.

Not long after this phone call, a friend of the Fisk family, Dan from Denver, passed a newsletter to Tami. It was the first Bulletin of MSI. The letter ended with the words: "Prayer is the vital foundation for all MSI services in China's needy inland provinces. MSI is looking for well-qualified short-term and long-term trainers in medicine, English & accounting to work side by side in field service."

Tami was intrigued. "What's MSI?" she asked.

"MSI stands for Medical Services International. It was only founded in 1993," Dan responded. *In 1993? That was my first year in China!* she thought.

"Take a look at this: it's the initial purpose statement of MSI in 1993, as written by Dr. James H. Taylor, Richard Chen, and Dr. Reginald Tsang, the MSI cofounders." Dan handed her the document.

Tami read it carefully. "Over the past decade, under the policy of four modernizations, China has welcomed 'foreign experts' from abroad to come and share in its opening and development. One of the critical areas for development is in medical services, especially in China's inland provinces, rural areas, and among the national minority peoples. We believe MSI can be a channel whereby skilled Christian medical personnel from the United States, United Kingdom, Canada, Singapore, Malaysia, Taiwan, etc. can serve the medical, physical, and spiritual needs of these areas."

Tami felt her heart pounding. These words echoed her vision! Inland provinces, rural, minority peoples, skilled medical personnel . . .

"But if it was founded only in 1993. Surely they can't be well established. Won't they lack the experience and necessary networks?" Tami objected.

"Well, you're right, it's new—but then, it's also old." Dan smiled mysteriously. "It's a long story. Do you have time?"

"Of course I have time. It's very important to me to know the full story." Tami tried to suppress her excitement.

"Well, I must admit I don't know it all. Talk to Dr. Taylor—Dr. James *Hudson* Taylor—about it. He knows far more."

"Dr. James Hudson Taylor?" Tami interrupted, her eyes widening. "As in Hudson Taylor, the founder of the China Inland Mission?"

"Indeed. Dr. Taylor is the great-grandson of Hudson Taylor." Dan smiled again. He continued, "This is what I know: the first foundation stones for MSI were laid as early as the 1940s when leaders of the China Inland Mission investigated possibilities to establish work among the Yi people. The Yi are a tribal minority in the extreme southwest of Sichuan, and they live in an enclave in the Great Cold Mountains. The mountains peak up to 14,000 feet in one of the most underdeveloped regions in China."

Mountains? Tami's ears picked up even further. She followed the story closely.

"I have been told that the forbidding mountains guard the territory on its western and northern sides, withstanding many foreigners' attempts to enter. Dr. A.J. Broomhall, a medical doctor with the China Inland Mission, arrived in China sometime in the 1930s. The plight of the Yi people deeply moved him. He tried everything possible to move up to the mountains to establish a hospital among the Yi. He finally succeeded in getting the approval and lived there from 1948 until 1951. His clinic attracted the sick from all these villages. He brought his family there, plus two single nurses. His youngest daughter was born there. To his great sorrow, his time was cut short in 1951 when every foreigner had to leave the country. He was grief-stricken, and the Yi mourned when he, his family, and the two nurses had to leave. They asked him to promise to return, and he did." Dan paused.

Tami was following every word from his lips. "And did he return?"

"Yes, sometime in the '80s. All his life, he waited to return. He was very old when permission was granted to visit his hospital again. What exactly transpired during his visit, I don't know. You'd better ask Dr. Taylor about the details. What I do know is that his visit ultimately led to the founding of MSI."

"Wow, that is awesome!" Tami exclaimed. She was quiet for a while as she tried to digest the information. "Is he still alive? Would I be able to visit him?"

"Unfortunately, he has died. If you want to find out more, you should contact Dr. Taylor."

"You bet I will," Tami said with her usual determination.

"Dr. Taylor lives in Hong Kong. Here's his address."

That very evening, Tami wrote a letter to Dr. Taylor explaining that she was interested in working in China's inland provinces as a medical doctor.

Chapter 6

TAMI JOINS MSI PROFESSIONAL SERVICES

"You would be the first doctor with MSI, Tami. You would be pioneering the work," Dr. Taylor told her on the phone after quite a busy exchange of letters and e-mails.

"The first?" Tami swallowed. Yet deep inside, the idea of being a pioneering doctor appealed to her. She asked carefully, "The first and only?"

"Yes, Tami, for the time being, you would be the first and only doctor. Of course, we are praying for many more doctors in the years to come. There will also be many short-term teams of doctors to come and assist. We have already sent out a lot of teams. But you would be the first long-term doctor we would place there."

"But not totally on my own?" Tami asked.

"No, we do not send staff on their own. We are currently interviewing two nurses—one from Taiwan and one from Japan. The three of you would be our pioneer team, God willing." He paused and then added, "Well, the first year or two, you would need to do full-time language study. But after that, if the doors remain open, we hope to send you to the Great Cold Mountains, as they are called in China."

"The same Great Cold Mountains where Dr. Jim Broomhall used to work?"

"That is the plan. You need to know, however, that plans can change anytime. China is changing and often unpredictable. No foreign doctor has worked there for more than forty years. We are not sure we will get permission for you, and we depend on the Chinese authorities. So far, they have welcomed us with open arms. But there are no guarantees. We are all taking each step in faith. Tami, if you indeed join MSI, you need to know that this is a step into the unknown, a step in faith."

Tami was pensive as she got off the phone. The biography of Dr. A.J. Broomhall had stirred her heart over the past weeks while communicating with the MSI office in Hong Kong. Was this indeed the organization God wanted her to join?

A phone call to Ellen, her friend from Rochester, put words to Tami's concerns. "Are you sure about this?" Ellen asked. "The first and only doctor? A relatively new organization? They are not sure yet whether they will indeed be able to place you? And you're seriously considering it. Tami, have you gone crazy?"

"I know, it sounds hair-raising. I usually am such a planner . . ."

"You are the prototype of a planner," Ellen interrupted. "How can you take all these risks?"

"Maybe God wants me to learn to trust Him more—to bring everything to Him in prayer rather than taking things into my hands, as I have done so often." She paused. "Besides, you should listen to the history of MSI, Ellen. It is such a story of God's working. Every time I read about it, I praise God. I'm simply awestruck by the life of A.J. Broomhall. When he was asked to leave China in 1951, he was despairing. Talk about plans being thwarted! He had prepared all these years to serve among the Yi, but God only granted him three years! After he left China, he never ceased to think of the Yi. He wrote several articles and books on them. I was able to get hold of one of the books, and I am currently reading it. Imagine, three decades later, he was still committed to the Yi. He prayed every day for them without fail. He prayed he would be able to return. When he realized that wouldn't be possible, he prayed that others would return. Isn't it an awesome thought to be following in his footsteps? His dreams might be fulfilled through me, Ellen."

"Thrilling," Ellen said. "Truly. But what does all that have to do with MSI's founding?"

"Plenty. I heard the story from Dr. Taylor. Dr. Broomhall apparently received a letter from China during Christmas in 1986. When he opened the letter, he found a handwritten note on a piece of flimsy rice paper, written by two men from the village he used to work with in the Great Cold Mountains. I can't remember the exact name of this village, but it did start with a 'Z.'" She continued, "In this letter, they invited Dr. Broomhall and his family to return to China, stating that China had opened up to foreigners. One of the two writers was a Communist cadre who promised to get all the necessary paperwork including a visa and travel permissions to enable him to visit the village. After much prayer and planning, in 1988, at the age of seventy-eight years, Dr. Broomhall finally embarked on the long-awaited return trip to China. Joy, his youngest daughter, joined him. And there was also a nurse who used to work alongside him there. She must be in her seventies now. Can you imagine the anticipation they must have felt? Dr. Broomhall had not set foot there for more than thirty years."

Tami paused as she recalled her conversation with Dr. Taylor. "I was told they were welcomed and treated as long-lost friends, even as royalty. They must have been so thrilled. Public security officials granted them a three-day visit to the Z village."

"That all sounds really incredible, I must admit," Ellen said.

"Well, back to the story. This first trip opened doors for more visits. According to Dr. Taylor there is another city, a much bigger city, in the foothills of the Great Cold Mountains. It's hard to pronounce, but it sounds something like Shee-tsang—it's spelled X-I-C-H-A-N-G. You have to go through Xichang to get to the Z village. All the important Chinese authorities are based in Xichang. Well, during their second trip, team members were asked to teach English in Xichang. This apparently marked the start of many more English teaching courses to follow. Surgical procedures were performed at Xichang Hospital. And this impressed local authorities. They shared their desire to develop a program of continuing medical service. Dr. Taylor said that he could recruit doctors and nurses to offer medical services. The Chinese authorities liked the idea. I guess it was the combination of their respect and fond memories for Dr. Jim Broomhall, the surgical skills, and the English teaching that ultimately led to the foundation of Medical Services International."

The rest of the story didn't take long to tell, though it covered a lot of ground. Negotiations with the Sichuan Public Health authorities commenced. Contracts were drawn up. In 1993, Dr. Taylor met a businessman in Hong Kong and later Dr. Tsang, a medical doctor and professor based in the United States. Together they drafted their first vision statements and drew a Memorandum of Understanding.

"That's the story," Tami finished. "What do you think?"

"I'm starting to understand why you are drawn to MSI. And to be honest, you would fit. You'd be exactly the right fit for MSI."

Tami laughed. "I'm really excited about it all. I'm busy filling out forms—millions of forms, by the looks of it! If everything goes well and they accept me, I'll fly out this summer. First I have to do a kind of orientation course, and then a language course. I'm just praying that indeed, only *His* will be done!"

꒱

Tami was accepted. The agreement was that she would initially do three years in China with MSI, then undergo further medical training in the U.S. before she would return for an unlimited time, if not a lifetime.

Several more months of preparation passed, and then July 1995 finally came. When she boarded the airplane for Hong Kong, a sense of relief came over her. At last she was on the journey she had prepared for all her life. The farewells had been painful, with many tears shed. But the joy of anticipation and sense of purpose were stronger than the sadness. There were many supporters, and she was thankful for that. She promised to write letters regularly. Her debts had all been paid off. And she felt she had already laid some groundwork in Chinese.

Dr. Taylor and various other MSI leaders met her in Hong Kong. After so many e-mails, faxes, letters, and phone calls, Tami was really looking forward to meeting Dr. Taylor in person. He was small in stature, with gentle and bright eyes; a little reserved perhaps. She could immediately sense he was a humble servant leader, yet a leader with a strong vision, a leader she could trust.

"Tami, welcome! *Huang ying ni,* as we say in Chinese. We have waited for you and prayed for you in great anticipation." Dr. Taylor warmly smiled at her. "Tami, may I introduce you to Dr. Reginald Tsang?"

"Call me Reggie!" A bright smile came forth from this dynamic Chinese professor. He had given up his full-time position as Professor of Pediatrics at the University of Cincinnati to focus on mobilizing doctors to serve in China.

Looks like a bundle of energy, Tami thought.

"And this is Richard Chen. Richard is a businessman from Hong Kong. He was really instrumental in setting up MSI," Dr. Taylor said as Tami shook hands with the third man.

MSI orientation was a one-week course on getting to know one another and learning about China and MSI. Sharon and Tomoko, the nurses Dr. Taylor had mentioned who would work with Tami in China, were also there, together with some other interested folks. From morning till evening, they studied the history and political system of China, including the limitations and restrictions for foreign professionals working in China. Dr. Taylor, Richard, and Reggie, the cofounders of MSI and the main teachers during the course, conveyed deep insights into China and a genuine love for the country. It was a thrill to listen and absorb.

"We would like to teach you a song," Dr. Taylor announced one day to the first small group of workers with MSI.

"Ai shi heng jiu, ai shi . . ."

Tami did not understand all the Chinese words, but as the song proceeded, she recognized a few. It slowly dawned on her.

"Are these the words from 1 Corinthians 13?" she asked as the song ended.

"Yes, Tami," Dr. Taylor answered. "They are the words of 1 Corinthians 13:4–10: 'Love is patient, love is kind. It does not envy, it does not boast, it is not proud. It is not rude, it is not self-seeking, it is not easily angered, it keeps no record of wrongs. Love does not delight in evil but rejoices with the truth. It always protects, always trusts, always hopes, always perseveres.' MSI has chosen this song as its theme song."

The joy of conviction poured into Tami's heart at that moment. She now knew she had joined the right organization. There could not have been a stronger confirmation from God than those words from 1 Corinthians 13, "her" words since early childhood.

Dr. Taylor continued to tell the MSI story. "As you know, 1993 was the defining year for MSI's development; it was the year when we wrote the vision statement. As the year progressed, it was almost uncanny to see others expressing their interest in medical service in China." He paused, and then, visibly moved, shared words spoken by a Chinese official in 1994.

"'These people come to you in the spirit of Christ.' Yes, these were the words the Chinese representative of the Alumni Association from Beijing used when he introduced MSI to the Sichuan Provincial Public Health Bureau leaders in Chengdu. Can you imagine such words spoken in a country that for decades had banned anything to do with Christianity? It was March 1, 1994. The MSI team of eight was sitting face to face with public health leaders in a large conference room discussing partnership in medical services. After several speeches, the Governor of Sichuan, responsible for the most populous province in China, gave his approval. The historical moment came when we signed the Memorandum of Understanding between MSI and the Sichuan Public Health Bureau. The initial welcome was followed by a banquet and then visits to several places in Sichuan and Yunnan where MSI could potentially start work. The week of visits ended with a wrap-up evaluation and the usual banquet. We had the largest round banquet table that I've ever seen."

Dr. Taylor paused again, recalling the events of that evening. "After some formal opening words of appreciation, I decided to open my heart to our hostess and the gathered officials. I shared with them that I had been born in China and after an absence of thirty-four years had returned in 1980. At that time, all foreign tourists were obliged to travel with a tour group. Only overseas Chinese were permitted to travel on their own. To our mutual surprise and delight, our tour guide and I discovered that we had both been born in the same province and city. In Chinese culture, that gave us a special relationship. He agreed to help my mother and me visit Kaifeng, the city of our birth. We got clearance from China Travel for the change in our itinerary. Tears coursed down my cheeks as the thrill of being home overwhelmed me. The only permission that was still required was travel clearance from the Public Security Bureau. The group around the banquet table listened spellbound as I recounted the ensuing events. The police officer accompanying me couldn't have been more creative and accommodating."

"'He was born in China and now lives overseas,' the police officer said. 'We will consider him an Overseas Chinese.' Approval was given to visit Kaifeng. I described to my audience what seeing her old friends and town had meant to my eighty-two-year-old mother.

"In a flash, the atmosphere in the banquet hall was transformed," Dr. Taylor continued. "Our hosts began to sing some well-known patriotic songs. When they turned to us and said it was now our turn, we were dumbfounded. This was a new medical initiative. No one had dreamed of being called upon to sing. Several from our group volunteered to sing. A couple from Taiwan, Dr. and Mrs. Hsu, rounded out our singing. They chose to sing 'The true meaning of love'—1 Corinthians 13. You could have heard a pin drop. In this way, the banquet ended. But it was not over. Turning to me, our hostess said, 'I have never been to a banquet like this.'"

Dr. Taylor chuckled. "Well, I hadn't either. The hostess continued, 'I will never forget the last words of Dr. and Mrs. Hsu's song.'"

Tami's throat felt all choked up. She looked around the small MSI office. Next to her were Sharon and Tomoko. They were also visibly moved. She looked forward to getting to know them better in the near future.

It was a small MSI team. They sensed the responsibility and huge task ahead of "coming in the spirit of Christ" to serve in China. They sang the "Love Song" together several times. Within days, Tami had memorized the Chinese words, and she was soon able to sing it by heart. She hoped she'd be able to sing it often in China. Her heart quickened at the thought that, by the end of the week, she would leave Hong Kong and arrive at her destination.

Tami at 5

High School Senior Tami

Wheaton College Graduation

Emory Graduation with family

The "Four Med-Peds" residents—Tami, Dr. Schuster, Cathy, Ellen and Gary

Tami hiking Colorado "Fiourteeners"

PART
two

JOURNEY
TO CHINA

Chapter 7

ARRIVAL IN CHINA

'm really here! I'm really here! Tami had to pinch herself as the plane from Hong Kong landed in Chengdu. _I'm finally in China! After all these years of preparation._

At the immigration desk, she handed her passport to the officer, thinking, _This is not just a visit, but the beginning of a new phase in my life!_

"_Huang ying_—welcome, Dr. Fisk."

The representative for international relations of the Sichuan University was waiting for her at the exit of the Chengdu Airport. Driving into town in the university van, Tami immediately absorbed her first impressions. All around her were people, people, and more people. This was a large city, buzzing with a multitude of cars, motorcycles, and bicycles. Countless construction sites lined the main road from the airport to the university. The traffic was chaotic.

"We'll take you to your student dormitory. You will be sharing your room with another international student," the official informed her.

Arriving at the university, she saw that the campus was teeming with students.

"We have more than fifty thousand students in this university," the representative said proudly in her heavily accented English. "Sichuan University is one of the biggest universities in Chengdu, but it is not the biggest in China. Cities such as Beijing or Shanghai have even larger universities." She led Tami up the steps to her new room in the student dormitory.

Not too bad, she thought upon entering. The room was clean and had carpeting. It even had an en suite bathroom.

Shortly afterward, her roommate entered and introduced herself. "Hi. My name Naara. I from Mongolia."

Tami introduced herself and added, "I'm looking forward to sharing the room with you."

Upon which Naara replied, "My name Naara. I from Mongolia. English no good."

I will need to improve my pantomime skills, Tami thought. As Naara looked like a really nice person, she was looking forward to getting to know her.

After unpacking, she took a shower. Showering was a challenge. The drain wasn't at the lowest level of the shower floor, either because the builders wanted a more challenging showering experience or because the building had settled differently than expected. In order to prevent flooding, she had to constantly push the water toward the drain with one foot while showering. "This makes for an interesting little dance, if anyone could see me," she chuckled. Afterward, she swept the rest of the water down the drain with a little broom.

In the corridor on the way out, she met an American student in his second semester of Chinese studies. Driving through the city, she had noticed that thick gray clouds smothered Chengdu, clinging to houses and reducing visibility to a murky one hundred yards or less. She was used to the clear blue skies of Colorado. "Where is the sun?" Tami asked the student jokingly.

He smiled, but answered her question seriously. "Rapid industrial development has transformed the natural gray-white clouds over Chengdu, which are here for most of the year, to dirty smog," he explained. "The dirty air stains all it comes in contact with. Try wiping your nose at the end of the day. You'll be in for a surprise!"

At the end of the day, Tami remembered to look at her handkerchief. It was stained black. The white collar of her shirt had also turned to gray. *This will be difficult to get used to,* Tami thought.

The next day, Chinese class commenced. After the introductions, the teacher started to explain a little about Chengdu. "This is an industrial city. It is the fifth largest in China in terms of population, just behind Shanghai, Beijing, Tianjin, and Chongqing. As you explore Chengdu, you will notice it has a strong industrial base, with light and heavy manufacturing industries including aluminum smelting and chemical production plants. It also has an ancient textile industry which remains important and is fueled by cotton and wool milling and traditional silk brocade and satin manufacturing in the surrounding countryside." The teacher went on to distribute the language books for the new term.

At the end of her first week, Tami sat down to write a long letter to her parents.

I'm a little confused, a little numb, and a little overloaded with all the new sensations. I've walked through busy markets selling everything from clothes to raw meat on hooks, from light fixtures to vegetables and fruits, some identifiable, some not. The most popular sidewalk sale item is China's version of a Chia pet (called a grass dude), and the second most popular item seems to be elevator shoes— every possible style. Stores selling tapes and CDs blare their music out onto the streets, adding to the orchestra of construction music from the many building sites around. One should really say *destruction,* as most are still at the "big hole in the ground" stage. My first week in Chengdu had several adventures. First, there was the Great Banking Adventure (or "how to kill an entire day finding the right line in the right bank to cash a U.S. check and convince the bank staff to do it"), followed by the Great Phone Call Adventure (or "how to see half the city and kill a whole day trying to phone the U.S. using my MCI card"). Next was the Great Laundry Adventure (or, "how to kill a whole day . . ."' No, just kidding; we have semiautomatic washing machines in our dorm). Later in the week, I was the unwilling star of two minidramas set on the streets of Chengdu: "Foreigner buys a bicycle," followed quite closely by "Foreigner gets her new bicycle fixed." The rest of the cast consisted of a varying number of extras whose only line was "hello"!

Riding a bicycle in Chengdu was scary at first, but Tami soon adapted. Just to cycle to the building where her language classes took place, she had to weave her way through seemingly impenetrable masses of cars, scooters, bicycles, and pedestrians. When perched up high on her bicycle seat, she felt as though the sea of bobbing black heads engulfed her like an island, extending as far as her eye could see. *Being much taller than everyone else finally proves to be useful—at least for navigation on a bicycle!* she thought.

Foreigners were a rare sight in Chengdu, although the campus itself had quite a number of international students. The little kids in the streets thought Tami was the funniest-looking creature they'd ever seen. They stared at her, and she stared right back! They often pointed to her nose or played the game of wanting to grab for her "big" nose. In China, foreigners are sometimes called *da bize* (big nose). Many people shouted after her, *"Lao wai!"* or *"Wai guo ren!"*—terms used to describe a foreigner. Sometimes, Tami could not resist turning around and uttering back a response in Chinese, whereupon the Chinese would cry in embarrassment, "Oh, she understands Chinese! A *lao wai* that understands Chinese . . ."

Close to the university campus, the brown river meandered by. Here old men gathered, often whiling away the time by fishing with nets made out of bamboo. Nearby hawker stalls attracted students to eat "hot pot" (Chinese fondue) on the river's banks. Stretching along this part of the riverbank was a string of restaurants offering inexpensive but very tasty food. Food stalls opened early in the day and stayed open till the small hours of the night. Food was so inexpensive and abundant that eating out quickly became part of everyday life. Tami's favorite restaurant was called "Italian" for no apparent reason—they only served Chinese food. For dinner, she usually chose from a variety of stir fries, either in the university dining hall or at one of the nearby restaurants. For lunch, noodles were the clear favorite. She soon discovered that each restaurant had its own particular variety of spicy sauces. Various snacks were sold at little stands along the street. "Street food," she named them. One round bread-like item attracted her attention. Pointing at it, she asked for its name, trying to apply her Chinese in everyday life. "Guokui" was the answer.

Guokui (pronounced *Gwoe-quee*) was plain fried bread with either plum or meat sauce, served with onions and a variety of spices. Near Tami's dormitory, an older couple ran a booth where excellent guokui was made. She stopped by every few days for a quick (and very cheap) breakfast or lunch. It was fun to watch the couple preparing the food. He was especially fast. He made balls of dough, worked in some shortening, pulled and rolled them into strips, added the filling, rolled them up, smashed them down, and then rolled them into pieces. Then his wife took over. She fried the pieces on a flat wok until golden and then placed them underneath the wok in the little space around the charcoal fire to keep them warm until they were bought.

"The food here is so addictive!" Tami wrote in one of her letters. "If I do not get my guokui in the early morning, I will have breakfast in the dining hall, which means peanut-butter cookies and green beans! Although having said that, I can also have meat-filled dumplings, rice porridge, or eggs. But rice porridge is definitely not my favorite."

Culinary adventures were high on her priority list. Hesitant at first, with time Tami became more and more courageous in trying out all the local foods. Sichuan's food is known to be very hot. One of the most famous dishes in Sichuan is *mapo dofu*—a dish that is not merely hot, but numbing. The spices literally numb the tongue and lips. But Tami loved it! "She can even take spicier food than we do!" one Chinese student commented admiringly. Noticing that food was a real icebreaker into Chinese culture, it soon became her ambition to try every exotic dish in Chinese cuisine.

"Deep-fried watermelon anyone? How about some pig's tongue?" she wrote in her newsletter.

Welcome to "the great dining adventure," brought to you live (not really—count your blessings) from Sichuan. Yes, I have indeed sampled from both of the above "delicacies" . . . One night at a local restaurant, I thought I was ordering bamboo shoots—*zhu shun* ("zh" is pronounced like the "g" in large; "u" is pronounced "oo"). Between my tone mistakes and the differences between Mandarin and Sichuan dialect, the waiter thought I ordered pig lips! (Mandarin: *zhu chun*; Sichuan dialect: *zhu sun*). Pig's tongue was the closest thing available, so he served us some the next night again. Talk about having to eat your words! Watermelon is not meant to be cooked (no surprise here).

On weekends, Tami went exploring. Chengdu was a sprawling city of nearly ten million people. As she set out to discover it on her bicycle, she was struck by how rapidly the city was developing. Chengdu, already busting at the seams, was extending in all directions. Large avenues crisscrossed the city, and several ring roads circled it in ever-increasing circles. Tami passed many family planning posters prominently displayed, mounted on large billboards showing a Chinese leader welcoming the birth of a baby girl. The slogan underneath pronounced "China Needs Family Planning." At the foot of modern high-rise buildings were old-style markets with fresh meat hanging off large hooks, attracting clouds of flies.

With its long and colorful history, Chengdu had a number of Buddhist temples set in pretty parks. Some of these had been adapted to "tea drinking houses" where families spent the day eating, chatting, smoking, and snoozing.

Strolling through one park, Tami observed several small groups of people watching a delicately performed operation done by one person to another in the middle of a cluster. To her amazement, the person in the middle of the circle was having his ear cleaned! It wasn't an uncommon sight. The typical ear cleaner was a little old man armed with small spiky metal sticks and cotton swabs. These ear cleaners could often be seen wandering around, offering their services. She shuddered at the thought of a sudden head movement during the cleaning with those sharp pointed sticks.

Chengdu had already lost many of its historical walls and gates. Judging by the rate at which things were changing, it would soon lose even more. The need for more housing space, shopping malls, and infrastructure development was too great. Heading towards the center of town, Tami was struck by the towering statue of Chairman Mao, greeting her with his raised, outstretched hand. Her friends had told her that this was one of the few remaining large cities in China to display a statue of its Communist founder.

Mao's appreciation for the poetry of Du Fu meant that the cottage of the poet from the Tang Dynasty was now a national shrine. The cottage was situated in a beautiful park in the middle of Chengdu. When she entered the park, Tami noticed two different entrance fees—a high one for foreigners and a low fee for locals. *A bit unfair*, she thought. *I am only on a small student budget here.*

When she asked, she was told that the tiered entrance fees applied to the majority of parks and museums in China. Strolling through the grounds of the old-style Chinese cottage, Tami watched the people. Her eyes were caught by a couple. The man had just lit a cigarette, which was limply dangling from his lips. He was cradling a suitcase-sized hi-fi with his eyes closed, absorbed by the screeching thumping noise it emitted. The young woman next to him, presumably his girlfriend, was struggling with high-heeled, pointed, shiny shoes, probably newly purchased from one of the nearby glittering department stores. *Modernity and old traditions are all muddled here*, Tami thought.

☙

The constant gray weather started to weigh on Tami. As soon as the sun peeked through the heavy clouds, she would quickly pack up her books and skip language classes, trying to catch up on sun exposure! On one of the rare sunny days, she walked to the other side of campus where many of the Chinese students lived. As she walked between the densely packed dorms separated by winding dark pavements, she thought she could hear a great commotion ahead. As she turned the corner, she realized where the noise was coming from. She had entered a small square, walled off on all four sides by high brick walls and packed with people. Everyone was shouting at the tops of their voices as they bargained with one another over food and textile items for sale.

On a weekend when the sun seemed to stand a chance of peeking through the clouds, she decided to take a bicycle ride out of the city to visit a Buddhist temple. The traffic on this side of the city was crazy—dense with bicycles, people pushing heavy carts, others carrying ducks, chickens, or other livestock, trucks parked in the bicycle lane, and of course the steady traffic of water buffalo. As the bicycle lane was already pretty narrow, navigation was tough and demanded constant alertness. Suddenly, she noticed a large piece of wood on fire rolling around the bicycle lane. She quickly jerked her bicycle around, narrowly missing the hazard. Once past the outer Chengdu ring road, the traffic loosened up. For a while, there were still stores on either side of the road, but then they became farther and farther spaced.

It was nice to get out of the densely populated areas and venture into the countryside. The rice fields had all been plowed under for the winter, but there were still lots of green areas, growing leafy vegetables, and sometimes melons. Once she arrived at the village she was looking for, it was pretty easy to find the monastery. A whole street of shops selling candles, incense, fruit for offerings, snacks, and trinkets lined the way to the temple. After the twenty-mile bike ride, she was famished. She stopped for some spinach soup, spicy tofu, pickled radishes, eggplant, and a vegetable "sausage" at the corner restaurant.

In the temple, there were two golden Buddha-type figures, round pillows on the floor for prayer, and traditional scroll paintings on the walls. Some of them were pretty, she thought, but some were more like "Picasso meets the Qing Dynasty." Each temple had central idols, with artifacts and paintings along the sides. In each courtyard were huge metal basins for burning incense and candles. Monks wandered around the complex, guarding certain doors. One monk was fishing out the money that tourists and pilgrims had dropped into a basin. Although the majority of the pilgrims were older women, she was surprised to see young couples bowing down and praying, and children being told by their parents to kowtow to the various figures. Some of the figures were dreadful to look at, even frightening, and all were dead stone. It broke her heart to see people praying to them.

After she returned home, she sat down to pray about her desire to join a Sunday fellowship where she could worship and fellowship with other believers. Not long after, she was introduced to Linda and Gary and their children. They were Americans and had been in Chengdu for several years studying Chinese.

"Tami, why don't you join us on a Sunday morning? We are a small group of believers and meet at our student apartment on campus. You need to know, though, that you cannot bring any Chinese friends along, as that is against the law. Furthermore, our apartment is bugged, which means the Chinese authorities listen to what we say and sing. We don't mind that much, as we really have nothing to hide, but sometimes we do have to be sensitive about what to say and what not to say."

Tami soon found new friends and prayer partners in this small but close fellowship. It felt strange to know that they were regularly being spied upon. But then, the feeling of being followed was not altogether new to her. She had sometimes noticed that she had been followed in the streets, and once, she was sure her apartment had been searched.

In her daily readings, Tami was reading from the book of Isaiah. She was struck by how often the word "peace" was mentioned. "The peace mentioned in Isaiah has been a good reminder," she wrote home. "Here, there is so much that steals away peace. Many days, there are senseless annoyances, like having to argue for an hour to get two sheets for my bed or buying something and later finding out that they cheated me on the price. This is definitely not a city of peace—there is so much noise, frequent arguments, lots of anger. Tempers here are often as hot as the food! I'm learning to turn more and more to the inner peace from God that doesn't depend on circumstances. Don't get me wrong—I am actually enjoying living here and am feeling more and more at home all the time, but there are *some days* . . ."

Chapter 8

CHINESE:
THE ETERNAL LANGUAGE

Tami plunged into Chinese language learning with her characteristic energy and discipline. She had some experience in language learning. She had progressed well in German and had a good try with the African tribal language spoken at the hospital in Zambia. However, Chinese proved to be more of a challenge.

First, there was the Chinese script. Chinese characters constitute a system of writing so obviously different in appearance from Western scripts. They originated as pictographs—literally as pictures that were used to record the history and culture of the civilization. Though they were now highly stylized, with a bit of studying, Tami learned how they were related to their origins. The challenge was not only to read them, but also to write them. Chinese characters are constructed from basic units called "strokes," with three general categories of strokes: dots, lines, and hooks. Tami first practiced the basic strokes and then combined them to form characters, bearing in mind that the strokes had to be written in a proper sequence. There were rules such as "top before bottom" and "left before right." The next learning step was to vary the size of the strokes so the total effect would be a pleasing balance. She used paper ruled into squares of an inch on each side for practicing the art of writing.

As she and her classmates progressed, her teacher explained, "You have now all mastered the basics. The more advanced step is to learn compound characters. This is by far the largest category of Chinese characters. To understand the Chinese system of writing, there are some principles of formation. First is the pictographic principle. This can be illustrated by the well-known examples of a circle with a dot or horizontal line inside for 'sun' and a crescent with one or two lines for 'moon.'"

She drew on the blackboard. "Next is the compound indicative principle: meaning is derived by combining the meanings of constituent parts. An example is the combining of sun and moon to form the complex character indicative of the word *ming*—light. Another principle is the semantic-phonetic principle. This is an extension of the previous principle, in which the different homophonous words represented by the same character are differentiated by adding semantic elements to the common underlying phonetic element. The characters that result from this combination are referred to as phonetic compounds."

Tami's mind raced as she tried to absorb all this information.

"The teacher keeps commenting on how 'unattractive' my characters are. Guess I need even more practice," she wrote to her parents. "Aesthetics plays an exceedingly important role in Chinese writing, more so than in any other system of writing. Calligraphy has been elevated to an art form. In scrolls displayed as wall hangings, the characters are often executed in such a way that they resemble graphic designs rather than easily recognizable symbols."

It's a good thing the pinyin system has made Chinese so much easier to learn, she thought. The pinyin system is the Latinized version of Chinese, and it helps students learn pronunciation. At times, she wished the characters would all be abolished and replaced with pinyin. However, she knew that, given the esteem for the role of Chinese characters in the history and culture of the country, it would be almost sacrilegious to suggest such a thing. Had not Zheng Ziao, who lived 1104 to 1162, said, "The world is of the opinion that those who know Chinese characters are wise and worthy, whereas those who do not know characters are simple and stupid"? Tami smiled at the thought of quoting this to her friends and family back home.

Then there was the challenge of the tones. Chinese has four tones. These are not fixed notes on a scale, but relative sounds that vary according to the normal vocal range of individual speakers. Tone 1 is high level, Tone 2 high rising, Tone 3 low dipping, and Tone 4 high falling. A change in tone, despite keeping the same syllables, would mean a total change in meaning.

"Some days I feel like I'm making lots of progress, and other days I feel like an imbecile. I get very proud, especially when I understand the major part of a conversation, and then am immediately humbled when I miss something completely or someone doesn't understand my Chinese because I'm using the wrong tone or pronunciation," she wrote to her parents.

Her teachers at the university gave her the Chinese name of *Tian Ni*, a phonetic resemblance to Tami. The meaning of Tian Ni was "girl of the fields or countryside." Tami really liked it. She felt she *was* a girl of the countryside. She frequently wished she was there, as the smog of the city often depressed her.

"We had a test in our main Chinese class last week," she wrote home.

I did well on the grammar and vocabulary. The first time I read a passage, it was sort of like a game—figuring out the new characters piece by piece, guessing them from the context. After that, though, going back and memorizing the characters and practicing writing them is not nearly as much fun. I get called on frequently in class, partly because my Chinese name is a fairly common Chinese first name, so the teachers remember it easily. That's good, I suppose—it really makes me prepare for class. I still don't know how I'll be able to function entirely in Chinese in a hospital next year. Too early to worry about that, I know . . .

I had another "dining adventure" (after all these banking, phone call, and laundry adventures). I tried hot pot with a Chinese friend. We ordered chicken feet and something or another, which she assured me were a form of mushrooms (and they were). But I misunderstood what she was saying on another item. I thought it was also some kind of mushroom or vegetable and was startled, to say the least, when they brought small pig brains to our table. She convinced me to go ahead and try them. Not bad—a little slimy, and with a taste vaguely reminiscent of the smell in the anatomy lab, unless that was my imagination—but not something I'm dying to have again.

For lunch, she frequently met up with Linda, her American friend living in the same university compound.

"Tami, you appear discouraged today," Linda said one day.

"Yeah," Tami sighed. "I'm so discouraged with my slow progress in Chinese."

"Slow progress? Tami, you are way ahead of all of us! Isn't it enough that you started in a higher class because you'd already studied Chinese back in the U.S.? And then they moved you from Level 2 to Level 3 because of your amazing progress. It took me three years to get to Level 3!"

Tami sighed again, poking at her food. "It's just that I can't wait to get back into medical work. Any difficulties in language learning mean a delay in getting out there." And then she added, "My main frustration is that the locals here don't speak the Mandarin we're studying in class."

"Yes, the Sichuan dialect is pretty heavy here. It makes practicing really difficult," Linda agreed.

"Sometimes whole words are different. Or the same word has a different tone. It's really confusing. The other day, I was at the local market. When I used the standard Chinese word for *small child*, people were looking at me funny—some were laughing at me, I know it. Come to find out later that in Sichuanese, the word means *small shoe!*"

Linda laughed. "My only comfort is that Chinese words are all mono-syllabic. The grammar is pretty straightforward too—no conjugating or declension."

"But Linda, don't you feel like you're learning three languages at the same time? There's a sound, tone, and character to remember for every word!"

"True. God obviously wants to teach us patience, as Mandarin takes three times longer to learn than any other language!" They both laughed.

When they finished their lunch, Tami said, "I feel a lot better. You've really encouraged me. Thanks, Linda. Would you like to have regular prayer time together?" And they did.

With time, Tami's memory retained more and more of the characters. But the Chinese classes became harder and harder too.

"Trivia quiz: what is a camlet? What is a junket? The last few lessons of my Chinese book have been pieces of eighteenth- and early twentieth-century literature, and these are some of the words I found on the English side of the dictionary when I looked up the Chinese words in my dictionary!" Tami wrote to her friends. "Well, if you really want to know what *junket* means, the French column in the vocabulary list translates *junket* as *butter*. Recently, I found the same character in my newspaper textbook and realized that in Chinese, Kentucky Fried Chicken is described as tender on the inside, junket on the outside. My class teacher also brought in some cookies to demonstrate the flaky/crispy texture which he described as junket. I suppose the connection with butter or this flaky/crispy idea is how the dictionary got *shortbread* as an additional explanation for the word." Tami jokingly added, "Next time you want any more clear, erudite explanations of Chinese words, let me know."

Tami found that the classes on classic Chinese literature were not really helpful for everyday Chinese. So after one really tough week, bolstered by advice and prayers, she gingerly approached her teacher. This teacher had frequently scolded students for missing even a day of class. Tami carefully explained her dilemma—many of the words they learned during this class were impractical for her future use in medicine. To her surprise, the teacher responded positively. She suggested that Tami should stop attending class in classical Chinese. Tami was joyous; her prayers had been answered. Instead of the classical Chinese classes, she hired a tutor to help her study Chinese medical terminology.

Conversations with her roommate, Naara, were slowly getting more meaningful, mostly because they were both improving in Chinese. Once when Tami had a stain on her dress, Naara showed her a little trick for removing it using her toothbrush. This caused Tami to write in her newsletter that month, "And now, what you've been waiting for: The first edition of 'Household Hints from Outer Mongolia.' To get stains out of clothes, rub stain remover into the cloth with an old toothbrush."

The weather in Chengdu was turning to fall. "I haven't figured out the fall weather here yet," she wrote at the end of one of her newsletters. "One day it's rainy and cold, so I pull out the sweaters and the poncho, and then it gets warm and sunny and I'm back in shorts. Some days I guess wrong, or the weather changes, so I end up changing clothes several times."

Tami also noticed the peculiarities of the Communist public system. In the middle of fall, the mayor of Chengdu suddenly ordered a period of "clean-o-mania" in preparation for an inspection from Beijing. "We were told the mayor wants Chengdu to be the cleanest city in China, at least when the inspectors are here," she wrote. "In the process, they kicked out all the sidewalk merchants, plus they made all the Chinese people leave their jobs for half a day or so to help sweep the streets (in high heels or business suits, no less). As much as I hate to admit it, the city is cleaner, but I'd gotten used to buying from certain vendors who are suddenly gone."

At the beginning of many a conversation with locals, the question, "What do you like about our country?" was often asked. "Food!" was always a good answer!

"Why did you come to China?" was another frequent conversation starter, or if the person was already acquainted with Tami, "You are a doctor and could make so much more money in the U.S. Why are you here?"

"Because I love China," Tami would answer simply.

"Could you teach me English?" Many Chinese students on campus and in the city wanted to practice their English. Tami loved to teach and did so often. She started teaching English at the medical school to a group of local nurses and doctors. At times, however, the demands for English teaching were so overwhelming that Tami pretended to be a German speaker. She could converse well in German, as she had spent some time studying it in Germany during her high school years. She could even put on a Southern German accent.

⤳

"Could you please share about Christmas?"

Christmas attracted a lot of attention. One of the language teachers had a friend who ran a private school for eight- to eleven-year-olds. Tami had a handmade stocking with a nativity scene. With the help of a dictionary, the New Testament, and a few corrections from her language tutor, she put a presentation together all in Chinese. She told the kids about Jesus' birth and the visits by the shepherds and wise men. Of course, they also wanted to know about Santa Claus, traditional foods, and the Christmas tree.

It was her first Christmas far from home, in a totally different culture. Her mother had sent her a parcel that included homemade marzipan cookies filled with raspberries, but to her disappointment, the parcel never arrived. She felt so homesick. As Christmas was not a public holiday in China, language classes went on right until Christmas Day and restarted the very next day. But several parties with her close friends from the fellowship over the long weekend, plus lots of eating out, made up for it—at least a little.

Tami did not usually visit the Three-Self Church in Chengdu. But as it was Christmas, she decided to do so. To her surprise, many Chinese turned up for the Christmas service. People literally crammed into the church. Not everyone fit into the building, and the people outside were squashing against the windows to get a glimpse of what was going on during the Christmas service. Because the preaching was all done in heavy Sichuan dialect, she found it hard to follow the sermon. But she delighted in studying the Chinese faces. A child was crying; another had a dirty face with a runny nose. Some old women were falling asleep. There were so many old people here, and also small children.

But where are those between twenty and forty years old? she wondered. Were they the people who thought the Christian faith was for the uneducated, the old, the poor? How could she convince them that the God of the Bible was the true living God who offers fulfillment, peace, and joy to everyone?

On Christmas morning, she joined the twelve singles and families who usually met on Sunday mornings at Linda and Gary's home. Over the past months, they had become a second family to her. Gary delivered the message that Christmas Sunday. It was a very thoughtful and challenging sermon.

I don't get such meaningful preaching that often in the United States, she thought. But here, in an unexpected corner of the world, among a small group of committed Christians who had all given their lives fully to the Lord, she learned so much more about the true meaning of Christmas. The songs did not have the sophisticated accompaniment she was used to from the States, but everyone sang with deep conviction. "I have to say that this Christmas, my first Christmas in China, was one of the best Christmases ever," she confessed to her journal.

Chapter 9

CULTURE SHOCK

The new year started roughly as winter descended on Chengdu. Frequent power cuts meant that Tami could not heat her room, and the classroom was also often left unheated. The cold was pervasive, and Tami, together with the other students, had to resort to constantly wearing winter jackets, gloves, and hats during class, since the teachers preferred to keep the windows wide open.

Why keep the windows open in the middle of winter? Tami wondered. *It's some kind of fresh air fetish. Crazy! This is one thing I will never get used to here!*

The cold was damp, carried around by the dense fog that clung to the buildings outside. Sometimes, the game with electricity seemed like a no-win situation. Turning on the heaters when the electricity was working frequently caused the electricity to cut out again. If this happened at night, one could watch the lights in the surrounding blocks go off all together as whole sections of the city descended into muffled, cold darkness.

The noise among the foreign students in the dormitory was often nerve-racking. Wild parties kept Tami awake at night. Angry notices on the dormitory notice boards soon triggered cultural tensions between some of the Korean and American students. Fighting an upper respiratory infection, Tami had to cram for her language exams. The combination of the Christmas distractions, studying irrelevant material for the exams, and the noise and atmosphere in the dormitory on top of her infection resulted in a bad exam outcome.

"Never have I failed so miserably on an exam in my whole life!" Tami cried out to Linda. "It is so humiliating!"

Linda tried to console her. But Tami was really discouraged.

"Just to add to that, Linda, some major prayer concerns have not been answered. Naara had some financial difficulties, and she had to move to another university that charges lower fees. She left the dorm before I was able to effectively share my faith with her, and that hurts. The friend from the medical university to whom I taught English some time ago initially showed some interest in my faith—but her interest has completely dried up. I feel so useless just studying the language. My only medical work so far was for this drunken American student who vomited in the dormitory and called out for a doctor at two in the morning."

"Tami, there is a time of preparation, and a time for ministry. There are times when we sow the seed, but it is scattered among thorns. There will be a time when the seed will grow."

Tami was pensive. "I guess I have still many lessons to learn," she sighed.

That semester, there were further ups and downs. Although she was developing the Chinese language skills she had been praying for, real-life irritants never went away. Often there were phone problems, schedule changes, and surprise dorm hygiene inspections that disrupted planning and everyday life. Particularly bitter was the day when Naara had to leave Chengdu. She had to return to Mongolia because of ever-increasing financial problems.

"I will miss you, my friend." Tami hugged her at the airport. "Will you continue with the habit that we developed together?"

"You mean reading the Bible? Okay, I promise."

They waved good-bye, and Naara vanished behind the checkpoint. Tami wiped away a tear and silently prayed for her while trying to catch a cab to return to the city.

"How are you, Tami?" Linda asked when she returned. The American woman had become her best friend, and Tami was more glad to see her than she could say.

"Linda, it was so hard to see Naara leave. And there have been so many other disappointments lately. It's just such a roller coaster. One day, I feel high because I think I've arrived at the place God wants me to be. The next day, I'm low because nothing is turning out as I'd expected."

"Welcome to the world of culture shock, Tami," Linda said simply. After more than three years in Chengdu, she knew what it was all about.

"Yeah, that's it," Tami agreed. "I guess I've got all the signs and symptoms!" Tami looked forlorn for a while, but quickly her usual sense of humor returned.

"Culture shock? I can tell you a story of *real* culture shock! The other day, I went to a restaurant and found something that was listed on the English menu as 'beehive.' Out of curiosity, I ordered it. Well, it turned out to be not the hive, but the residents—deep-fried bees! Once I got past all those little legs and eyes everywhere, the taste wasn't so bad! I decided that deep-fried bees taste like deep-fried anything. Next time I'll bring ketchup!"

They both laughed heartily.

"Tami, would you like to come by our apartment for dinner? Afterward we can watch some movies I brought back with me after our last visit to the U.S."

"Linda, I'd love to! It's been ages since I watched an American movie! I'll bring along some chocolate. Actually, it's Naara's chocolate."

"Can't wait to hear that story," Linda replied.

"I'll tell it to you. Tonight. See you then, Linda."

They got on their bicycles and headed for language classes. "I'm on my way first to the bicycle repair stand at the corner of the street," Tami said just before they parted ways. "The guy there already knows me really well—I'm there almost every other week with something that falls or rusts off my bicycle. This time it's the basket. Let's see which other parts will be overwhelmed by gravity in the future!" Laughing, they waved and departed.

That evening at Gary and Linda's home, they enjoyed an American movie after dinner. They chatted and laughed while eating chips and cookies and Naara's chocolate.

"So what's the story of Naara's chocolate?" Linda reminded Tami.

"Well, Naara returned to Mongolia for the Chinese New Year break, and she brought these chocolates from Mongolia back with her—so this is our first Mongolian chocolate experience! She also brought me some beautiful traditional Mongolian clothes, a blue silk robe handmade by her great aunt. It meant a lot to me. When I was trying it on, she read a traditional poem to me. So now I'm apparently an adopted Mongolian." Tami chuckled at the thought of it.

"See," Linda added. "Your time with Naara was not for nothing."

"I guess you're right. We always need to count our blessings." Her eyes sparkled. "By the way, Naara also brought some less-than-delicious Mongolian snacks. Something like peanut butter, but made with fermented goat's milk. She recommends we put it in coffee or on crackers."

They both shuddered at the thought. "I'll tell you some other stories of culture shock. This time it's culture shock within the *foreign* community." Tami shifted on the couch, happily in the mood for stories. "To live with so many different nationalities in one dorm can be really amusing. We are divided by a common language," Tami explained jokingly. "For example, the British say, 'After tea, I shall get my fringe cut.' You know what that means? 'I'll get my bangs trimmed after supper.' And I'm often amazed at what people eat for breakfast—from noodles to kimchi to Marmite."

"Marmite?"

"Marmite is this awful stuff from Britain that you spread on toast. It's black and smells worse than any food I've so far encountered in China. And then there is this weird cereal the British fellow students prefer to eat for breakfast. 'Wheatabix,' they call it. And just imagine—it gets soggy if milk is even in the same room."

Linda laughed—Tami was a great storyteller.

"You know what Australians call an infant car seat? A 'baby capsule.' And 'baby grinder' is the Swiss word for those manual grinders to mash table food for infants. I keep begging the Swiss couple not to put their baby in there!"

It was a wonderfully relaxing evening. On her way home to the dorm, Tami realized it had been helpful to immerse herself in her own American culture to ease her culture shock. What if she did it regularly? That night, she sat down in her little flat and jotted down a letter to her parents. "Please send me the bestseller list periodically, Mom . . . What about the latest movies? . . . I miss those marzipan and Italian almond cookies . . . Dad, could you send me the latest David Meece CD? Is there anything new from Amy Grant apart from *House of Love*? Could you please send me something other than *Heaven in the Real World* by Steven C. Chapman?"

The following months continued to be an emotional roller coaster, with the ups and downs of adapting to a new life in China. Because Tami was able to take more private tutoring during the Chinese New Year break, the language school decided to allow her to skip another semester. But being upgraded to a higher level also had its disadvantages: it meant increased class hours and much more preparation time. Tami was struggling to prioritize her time between studies, local and foreign friends, patients, tutors, errands, exercise, and personal time. By now, word had gone around that Tami was a doctor. Foreign students and expat families called upon her at any time of the day and night with their minor—and sometimes quite serious—medical problems. There were many demands. Tami was starting to feel exhausted.

"I do my house calls on my bicycle," she told her parents. "I really get around Chengdu a lot these days."

Three new MSI team members joined her in Chengdu. Tami's new task was to initiate them to life in Chengdu. "It is kind of playing mother hen to the newcomers," she described in a letter.

But it is also great fun taking them around Chengdu and rediscovering the city through three pairs of new eyes. I notice afresh the things that have become routine to me. For example, people riding by with live fish (swimming in a bag of water) in their bicycle baskets. Or the way things are sold in Chengdu. We cycled around for hours to find some rope for clotheslines, until we finally found the *one* street where *all* the stores sell it. They also have entire streets where they sell only bicycles or only kitchenware or only clothes. I *love* the street where they only sell Chinese dumplings. Most streets advertise their wares by making sounds. The street that sells hardware such as pots and pans makes sure that everyone knows their product by banging them together. The distinctive sound communicates what the product is. A lot of noise, but now even I can now identify the products by sound alone!

There was an official kite-flying holiday coming up, so everyone was soon out practicing and enjoying the March winds and breezes. The colorful kites were spread out on the sidewalks for sale, and were often seen held by kids riding on the backs of their parents' bicycles and decorating the sky (and the trees and telephone wires). Tami enjoyed pointing out the various peculiarities of the city. The two new Americans were particularly intrigued by the markets. In narrow rows, whole lambs or pigs were hanging upside down, sometimes halved, and covered with flies. When her American friends emerged from the markets with pale green faces, Tami realized how much she had already gotten used to China. In fact, she noticed how much she really liked the atmosphere of the old Chinese markets. There was so much happening, so many smells to sample— noises, colors, life everywhere.

The annual lantern festival was soon to take place. Huge mobile dragons and mermaids were displayed in the lake in the center of the park. The boats were covered with colorful lights, as were the amusement-park rides which ranged from Buddhas to animals to Snow White and the Seven Dwarves. Loud music blared from public loudspeakers, each playing its own music, resulting in a cacophony of bright sounds. People were performing songs, dances, and skits. Close by, there was an area of fairly realistic animated dinosaur figures. One set of huge dragon and phoenix figures glowing with lights was decorated with an incredible number of small white silkworm shells. Tami explained and interpreted to her friends as she introduced Chengdu to them. Although she had been in Chengdu for less than a year, it seemed like she was already an insider.

Chapter 10

WHAT GOD
HATH WROUGHT

Tami had been doing intense language studies for more than nine months when Dr. Taylor asked her to fly to Hong Kong. He had arranged for the team to come together for a week at the MSI office to discuss the plans for the next year. Sharon and Tomoko were also there. Dr. Ted Lankester and his wife Joy had flown in from the UK especially for the occasion. Joy was the youngest daughter of Dr. Broomhall and had been born in Zhaojue, the village in the Great Cold Mountains of Sichuan Province. They had recently visited Zhaojue to assess the situation and provide consultancy to MSI. Tami was fascinated by the stories they had to tell.

"I accompanied my father on all his recent trips to China," Joy started off. "We were all so excited to return to the place my father loved so much. It was 1988, and my first chance to visit the place where I was born. Lots of things have changed, of course, but some older people still even remembered us! Some showed us pictures of old times. We planned our next trip to Zhaojue in 1991. Unfortunately, my father suffered a stroke in March 1991, which resulted in paralysis down his right side and loss of speech. Not wanting to give up, he was very disciplined in physiotherapy and speech therapy. He made a remarkable recovery, regaining his speech in part, and he joined the trip in a wheelchair in June 1991. It was an incredible sight! An old white man in a wheelchair in the mountains of China's inland! Again, we were given permits without difficulty. We were driven to Zhaojue in a minibus provided by the hospital. As a welcome, a huge bonfire was lit in our honor in the grounds of the hospital."

Joy took a deep breath. "My father's prayer had always been that the work among the Yi would continue. God only granted him three years among the Yi.

At times, he wondered why. His background—having been born and brought up in China, with a deeply-rooted love of the country, its sights, sounds, and fascinating people—left little doubt that he should return eventually. He waited more than thirty years. To be so welcomed in Zhaojue meant a lot to him, as you can imagine. The bonfire that night was the highlight of his life. I would like to read some passages of his book to you."

And then Joy read, "The way in which God has directed the details of my life is a constant source of amazement to me; at times when it has seemed that preparation for the mission field was a great mistake. He has given such firm conviction that He has no other purpose in view, that the statement, 'Ye are not your own, for you are bought with a price' has been clearly demonstrated in my own experience."

Joy was in deep thought for a while. Then she continued, "God's ways are indeed beyond our human understanding. During his second trip, when he was in his late seventies, my father met Dr. and Mrs. Taylor and their son Jamie in Xichang. God was bringing together the Broomhall and the Taylor families again, and this in the middle of China. To understand the immense historical and spiritual significance of this, we need to dig deeper into the early history of the China Inland Mission.

"The China Inland Mission was founded by Hudson Taylor in 1865, as you probably all know. The Broomhall and Taylor families had enjoyed close connections ever since the early history of the China Inland Mission. Jim Broomhall's grandfather, Benjamin Broomhall, married the sister of Hudson Taylor, Amelia. Benjamin and Amelia Broomhall supported Hudson Taylor from their home base in England and mobilized hundreds of missionaries for China. Five of their children became missionaries to China. One of them was Dr. Benjamin Broomhall Jr., my grandfather. He lived in China for almost thirty years of medical service. During this time, my father was born. He also took up medicine and returned to China for lifelong service sometime in the 1930s, lived in Zhaojue in the late '40s, but had to leave in the early '50s. To see how God led these two families together again in the '80s is indeed a testimony of how our Heavenly Father leads."

"How God hath wrought," Dr. Taylor added, quoting a phrase from Broomhall's writings.

Joy continued the story. "After his second trip to China, my father's health was failing rapidly. Dr. Taylor was keen to let him know that the memorandum between MSI and the Chinese officials had been signed. When he heard the good news and knew that his life's work had not been in vain, his face was transformed by a sense of joy and peace. God had answered his prayers. The work in Zhaojue would continue. He died peacefully on that very evening."

Joy looked at the small team. With tears welling up, she said, "And now indeed it looks like my father's work will continue. It will continue through you." She smiled. "You know, my father prayed for men to work alongside him in the early years in Zhaojue. But God sent him two women, Joan Wales and Ruth Dixon. Now, God is sending again a team of women to Zhaojue."

Dr. Taylor added, "Ruth has since died, but Joan is still alive and now in her late seventies. Without any doubt, you will meet her one day. She will try everything to get back to Zhaojue! She is a woman of extraordinary energy and love for the Yi."

Tami thought how much she would love to meet Joan Wales and listen to some of the firsthand stories from Zhaojue. Thoughts of her own little problems with culture shock crossed her mind. How they paled against the big picture!

Ted shared his vision for community health work in Zhaojue. He and Joy had visited Zhaojue not too long ago with the purpose of consulting with MSI as to the next best steps. Tami liked Ted's down-to-earth approach.

"I was struck by the beautiful scenery on the windy road up to the village. We often stopped to look at the flowers. We even discovered edelweiss! Zhaojue is a quaint Yi town, surrounded by many small Yi villages. There is a hospital and a good number of medical doctors and nurses. The problem is not so much the lack of medical care, but that the poor Yi patients cannot afford it. The main focus should be on raising the economic level."

Dr. Ted Lankester's extensive experience included many years of community health work in India, and he taught the team how to prepare for community-based health programs. The challenge was to get communities involved. "Only if communities participate, identifying their own problems and finding solutions for them, will there be sustainable development," he explained.

At the end of the week's training and team formation exercises, Dr. Taylor announced, "MSI has decided to take up Dr. Lankester's suggestion of helping to alleviate some of the immense poverty among the Yi. So we have come up with a strategy. A sheep farming expert from New Zealand—Peter Feickert, who has previously visited Zhaojue—has come up with the idea of raising sheep among the Yi in an effort to raise their economic standards. Well, in response to his idea, MSI has purchased two hundred and ten sheep, and we will be donating them to a group of Yi in May. I would like to invite you to join our team to witness the first sheep donation."

Chapter 11

SHEEP AND A PIG'S HEAD

Down the slope came hundreds of sheep, herded by the sheep-rearing expert Peter Feickert from New Zealand. Everyone stood up to see what was happening. Cameras clicked. Ten Yi farmers stood to attention with their shepherd's rods held high, solemn but beaming. They were the proud owners of the first MSI sheep delivered to a small village just outside of Zhaojue. Dignitaries from the provincial government, prefecture, county, and district all watched the drama unfolding with excitement, together with twenty-six MSI team members. The sheep, bleating as they ambled in, milled around the official courtyard looking bewildered, but no doubt impressed, by the amount of attention given to them.

Peter took out the shearing equipment. Quick as lightening he had a kicking sheep on its back, and he sheared it in three minutes flat, much to the joy and amazement of the onlookers and the embarrassment of the now-naked and bleating sheep.

As she watched the scene unfolding, Tami thought how each person at the ceremony would take away a different message. To the Yi farmers, this was a business opportunity: each farmer was given twenty ewes and one ram to start a flock to provide for wool and a chance to raise his family from poverty level. To the officials, it was a confirmation that MSI was serious about its commitment to help in the economic recovery of the town. To the government of Sichuan, MSI had come in the "spirit of Christ," in the spirit of sacrifice and involvement. Money, the officials said, was helpful, but more important than that was the spirit brought to Sichuan in that skilled MSI personnel were willing to come on their own expenses and time to work side-by-side with the people of Sichuan. To Tami, the biblical parallels were clear: the Lord, in the parable of the hundred sheep, had revealed His passion as a shepherd by investing so much to find the one lost sheep.

Tami was part of the team of more than twenty physicians, administrators, nurses, and sheep-rearing experts who descended upon the Yi autonomous region in the Great Cold Mountains that May in 1996. Most of the team came from Singapore, Hong Kong, and the United States, and the sheep experts were from New Zealand. Tami quipped, "At the end of the trip, I'm sure the local officials will think that the sheep are easier to herd than we were!"

It was the first time Tami saw where Dr. Broomhall had lived and worked forty years ago. She was fascinated by the Yi people, and there was much mutual staring. They stared at Tami's tall stature, her blue eyes and brown hair; and she stared back at their beautiful faces weathered by the sun and wind, often marked by deep furrows from years of hard toil and exposure to the harsh elements of nature. It was obvious that they were poor, poorer than most of the local Han Chinese. Their clothes were well worn, covered in patches, and torn. Shoes showed gaping holes, exposing thick rough socks or sometimes even the bare flesh of the feet. The Yi stood out from the Han Chinese with their dark skin, taller stature, and rounder and larger eyes together with their prominent noses. Tami could not but help notice that the Yi were a proud people.

The team visited the local hospital, finding it in a sad and dilapidated state. There were no toilets in the hospital, and patients had to either venture downstairs to the courtyard to the outhouse or use bedpans. Plaster fell from the bare walls, and there was no heating. On a more critical note, medical equipment was missing or out of date and in poor condition.

While donating sheep was the main purpose of the team's visit, they were also exploring to establish whether Tami and her teammates could work there in the near future. Tami felt like Dr. Broomhall forty years ago, visiting the towns and hospitals and meeting with the officials. Dr. Taylor, Dr. Reggie Tsang, Tami, and others presented proposals to the Chinese officials discussing how the hospital could be improved, what training would be needed, and what MSI could contribute. Dr. Taylor suggested that MSI place its first medical team. The officials welcomed this idea, and together they continued to discuss the details of moving the first MSI long-term team to the area. One important matter to be sorted out was that of Tami's license as a medical doctor.

"We had meeting after meeting," Tami wrote. "It was most encouraging to hear some of the Yi and Chinese officials speak warmly about Dr. Broomhall, and this helped in the discussion of the plans for the first MSI long-term team. As the speeches got longer, speakers' Sichuan accents and Yi accents got thicker, and my brain got more and more tired, I understood less and less. For the last hour, I was dying for a break—like the kid in the Far Side cartoon who asks his teacher 'Can I be excused? My brain is full.'"

Dinner was in traditional Yi style. Tami, as the future team leader, was seated at the head table next to Dr. Taylor. The feast was artistically spread out before them. Their hosts used raw vegetables, cherries, and small pieces of meat to create colorful dainty borders on the plates and to make various shapes. A fish was made of cucumber slices and a bird of radish slices. They had good-sized crabs served with sesame oil and garlic dip. Soup was served with small chunks of meat still on the bones floating on the broth. The Canadian short-termer next to her said it was pigeon soup. When Tami asked her how she knew, she whispered, "Because I have the pigeon head in my bowl! Whenever I tried to pass it on, they passed it back to me." Even though the waitresses changed their bowls and plates every few minutes and cleared bones, crab shells, and other debris, they left the Canadian's pigeon head behind until she hid it really well under a pile of other leftovers.

Another huge plate brimming with food was set in front of Tami and Dr. Taylor. Tami could not believe her eyes. As honored guests, they had been presented with half a pig's head! Yes, a pig's head, with everything still on it—eyes, ears, skin, hair, fat. Tami wondered how it would look if the half was turned around, revealing the insides of the head. Half a tongue, half a brain? After everyone marveled at the pig's head, it was taken away—and then, to Tami's shock, returned to the table in smaller portions, basically chunks of pork with skin and hair and all. Fortunately, Dr. Taylor leaned over to Tami and told her in a low voice that it was perfectly polite to pull the skin, hair, and fat off the pork and return it to the pot for someone who appreciated it more! And that was exactly what Tami did. She liked the buckwheat cakes, the staple food of the Yi. Quite bland and filling, but definitely safe! With their hands, the guests broke off the buckwheat cake and dipped pieces into the sour vegetable soup which Tami thought tasted like chicken or pork stock with various greens and pickled vegetables.

After dinner, the Chinese and Yi officials invited the international team to sing. The Chinese sang first. Then it was the turn of the MSI team. Tami joined in as they sang the 1 Corinthians 13 Love Song in Chinese. After each team had taken several turns singing, the MSI team started to sing "He lives! He lives!" and Tami saw that several of the Chinese officials joined in the singing. This is what she had so much wished for! She blinked away joyful tears, moved and almost in disbelief that she was part of this historic exchange!

One night they were treated to a traditional Yi dance around a big bonfire in the hospital compound of Zhaojue. Tami wrote,

> Despite the fact that I always seemed to be on the wrong foot or heading the wrong way—the rhythm of their music is so different from anything Western—I still had a blast. A big handicap is that the women wear such long skirts that one cannot see their feet. In contrast, I was wearing pants and—formerly white—running shoes, so my footwork mistakes were glaringly obvious! Some of the men wore skirt-like wraps, too, but if I could stand near one in pants and watch his feet, that helped. At one point, I broke out of the semicircle to take pictures and rejoined at a different point so that I would be stepping on other Yi people's feet for a change. Between now and my time until I move to Zhaojue, I need some private lessons—or a long skirt like theirs to hide all the mistakes my feet make! The pearls hanging from the girls' headdresses and the gold-colored threads embroidered into their vests sparkled in the firelight, and their patient smiles warmed my heart. I couldn't help hoping that someday we'll be dancing like that in heaven, with Yi brothers and sisters by our sides.

At the end of the two-week trip, the plans for the rest of the year had become clearer. An understanding had been reached between the MSI leadership and the health authorities. The exact details were still somewhat fluid, but several important facts had been established: The Xichang authorities welcomed a long-term cooperation with MSI focused on raising the medical standards of the region. A medical team would be placed in Xichang in the second half of the year. And Tami would be part of this pioneer group. With time, the medical work could extend into the poorer surrounding villages where the majority of inhabitants were native Yi people.

Tami returned to Chengdu with a quote from Charles Dickens: "It was the best of times, it was the worst of times." The best of times: fellowship with like-minded believers, seeing the place she would soon move to and work. The worst of times: being brought face to face with her own inadequacies. In a letter she shared with her friends, she wrote, "I had trouble adjusting to the living conditions. I struggled to understand the Sichuan dialect. I did not feel like I was being an effective team leader, especially when I was tired, sick, and crabby. Through His Word, God graciously reminded me that He alone is my source of confidence and competence (2 Cor. 3:5–6; He has made us competent as ministers of the new covenant)."

Returning to Chengdu made her realize what a sophisticated city it was in comparison to Zhaojue and Xichang. There were only a couple of months left till the move to Xichang, and Tami tried to use every minute to cram in as much language study as she could. One thing really worried her: her medical license had not yet come through. Many foreign doctors had tried in vain to get such a license, and getting one would be close to a miracle. She made it her daily prayer item. But even as she waited for an answer, the plans to move to Xichang were firming up rapidly.

In June 1996, the day arrived for her to pack all her things and move to Xichang.

"We will miss you here in Chengdu when you are out there in your Yi land," Linda said, smiling though her eyes were sad too. Linda and Gary had accompanied her to the Chengdu airport.

"I will miss you too, Linda! All your support, our prayer times together, our fun."

"To me, it appears that you're living life on fast-forward, Tami," Linda joked. "One year of language study in Chengdu, and now you are off to greater pastures."

"I will always remember how you said there was a time for everything," Tami responded. "A time for studying, a time for service. I pray that the next phase will indeed be more a time of service."

Linda smiled and paraphrased words from Isaiah 55: "God's word is like the rain that comes down and waters the earth, making it bud and flourish, so that it yields seed for the sower and bread for the eater . . . it will not return empty but will accomplish what God desires and achieve the purpose for which He sent it."

Chapter 12

THE GATEWAY CITY

As the small old Russian airplane rumbled through the air from Chengdu to Xichang, Tami reflected over the past year—but her thoughts soon moved to the time ahead. She was both apprehensive and excited. God was bringing her closer to her destiny. Although her time of preparation and language acquisition was not yet over, she had completed the first stage and could now begin her medical work. She had graduated from "language student" to "foreign expert."

The short-term plan was for the team to live in Xichang and commute from there to Zhaojue and other Yi villages to do community health projects. Perched on a plateau at sixteen hundred meters at the base of the Great Cold Mountains, Xichang was the ideal gateway to the Yi Autonomous Region and Zhaojue. Tami also planned to work in the hospital in Xichang in order to understand the Chinese medical system better and learn more medical Chinese terms. The long-term plan, however, was to one day move to Zhaojue.

She looked to her side where Sharon, her new teammate, was sitting. She was a nurse and had grown up in a poor family in rural Taiwan. God had clearly shown her that she should go and serve in China. Her fluency in Mandarin was a great asset; her energy and delightful smile were contagious. Tami was particularly happy about the fact that Sharon shared her passion for running and mountain hiking.

The Tami-Sharon pair was an intriguing sight, with Tami more than a head taller than Sharon. Tomoko, a Japanese nurse, would join the two of them later. These three would form the first long-term MSI team. Two English teachers, a surgeon, and an administrator had also joined the international team moving to Xichang that summer, as short-termers. Their plans were to stay for several months before returning home. Tami was the designated team leader.

"Language-wise I'm at the bottom of the totem pole," she chuckled. "It is a humbling experience, and I will constantly need to rely on God's wisdom and that of our many leaders and consultants."

As the plane descended to the "mile-high" city of Xichang, the western foothills stood out against the clear blue sky. Red soil peeked out from between the trees on the lower slopes, and dark green pines clothed the upper ridges. Bright sun sparkled on the snow of the higher rocky peaks just visible beyond the first range. *It feels as if I am returning home to Colorado.* Quietly, Tami thanked God for the confirmation in her heart that this was the place she was meant to be. She was filled with peace and joy.

The officials and directors from the Xichang Health Bureau and 2nd Hospital warmly welcomed Tami and her team. Waiting buses drove them along a flat, stretched-out valley with mountains on each side. The valley, checkered with lush green fields and rice paddies, was dotted with water buffalo, heavily-laden peasants, and adobe houses with tiled, curved roofs. As they traveled along the narrow, tree-lined road, the small rambling Chinese shop houses merged closer and closer as they approached the city.

Xichang was a city of half a million people, surrounded by mountain lakes, hot spring waterfalls, and beautiful valleys. The city was rapidly modernizing. High-rise buildings were mushrooming; new businesses sprouting. The main road through town was busy—motorbikes, cars, buses, and loud diesel trucks emitting huge plumes of black exhaust fought for space in the narrow city center lanes. Bicycles and horse carts shared the side lanes, and vendors and pedestrians jostled along the crowded sidewalk. Here and there, Yi people, dressed in their traditional colorful vests, capes, and scarves, sat sprinkled along the sidewalks eating, chatting, and smoking. Along the main road, past a wide bridge over a mostly dry river, was a huge statue of a Yi man and a Communist soldier standing arm in arm and smiling. Tami was reminded that this was still Communist China.

༄

"Dr. Tian Ni, could you please give a speech at the hospital meeting?"

It is one thing to have mastered conversational Mandarin, but another to give a formal speech in Mandarin! Over the next few days, Tami painstakingly prepared every single word with Sharon patiently helping her. Great care had to be taken to use the correct tones. For example, the word *ma* can take on the meaning of *mother, horse,* a generic question, or a cursing verb—definitely a mistake to be avoided during a speech!

As it turned out, Tami did not just give one speech, but a whole series of speeches at official meetings over the following weeks and months. Planning meetings and speeches seemed to take over her life: there were banquets, staff meetings, and meetings with the Public Health Bureau and other government officials. But Tami was overjoyed as hospital work also began—the Sichuan Health Bureau had granted her a medical license to work in the hospital! Getting a Chinese medical license was miraculous; getting it so quickly unheard of! Other doctors had spent years wading through bureaucracy before being licensed. Tami knew that this was a major answer to prayer. It also reflected the increasing trust between health officials and MSI. God had provided.

⌇

"Dr. Tian Ni, this four-year-old boy has a heart rate of 140 per minute, and he is very weak. It could be heart failure. What shall we do?"

Whenever possible, Tami would join the doctors on their morning ward rounds for both internal medicine and pediatrics at the Xichang 2nd Hospital. Sometimes it was difficult for all of them to squeeze into a patient's room, especially if several family members were already sharing the four corners and the windowsills. The doctors would usually invite Tami to join them when examining the patient. A lively discussion would ensue as they discussed their findings and proposed management. Many of the tests and medications encountered in the USA were not available.

"Medically speaking, it's a fascinating place to work. It's a small hospital, but the variety and severity of diseases here rival larger U.S. hospitals," Tami wrote home. It was certainly not easy for the Chinese doctors to work within the limited resources, and motivation was often lacking. Tami suggested some therapy options for the four-year-old. Together they propped up the little boy to ease his breathing. But the restricted resources made Tami feel helpless.

One patient came close to breaking her heart. She was a ten-year-old girl with progressively worsening headaches, fever, and vomiting over several months. For the preceding three weeks, she had not eaten, and she had recently stopped talking. Her family had sought help from the resident shaman. When this failed, they came down from the mountains to Xichang to seek help from the hospital. This child was literally skin and bones. One could study skeletal anatomy just by looking at her. Her neck was arched back, her eye movements were random, and her legs were flaccid. Tami diagnosed advanced meningitis due to tuberculosis. How could she still help this little child? Sharon and Tami desperately tried to figure out how to provide basic medical support. They searched high and low for gastric feeding tubes so as to be able to feed her without causing her to choke. In the end, they had to settle for a urine collection bag turned upside down. All other tubing was either too stiff or too large in diameter.

After a ward round, a patient's husband sought out Tami and asked her to see his wife again. The medical team had seen her on previous hospital rounds. She had severe ascites (fluid in the abdomen) and peritonitis (inflammation of the abdomen) and was in a lot of pain. The Chinese doctors thought she most likely had advanced cancer of the liver, and Tami agreed with the diagnosis. Tami tried to encourage the attending doctors to broaden the antibiotic coverage and increase pain relief.

"It's not possible," the resident doctors responded. "The patient cannot afford any further medication, and the family already owes the hospital quite a sum of money. And, like many previous patients, she and her family would probably not be able to pay a cent."

Sharon tried to keep the woman hydrated by giving her frequent sips of water, but she could not hold it in. The patient's husband then confided in them that before he had brought her to the hospital, he had consulted the local *bimu* (witch doctor). The bimu asked him to sacrifice twenty sheep (one sheep a day for twenty days) to ensure a cure for his wife. Every day, he had offered one more sheep, but despite that, his wife steadily worsened. After the last sheep had been offered, the family decided to bring her to the hospital as a last and desperate measure. At this stage, however, he had spent all the family fortune and was not able to pay any more of the medical fees.

Over the next months, Tami discovered that similar tragedies were to be a recurring story. *How frustrating,* she thought. *Although medical treatment is available, many of the patients who need it most just cannot afford it.* Too many patients sought treatment at the hospital far too late, as a desperate last measure, but all too often at that late stage, there was not much more that could be done. This explained why many would either not come at all, or if they came, would need to leave when their money ran out.

Fridays were hospital cleanup days. After ward rounds, staff took hold of brooms and would sweep their assigned parts of the hospital grounds. "Shall we?" Sharon asked. "Sure!" Tami responded, and they each took a broom and pitched in. The hospital staff was so intrigued by the willingness of the foreigners to participate in the hospital cleanup that their story and picture was featured in the next edition of the local newspaper!

Tami treasured her hospital work, and she loved talking with patients and their relatives. "If they speak Mandarin instead of their thick Sichuan dialect, I can chat with them on my own. If they speak the Sichuan dialect, Sharon is able to translate. But if the patient speaks Yi only, both of us need a translator."

Unless there was a medical need, Tami spent most afternoons studying medical Chinese or preparing for lectures and speeches. Her progress in the language was fast, and she continued to pick up the Sichuan dialect as well.

Tami and Sharon, as different as they were, soon forged a strong team. "How about writing a prayer letter together?" Tami suggested.

So Sharon, in her Taiwanese English, wrote about Tami:

The more I stay with Tami, the taller she looks. I am only 5.0, she is 5.8. A friend said that the two of us look like Don Quixote and his little friend Sancho Panza. Tami is a born health care giver. No matter how busy she is, she is always running around town to see patients. Her brain contains ample medical knowledge; whenever I have questions, she is my dictionary. Amazingly she really likes Chinese food and can eat even spicier food than many locals. She is willing to learn the Chinese way of thinking and doing things. We can't work without each other. Though she is the leader, she accepts a lot of suggestions and advice from me, and tolerates my Chinese ways. The more we work together, the more we feel that we are one in Christ and that He has His purpose for both of us and wants us to fulfill a special task in this place.

Tami was equally full of praises for Sharon.

Her love for the people here and joy in serving are evident to all, and this has given her opportunities to share our faith with the

hospital staff, patients, and local officials. She has the daily burden
of translating much of the medical terminology and also portions
of conversations with officials and friends for me, and of trying
to help me adapt what I know of Western Medicine to this very
different setting. Sharon shares her faith so easily, quickly finding
words and analogies that the people here can identify with and
remember. Her musical skills brighten our worship, and her talents
in calligraphy have added much to our gifts to the people and to
the trainees' medical kits.

In the evenings, Tami and Sharon often went jogging out the back gate
of the hospital complex and down the dirt road toward the river. As they ran
down the dirt road, it soon narrowed to a path between corn fields. They
crossed a small creek and then found another road that led past rice fields,
which were bright golden as they were near to harvest. Further on, they ran to
a river where clear water rushed over dark red rock. The hillside before them
had terraced rice fields partway up and was topped with deep green trees.

On their way back, they could look back past the town to the even higher
mountains on the other side. They passed small children leading huge horses
and water buffalo home from the fields and adults carrying empty baskets back
from a day in the town market or burdened with piles of sticks and branches
for fuel. It was wonderful to be able to explore different routes through the
fields, along the river, or up the hillsides to breathe the fresh air and see the
blue sky and high clouds above the distant ridges. Both agreed it was much
better than running through the smoggy streets of Chengdu.

Chapter 13

TORCH FESTIVAL

"**D**r. Tian Ni, we would like to take you out to see the Torch Festival," the senior doctor from the hospital said one day. "Have you ever heard of the Torch Festival?"

"No, I haven't."

"It is a celebration of the Yi people and is the most well-known and important traditional event in this area. People travel from all over China to see it."

"I would love to see it. Thanks for the invitation. May I ask why it is called the Torch Festival?" Tami asked.

"It is called the Torch Festival because the local people hold torches and parade up and down the street and then throw their torches onto one big pile. There are also lots of fireworks. The people sing, dance and gather around big bonfires."

Officials from the Public Health School and the Public Health Bureau (PHB) took Tami and her friends in their bus. As they followed the paved road up into the mountains above the lake, they noticed more and more people walking alongside the road, heading for the festival. Some were herding cows and sheep along the path to sell at the market. Children and women wore bright and colorful costumes, often donning hats or other elaborate head decorations.

Suddenly, the bus pulled off the road to the right, careening down a steep, pot-holed pathway. After a few tense moments, Tami realized they were heading for a large natural plateau amidst the pine forest. In the middle of the plateau, the ground gently dipped to form a natural bowl. The sun was now setting and the mountains starting to light up, giving off an intense orange glow. More and more people were arriving and congregating on the hillsides on each side overlooking the bowl, which served as the entertainment and competition area. Women in vibrant clothes formed brightly colored patches amid the green of the grass and bushes.

It was still early evening, and the festival was to start one or two hours later. Some of the PHB staff approached Tami and her friends. "Would you like to come and see how the people here live?" they asked.

"Sure," Tami replied, and off they went on an impromptu tour of a Yi house close by. The door to the house had a rough-cut opening in a mud brick wall topped with sticks. In the center was a small muddy courtyard. Six little pigs, cute little fellows, came over to check out the visitors, while their more reserved—and anxious—mother lingered in the background. The house's owner, a woman wearing a large tatty turban and a hand-stitched Yi vest and pants, entered the courtyard. She gave a few sharp commands, and the pigs, both large and small, obediently scurried back into their little house. The woman beckoned the visitors into her house, which had one dark room mostly filled with firewood. The house was quite big by Yi standards, more than twenty square meters. In the center of the room was the hearth, which in true Yi style was without a chimney. In the corner, Tami could see an additional Chinese-style charcoal pit with a complete cooking wall in one corner. The only noteworthy pieces of furniture were two large cabinets containing some simple handmade Yi lacquer work.

"To stay warm, the occupants of the house sleep close together in the same room, lying on the floor covered by their homemade wool capes," the official explained.

The woman let them take pictures. At the end of the visit, they all said "Zai jian, zai jian," the Chinese way of saying "See you again." Then the group went back outside to watch the final preparations for the festivities. They found some suitable rocks for seats on a slightly flat area just above the grassy, steep slope on one side of the bowl.

"Help me tear up these cardboard boxes," the bus driver said to the group. "We can use them to sit on."

Groups of Yi and Han Chinese were scattered all around them, smoking, talking, laughing, and often staring at them. Tami could see three young boys high up in a large pine tree overlooking the field—what an excellent vantage point!

Finally, at eight o'clock, the program started. Groups of Yi men, women, and children carried torches held high onto the field. They threw down their torches in the center and then moved off to one side to initiate the traditional Yi dances. Tami walked down to get a closer view and take better pictures.

Just off to her right, she saw a group of competitors doing cow wrestling. The first four cow pairs did not seem too interested in fighting. They just wandered around the field, occasionally sniffing each other and briefly locking horns. Then they would wander off again, despite enthusiastic prodding, clapping, and ground-beating by their owners.

Tami had brought along some buckwheat cakes to eat while watching. Soon she grew bored of the cow wrestling, and she walked partway up a hillside to reach higher grounds above the field. Here she watched the next event, bareback horse racing. The horses galloped at an amazingly high speed around the tight-cornered track, occasionally ignoring their riders' control and galloping off the track at either end where the hillsides were less steep. Moving on to the adjacent fields, Tami saw sheep wrestling, which was like cow wrestling only on a smaller scale, as well as cock fights. After a while, the whole group found their way back up to the road where the bus was parked, passing curious faces and small tables set up for selling buckwheat cakes, sweet rice, nuts, crispy snacks, and boiled or fried corn on the cob. Beverages were offered in little plastic bags, which could be conveniently carried around using the thin strings attached.

The PHB staff drove a little farther into a pine forest where supper was prepared over a fire. Between short rain showers, they snacked on fruit, throwing the peels to some very content pigs that were wandering around the field. After a short time, supper was ready. They sat on their cardboard pieces and enjoyed potatoes roasted in the fire and chicken Sichuan-style, blackened and spicy.

Tami took a token chunk of very spicy pork. "I like the spicy seasoning, but don't particularly enjoy having to search for the meat between the skin and fat layers and the bone," she told her neighbor, a young nurse.

"But the fat and the thick skin are the most tasty part of this dish," the nurse replied, somewhat perplexed.

There were also buckwheat cakes and fragrant soup made from pickled radish tops. Then it was time to learn a few Yi dances before heavier rain chased them back under their umbrellas. Whenever the weather permitted, they danced in a small circle on the pine-needle-covered ground, dodging roots and rocks. Tami found the dances easier to pick up this time.

"The Yi are poor and often lacking in basic needs. Only about one third of the Yi are literate, and most Yi have no written language," the PHB official explained; he was a Han Chinese himself. "They exist on less-than-subsistence agriculture with a per capita income of U.S. $40–50 per year." From her reading, Tami knew that most of the Yi were extremely poor, uneducated farmers living from small plots of land.

"What do the Yi people believe in?" Tami carefully asked the PHB official. She wondered what his answer would be.

"The Yi people are animistic," he told her, "worshiping the spirits of all natural things. They live in great fear of the demons and evil spirits they believe live all around them. They need to be educated in the Communist way of thinking and liberated from their old-fashioned beliefs."

The Yi were one of fifty-six minority groups in China. They struggled with heroin addiction, crime and violence, smoking, and the deep-seated roots in shamanism. As she ate by the fire and listened to the sounds of celebration, Tami was sobered by the burden of their great task. *Hidden away from the vast population and bustle of urban China—does anyone consider them or know they are out here?* she thought.

Since her first encounter with the Yi during the MSI trip to Zhaojue, she had been praying that God would help her love the Yi people more. Looking into their faces, she indeed felt a growing love and appreciation for the Yi. Their faces were so beautiful. They were notably different from the Han Chinese, with strong aquiline features and swarthy skin. Some remarked that they had Caucasian features, and even described them as "a black branch of the Caucasian race."

Despite, or perhaps because of their poverty, they were very proud of their traditions. As they walked around after supper, Tami observed the clothes of the Yi in more detail. Their tunics were adorned with bands of ornate embroidery threaded around their shoulders. Some wore high-rimmed headdresses, others mob-caps, all elaborately decorated with ribbons of fine needlework. Their ankle-length black cotton skirts were hemmed from the knee in wide concentric circlets; combinations of heavily pleated, vivid blue, green, pink, red, and yellow; generating extravagant swirls of material with the slightest turn of their bodies. Women and occasionally men displayed bulky silver earrings. Some of the men wore turbans, neatly wound around their black hair and coiled into a prominent horn pointing forward above the brow.

Late in the evening, they returned to Xichang. As the main street was still closed off to all vehicles because of the ongoing festival, the bus dropped them off just outside the main bus station.

As they walked toward the center of the city, the streets were still crowded. Many of the people from the surrounding villages and cities who had traveled to see the festivities decided to stay overnight. Despite the late hour, many people were still carrying the long thin bundles of branches they had brought as torches. In some parts of the town, they were still carrying the torches in two rows down to the center of town in procession style. At the end of the street, they threw down the torches on a pile, giving the town an eerily flickering, orange backlighting from the many bonfires. Crowds were still dancing around the bonfires to loud distorted music blaring from loudspeakers.

Tami and her friends managed to push their way through the celebrating crowd, and some tried to join one of the dancing circles. This bonfire was large. With any strong gust of wind, sparks were blown into the crowd, causing the people to surge back and pushing the rows of bystanders along the sides of the road. Soon they found another circle around a smaller fire and joined in. As she danced, Tami quietly prayed that one day, the Torch Festival would be a festival of light as a witness to God's truth.

A group of adolescent boys started getting wilder and wilder, pushing one another and those around with each dance step. Irritated and a bit menaced, Tami decided to call it quits and returned to her little abode in "Mister Hotel." Lying on her bed, listening to the noise and music in front of her home, she was unable to fall asleep.

In the past, Dr. Taylor had told her, the Yi were called *Nosu*, which literally means "black people." More than one hundred patriarchal clans lived in the region of the Great Cold Mountains alone, and all were fiercely independent of each other. The history of the Yi was one of violence and interclan warfare. For centuries, the Nosu had raided the surrounding villages and made slaves out of the prisoners taken, forcing them to work on their farms and homes. In the early literature Tami had read, the Nosu were sometimes referred to as the *Lolo*, in reference to the small baskets they carried around with them which supposedly contained the souls of their dead ancestors.

As Tami reflected upon all the events of the day, she found it helpful to sort through them by writing in her journal despite the late hour. What a day she had been able to experience! Soon she found herself praying for the Yi. Sharon, in the bed across the room, was already asleep. Tami felt a welcome wave of tiredness overcoming her. She yawned deeply and drifted off.

Chapter 14

CEMENTED IN FLEXIBILITY

During the initial months in Xichang, Tami and Sharon lived at the Mister Hotel facing the health school. With so many uncertainties, MSI did not want to go ahead and buy or rent an apartment in Xichang. To reduce costs, Tami and Sharon shared the same hotel room. There was little space for privacy or "time out." Tami's only private space was a corner above her bed with pictures of her family, her friends, and the Rocky Mountains. For lack of a balcony, the laundry was hung to dry in a tiny windowless bathroom. They shared a wok pan and small gas stove. The stove was placed on the floor in the middle of the hotel room, and they had to squat around it to prepare their meals.

Two women from two cultural backgrounds sharing the same small space, day in and day out, was bound to result in occasional frictions and misunderstandings. Tami was the more reserved of the two and often wished for more privacy, whereas Sharon was more outgoing and extroverted.

One day, Tami suggested, "I'd love to get a kitten. What do you think?" Since early childhood, she had loved cats, and she thought this would be a cute addition to their hotel bedroom.

Sharon responded, "Fine with me. How about a dog too?"

"Well, I'm not really crazy about dogs."

Sharon offered an alternative. "How about a pig, then?"

Tami hastily answered, "Okay, okay, we'll get a dog!"

And that was characteristic of their cross-cultural life together.

Telephone and Internet access were fraught with problems. Although the authorities had kindly placed international phone line access into the room, reliability was a major issue. Because no available phone wire would fit, Tami came up with the idea of using crocodile clips to help establish Internet connections. She carefully adjusted the clips to get the connection right for sending and receiving e-mail. After ringing into the server, she had to wait for a little cursor to appear in the center of a black square, and then, as fast as she could, she had to hit "enter" repeatedly. Quick reactions and high tapping speed were important; patience essential.

In her newsletter she explained: "Living in a foreign country has taught me new skills and requires a lot of creativity. My recently acquired skills include phone tapping (to connect my computer modem to a local phone line—no jacks in the older phones here), checking fuses, and doing basic toilet repair. We've been practicing gymnastics, too: crawling under the couch to snip off fabric to match curtain colors, perching half in and half out the window to hang up temporary curtains, and angling bookcases up the stairs." Another trick they learned was to hang a calendar from the light switch using dental floss!

Tami had always been a task-oriented person. However, the lessons she was now learning were different. The name of the game was not so much achievement of a task, but how to survive when all plans got changed!

"Ready for some stretching exercises?" Tami wrote.

Here we go. Up! Down! Up! Down! Around! No, this is not some new "workout by mail." This is the story of my life lately. I've been getting lots of practice in being mentally flexible, because that's the way our circumstances and plans have been going—Up! Down! Around!

Last week's lesson:

Sunday: You will still have to go back to Hong Kong to get your visa.

Monday: Maybe it can be worked out in Chengdu.

Tuesday: Maybe not.

Wednesday: Your visa will be processed in Chengdu. Get your passport over to the Public Health Department NOW.

This week's lesson:

Monday: We're going to Zhaojue on Friday, and we'll stay three or four days.

Tuesday: The officials have decided to let us go Friday and stay three months.

Wednesday: A bridge between here and there has been washed out by flood waters. We don't know when it will be fixed.

Thursday a.m.: Another section of road has been washed out. Repairs will not be quick.

Thursday p.m.: The officials want us to stay around here.

Friday a.m.: We may be going tomorrow.

Friday p.m.: We are going next week.

"Flexibility lessons," Tami called them. They also meant meetings followed by more meetings, and then re-meetings to discuss adaptation of plans as they constantly changed. It was time-consuming and tiring.

"My faith definitely grows day by day," Tami wrote home, "as I learn to trust God for the big things (work visa) and the little ones (water, biking, letters). Learning to live without being able to plan more than two weeks in advance, and knowing that even definite plans change within a few hours, are hard lessons."

What did God want to teach her through all this? She wondered and prayed. When telling a friend about her flexibility lessons, one friend jokingly commented, "You are truly cemented in flexibility."

Tami laughed. "That's a good one! Yes, we're indeed cemented in flexibility! The only constant here is flexibility!"

She thought of a letter she had written many years ago to her parents when she was a high school student on a student exchange in Germany. She'd had to wait in departure lounges and bus stations. Feeling frustrated, she had written, "I cannot stand waiting! It is one thing I will *never* get used to."

Tami laughed at her own words now. *I guess God is now teaching me to wait and to be flexible and not to plan.*

Tami and Sharon took turns getting sick. In the course of several months, Tami suffered from respiratory infections, bouts of diarrhea, and stomach ulcers. The red peppers and spicy foods she so treasured were not only scorching her throat but also the lining of her stomach. Her diet was now limited to small portions of wheat and rice noodles, well-cooked vegetables, bananas, and crackers. She missed the "good stuff"—coffee, chili, fruits, and Chinese spices. She felt it was hard to finally be doing the medical work she had longed to do and yet be held back from full effectiveness by her physical problems—and the language barrier. The initial challenge of giving official speeches in Chinese turned to frustration as it distracted her from her clinical work. Furthermore, she was often helpless because of language issues and was dependent upon Sharon, aggravating her self-perceived inefficiency at the hospital.

Sharon adapted to the local situation more easily and was soon integrated into the community. Fluent in Chinese language and customs, she was more effective in the hospital too. Tami felt jealousy creeping up. As a countermeasure, she quickly cited the all-so-familiar verses to herself. "Love is patient, love is kind, love does not envy . . ."

The strongest witness in a country where we cannot openly share about the gospel is love, she thought. *They are all watching us. Lord, if all else fails, love will not fail. Give me love and patience.*

Sharon and Tami had planned to move to Zhaojue as soon as possible. But again there was delay. The time in the Mister Hotel turned from weeks into months. Cemented in flexibility? It had become the headline of her life in Xichang. Sometimes she laughed about it; sometimes she was pained by it.

During her quiet time, Tami meditated on the word "cement." She knew that she was cemented in God's love, no matter what the circumstances, yet doubts crept up. She prayed that her doubts would be buried in cement. Was she really in the right place? Then why so many problems and obstacles? They had come to serve the Yi, but so far she had done almost nothing. She was still just waiting in the gateway city. The Xichang hospital—was she really needed there? She missed the African bush hospital where her expertise was desperately needed and appreciated, while here in China, there was an abundance of doctors. Furthermore, she had trained in hospital medicine, but over the months, it emerged that the Chinese wanted her input in community health work and village doctor training. Was she doing what she was really meant to be doing? She thought about her two electives in a rural African hospital. All of a sudden, the many dialects in Africa seemed a breeze compared to the heavy accents of the Sichuan and Yi languages.

The doubts kept nagging her. Sometimes she was almost angry with herself. Had she not been through the same doubts before in Chengdu? Had she not learned anything from her time there?

One evening, she shared her doubts with Sharon and an MSI representative from Beijing. It took courage for her to voice them in front of her team members. She did not want to sound critical or too doubtful. But once she had spoken, she immediately felt better.

Dr. Wang from Beijing was particularly understanding. "Tami, what you are going through is so often seen in pioneering work. The pioneer stage of any venture is bound to be hard and disappointing."

They shared for a while. Then he recounted the story of Nehemiah in the rebuilding of the walls of Jerusalem. "We are all here to build up the walls of a broken country. Each of us here is a stone in this wall. We may think that a little stone is only an insignificant part of the wall. But it *is* significant! Every stone counts. Every stone is needed to complete the wall."

The words struck Tami's heart. Yes, she truly wanted to be part of the rebuilding of the community here, even if that meant just being a small stone. God had led her here, so there must be a purpose, although she could not see much of it in the moment. She resolved that being just a small stone in the wall would be sufficient for her.

After she had shared with Sharon and Dr. Wang, she looked for a quiet place to write down her thoughts. Writing had always helped her work through issues, and so she decided to write a poem.

Sometimes
I'm still surprised to find myself
    Surrounded by Asian faces
        Instead of African
    In the middle of a noisy, bustling city
        Instead of a quiet countryside.
But then I look back and see
Your guidance
    From the earliest friends from this country
    You brought into my life,
    To my first visit here,
    Falling in love with this place, this people,
    As I saw them through Your eyes.
I see Your provision, too.
    You've raised up so many
    Who reach out to me in open arms
And then lift me up to You in prayer.
    My every need is met.
Sometimes

I've wondered if I took a wrong turn,
Boarded the wrong airplane,
     I've wished for an easier language to learn,
     A medical system that lacks doctors,
     A place where I can share You more openly,
And yet, in the times
When You fill my heart
With joy at just being here,
I know You've led each step of the way.
There are doctors here, too many doctors.
But if you ask one, "Do you love your patients?"
They'd say "Don't ask me. I just work here."
Friends here have been told all their lives
That You don't even exist.
Yet You do,
     And You love
     And You came
     And died for me, for them
     And You rose!
And as You left, You said, "So send I you."
So here I am.
     And I can love with Your love,
     Study to show myself approved, Your servant,
     And walk through the doors You open.
That they may know
That they may love
That they may be Your people too.

Chapter 15

WHAT COUNTS

As soon as she finished writing her poem, a sense of peace flooded her. *I don't know why God has sent me here, but I do know that He wants me here. And that is enough for me. I just want to do His will.* The next MSI short-term team would be arriving soon. Although short-term teams meant a lot of work with e-mailing, arranging work visas, accommodation, transportation, and often also translation as well as playing tour guide, every team brought along blessings—be they chocolate, cheese, or good coffee; the bolstering of their Sunday fellowship meetings with lively songs and preaching; or just some cultural reminders from other countries. The large teams of experts also increased the visibility of MSI and fostered good relationships with the officials.

Tami was particularly looking forward to this team. Joan Wales was among the ten team members planning to teach English in Xichang for one month. Dr. Taylor's predictions about her return were coming true! Joan was the nurse who had worked alongside the Broomhall family in Xichang and Zhaojue forty years ago. Now, at age seventy-nine, she wanted to visit yet another time.

"*Huan yin*—welcome to Xichang." Tami gave Joan a big hug. Joan was a petite lady with a most delightful smile. Her wrinkled face shone forth God's love in a bright, wide, and endearing smile. In the following weeks, Tami accompanied her whenever she wanted to visit the places she remembered from the past.

Tami shared with Joan that they were planning to run a village health worker training course in the mountains. The Public Health Bureau was very supportive and was busy preparing the permission letters for them to go up.

When Joan heard about the plan, she told Tami in her beautiful British accent, "When we took an evening stroll on the walls of Zhaojue fort—you know, forty years ago—the smoke of the Yi homes rose from distant hamlets all around us as they prepared their evening meal. We reckoned conservatively that within a three-mile radius, there were thirty or forty hamlets of twenty, thirty, or forty homes, altogether thousands of people who might need medical aid. Even if it had been possible to visit one Yi village per day, we would never have been able to reach every village in a month. That was when the vision of village health training was born. Dr. Broomhall always talked about training villagers from every village to do basic health care. Tami, I am thrilled that God is using you and Sharon to put this into practice now."

Tami was touched. That evening, Joan and Tami visited an old acquaintance in a remote village. Tami watched Joan's joy at the reunion. The old Yi lady's husband had died shortly after the Broomhalls and Joan had left the area. During the rebellion the Yi led against the Han Chinese, fifty thousand Yi had died, the woman's husband one of them.

Returning home that night, Tami asked, "Joan, would you mind telling me more about your early years in Xichang and Zhaojue?"

Joan looked up at Tami and smiled. Her eyes shone brightly as she collected her thoughts.

"In the late 1930s, Dr. Broomhall heard about the Yi people. At that time, they were actually called the Nosu—I still have problems remembering that I should call them 'Yi' now. Well, he had heard that this people group was notoriously wild, and in the past, feared as headhunters. He knew of their long-standing oppression by opium, gambling, and drinking."

"You know," Tami said, "drinking, drugs, and gambling are still problems here. Because of the drug problems, Zhaojue is not so safe. The MSI office has told me not to walk through the streets on my own, especially at night."

The deep furrows of Joan's brow raised. "They need the liberating gospel." She looked into the darkening horizon. "This was also Broomhall's simple conclusion. He declared, 'Our great commission has to include the Nosu people.' His heart was firmly set on bringing it to the mountainous people who had never heard the joyous message of Jesus Christ before. In June 1947, Dr. Broomhall conducted his first exploratory trip to Zhaojue. Initially, there was strong opposition from an important government official in Chengdu, but soon the way was cleared for them. But disaster struck early on, and the expedition almost ended when their truck overturned on the treacherous road to Xichang. Broomhall emerged from the truck unscathed and immediately attended to the injured. But the accident was really a blessing in disguise.

As the people saw the helping spirit of the foreigners, doors opened, and the team was able to make its first contact with who they found to be very friendly and helpful people.

"The highest officials in Xichang helped them buy horses, supplied them with maps, and promised every form of assistance in the future," Joan continued. "On the way into the heart of Nosuland, the rival chiefs even offered to attack anyone troubling or offending Broomhall or his friends. The different Nosu clans were rife with hate for one another. Yet, they unanimously agreed that patients of any clan could go, safe from attack, to the hospital where Broomhall was to work. This was way beyond Broomhall's expectations. He was eager to plunge in and develop the work as rapidly as possible. He hoped to obtain government approval for the purchase of a plot of land previously occupied by the Manchu garrisons to build a little hospital at the very center, both geographically and strategically, of the Great Cold Mountains."

"And then?" Tami urged her on.

"Dr. Broomhall at once felt the immensity of the opportunities around him. For many days, he rode with his Chinese companion and his young Yi interpreter through areas populated by the Yi, who hailed his coming and intentions with genuine affection and welcome. Some of the influential chiefs not only welcomed the establishment of medical work, but also the preaching of the gospel of Jesus Christ. It was estimated there were about two million Yi in these mountains with no chance of hearing the gospel of Jesus unless someone went to them. Reaching some of their territories required many days of travel by horse."

Joan paused to catch her breath. "Alarming news of the civil war in China continued to surface, and questions as to whether Broomhall would be permitted to carry on his work under a new political regime grew. But he carried on the work, and his medical skills were soon prized by the locals. By January 1949, the primitive little clinic in Zhaojue was almost complete, and the future Broomhall residence was in place. In April 1949, the whole Broomhall family moved into Zhaojue, with their three children aged six, four, and one. Together with Ruth Dixon, also a nurse, I moved up into the mountains with them. We all settled in the little mud barn which also housed the horses, cows, and other fowl as well as two homeless lepers whom the Broomhall family adopted. Soon Dr. Broomhall was known as Dr. Hai."

Tami thought of how she was called *Dr. Fei*—the closest the Chinese could come to pronouncing "Fisk"—or *Dr. Tian Ni.*

"How did you cope during these early years, Joan?"

"The initial two years were tough," Joan admitted. "Against the ever-present background of unsettledness and uncertainty of what the future would hold, the medical and spiritual work went forward slowly. The language barrier was almost insurmountable."

"That sounds so like my own situation," Tami said. She shared with Joan how she was so often frustrated at the slowness of the work. "Indeed, the language barrier is still insurmountable!" she lamented.

She told Joan about how people stared at her because she was a foreigner. Joan laughed out loud. "Yes, that happened to us, too! They touched us, our hair, our noses, our eyes, and pinched our skin—like we were aliens! They especially examined the Broomhall daughters with great care and pleasure. Not always to the pleasure of those little girls, though!"

"Joan, please continue your story," Tami pleaded.

"Day by day, we were besieged by men, women, and children wanting treatment. They lived by selling farm produce, and often simply wanted to see the family of foreigners, or our house, and of course the clinic. Slowly, their faith in us and our medicine increased; the news of a few tumors removed and a leper improving under treatment sometimes spread like wildfire. But they still trusted chiefly in their sorcery and ritual sacrifices, and they discarded our measures if healing had not been achieved within a week or less."

Joan sighed. "We were not able to further build up their trust as a people, but we did win quite a few friends. In 1951, we were told to leave the country. We were devastated. The work had just only started. It was one of the hardest times in my life." Tears came to the elderly woman's eyes as she spoke. "Our departure from Zhaojue was stirring. About two hundred Yi came to see us off. They escorted us for the initial two miles, many of them weeping, singing, and praying. We could hear them even after we had crossed the river. Their final question still echoes in my ears, 'Will you ever come back?' And we promised we would. And unbelievably, here I am! God is faithful!" Her eyes shone even brighter than before.

"When I turn seventy-nine, I hope to still be doing what you are doing!" Tami looked at her with a sense of awe. "And how you climb up the stairs to our apartment although we are on the fifth floor is just incredible!"

Tami made a cup of tea for Joan, and when she returned bearing the tea cup and saucer, she said, "You know, my Grandpa is now in his nineties. He refuses to use a cane or look like a ninety-year-old."

Joan chuckled. "Our only task is to let God do His work through us, at any age."

That Sunday, they sang the chorus, "Life—it doesn't matter how long or short it is; what counts is how you live it."

Chapter 16

TAMI IS A MARTIAN

"I have recently come to a startling conclusion. I am, in fact, a Martian. Let me explain . . ."

The first village health training had been arranged by the Public Health Bureau, and Tami and Sharon went up to Zhaojue for two weeks.

"Since being in Zhaojue, many people have gaped at me with looks that can only mean they've discovered a life form never encountered before. Whenever I do anything such as speak, eat, or buy things, they congregate around me, watch in awe, and discuss among themselves, probably commenting on how human (or not) my actions appear. Whenever I am in a place with windows, people would come in waves for a glimpse of this new creature."

Faith without laughter leads to dogmatism and self-righteousness, Tami thought. *A pinch of humor is healthy for me and will liven up my newsletters.* She grinned wryly and went back to writing.

"In Xichang, I attract stares and frequent calls of 'hello.' In the mountains, I'm even more popular. All I have to do is stand still in the center of the town, and within seconds, a crowd gathers around me. The crowd grows almost logarithmically the longer I stand there (three seconds: five people; twenty seconds: thirty people; two minutes: sixty people). When we go out to a more rural area, I think the entire village population squeezes into a tiny courtyard to get a closer look at my fellow Martians and me. Though to be fair, I'm equally fascinated with the Yi's faces, each of which tells a different story."

I will call my newsletters "Martian Chronicles" from now on, Tami decided, as she continued to write.

"My suspicions about the presence of Martian life in Sichuan were confirmed when I recently spotted an English portion of a sign stating: 'Aliens shan't be involved in various activities incompatible with one's status.' The other day when I stopped in a few stores to buy things I found that I was doing one of my better 'Pied Piper' imitations. Half the town's children were strung out behind me, giggling and pointing as they tagged along. I have learned that pulling out a camera is a good crowd dispersal technique. A few of the older women and some of the kids, though, were sufficiently fascinated with me (perhaps because I was the first Martian they'd met) to let me take a picture."

⨳

Soon the Yi students for the ten-day village health training course arrived, all in their long wool capes and carrying a small bag not bigger than most women's purses. *I should take packing lessons from these folks,* Tami thought as she watched them coming in.

They started the morning with a card game called "Heart Attack," meant to help them get to know each other and learn their names. At the end, the loser sang a Yi song with the others joining in later. Then Tami and Sharon started to teach topics such as management of fever, transmission routes of infectious diseases, tuberculosis, hepatitis, and smoking cessation. An exam was planned for the end of the course. After the morning and evening lectures, they reviewed the key points with the students, only to find out that most had forgotten even simple things like nonmedical management of fever. Several of them had an elementary-school education only.

"We need to repeat the material more often, and explain it in different ways," Tami said to Sharon.

"Yes, more role playing, and skits and dramas to act out medical situations," Sharon suggested.

"We can also give them some homework to do. The experienced ones can teach the new ones how to measure temperature, pulse, and respiratory rate. They need to be able to perform these skills before the final exam."

Practical problems arose. Keys were wrong, rooms needed to be changed, basic items had not been brought. Tami and Sharon loaned thermoses and wash basins and provided more notebooks. On the second day just before dinner, they borrowed their neighbor's bicycle and rode to one of the small stores for more items needed for the course. Tami pedaled with Sharon on the back on the way there, and Sharon did the pedaling on the way back—much to the amusement of everyone on the main street. When they needed to open a bottle of iodine, they did not have the right-sized bottle opener. Tami asked one of the men outside to help, and he got it partly open by pinching it in the hinge side of the door; and then he opened the rest of it with his teeth.

Between classes, patients were often brought to Tami. One child was obviously breathless, and another had abdominal complaints. Listening to the chest of the breathless child with a stethoscope borrowed from one of the Yi students, Tami diagnosed bronchitis with asthma. Treatment was prescribed, and deworming added for good measure.

During lunchtime, Tami sat down at the hospital gate to eat a bite. While eating, she watched the world go round. A tiny kid perched high on a huge ox rode by. A mother rode down a steep hill on her bicycle with an infant tied to her back and a larger child sitting astride the back of the bicycle. Then two women passed by, each with six live chickens tied upside down on their backs; each woman also had a small child slung in front of her. One man cycled through a flock of sheep on the main street, causing the sheep to disperse to the sides. She wondered who the young girls with their backs to her were. When Tami came closer, she realized they were her students in their long-fringed capes, all happily taking a cigarette break. Cigarette smoking—it was an addiction everywhere, and, in particular among health care workers! Tami decided that she had to tackle this issue with the health care workers first.

One day, the students went for midwifery training in a small village further away. The drive was beautiful. There were yellow trees alongside a waterfall, and fiery red sumacs let their leaves drift down past rocky walls on their way to the river below. The higher hillsides were dotted with red, gold, and yellow, sprinkled with the dark green of the pines. In the valleys, a low-growing plant with deep purple flowers mingled with the green sprouts and the red clay of the plowed fields. The driver had to brake often as the chickens, sheep, and pigs were determined to cross the road, never mind the vehicle or its loud, ever-beeping horn.

Out in that small Yi village, Tami again quickly drew a large crowd of children as she went to buy pans for the midwifery kits. They were simple ones made of aluminum, shaped a bit like pie plates. As the edges had been bent somewhat, the sales lady took a thick stick and did her best to beat them back into shape.

During one of the demonstration sessions, a Yi student took off his boots. While the student was lying on the bench to be examined, the aroma was just about overwhelming. "Never again will I examine a patient without his shoes on," Sharon joked.

At one point, they passed a Yi *bimu*, a shaman, on the street. Sharon whispered to Tami, "Don't take a picture of him—otherwise he will yell at you and put a curse on you." Tami caught a glimpse of him just as he walked by. He was wearing a big straw hat and woolen clothes with a series of small bags hanging around his waist.

Just before the exam, one student ran away, afraid to fail. Three students initially failed the exam and had to be coached and retested right up to the last minute before the graduation ceremony. Some of the exam questions drew unusual answers. One student advocated the use of caffeine to bring out the measles rash, as this would help in making a diagnosis. The funniest answer to a question on the nonmedical management of diarrhea was, "Stop smoking, stop drinking." Good answer, but the wrong one. Tami chuckled at the thought of how she could use this answer for smoking cessations, the most pervasive problem among all the Yi.

Another last-minute frenzy concerned the diploma certificates. The night before the graduation ceremony, Tami found out that they could not use the diploma certificates they had purchased in Xichang, so she hurriedly generated new certificates on the computer.

During the graduation dinner, the students shared their experiences and ideas. One Yi village doctor described emergency cases they often saw related to rat poisoning. One of the younger trainees shared that he still firmly believed in mysticism. He had been ill during his previous medical training course and took various kinds of medicines from the hospital, but his condition did not improve. He went back to his village and went through some superstition-based healing procedure and was cured. Tami tried to explain to him that he probably improved at that point because his illness was just getting better or because he had quit smoking while he was ill, but he was totally unwilling to accept this. Tami then told him about the problem they had seen in the Xichang hospital where patients spent all their money on shamanism and then had no more money to pay for anything in the hospital when they had given up on shamanism. But he was not convinced by this either.

At the end of the course, Tami spent the afternoon outside washing clothes. Washing everything by hand, especially heavy corduroy pants, was a pain, but at least it was a good excuse to be outside on a nice day. In the evening, they were invited to join a karaoke evening with friends in Zhaojue. Tami was persuaded to sing "Edelweiss" with shots of Egyptian pyramids and Greece in the background. They were served coconut milk, sunflower seeds, and pine nuts. The karaoke place was remarkably upscale for Zhaojue. There was a bar in one corner and a separate room for dancing. The décor was plastic grape arbor on the ceiling with red velvet curtains on the walls. Tami danced for a while with the principal of the school, and then with some female friends from the medical ward. It was fun to be included in their idea of a night out in town. But as several of the men got drunk, she got out of the karaoke room as soon as it was polite to do so.

♪

The students returned to their home villages with simple medical kits and certificates. Tami and Sharon hoped to visit each village and give the trainees some review and supervision. But because of the remoteness of the villages and the red tape involved, they only managed to visit part of one village.

"Our trainees are our only windows on life there," Tami shared with Sharon.

"Yes, for now they are our only way to reach the neediest areas in this region," Sharon agreed.

"Their deep-seated cultural differences still have such a significant influence on their physical and spiritual health, like smoking and continued reliance on shamanism," Tami added. "It will take so much time and persuasion to change."

"So much still remains to be done. How can the two of us do all this?" Sharon asked. "And neither of us are well-trained in village health training."

It seemed that their thoughts were heard even before they expressed them to the MSI leadership. Not long after, they received an invitation from Dr. Ted Lankester. He had arranged for a study visit for Tami and Sharon to the Jamkhed program in India. As he had worked in India, he had the right connections. The intention was to train Tami and Sharon further in community work and village health training.

Thus, Tami and Sharon found themselves spending eight days in rural northwest India, learning from a well-developed community health and development program. The area had once been drought-prone, with almost one child in five dying before a year of age. Over the last twenty years, an incredible transformation of many of the very poor villages had taken place. Infant mortality had dropped to a level comparable to that in the U.S. Healthy, well-fed, and happy children often entertained them with health-related songs and showed that they, too, knew how to manage common illnesses like fever and diarrhea. Women's clubs sang songs about freeing themselves from oppression and poverty with the power of knowledge and unity. Workers shared that they were now free from the fear of the thousands of Hindu gods, and that they had come to know the One Living God. Women from the lowest castes had become health workers and leaders in their villages, learning and then sharing basic health care information and spurring on changes in water and crop management.

"It is all about not giving them fish, but teaching them how to fish," Tami commented to Sharon after listening to the talks of the Jamkhed leaders and the sharing by the villagers.

"You know, 'Don't give me fish, but teach me how to fish' is actually a Chinese saying," Sharon responded. "This approach should work in China, shouldn't it?"

"Seeing this program has given me hope that similar changes can be brought about in the Yi area," Tami agreed.

"But we face a different set of barriers than they do here in India," Sharon said. "Since we have limited chances to visit and work in the villages directly, we need to be creative in different ways."

Tami agreed, and they started brainstorming on different options.

꒰ꜟ꒱

It was Christmastime again. Just before Christmas, Tami visited a new MSI couple in Chengdu. They had just arrived with their two-year-old son to study Chinese.

"Tami, your Chinese is so much better than ours. Can you help us?" they asked one day.

"Sure!" Tami responded.

"Our *bao mu*, our Chinese helper, has expressed interest in our faith. But we can barely share our faith with her. Would you mind explaining the gospel to her?"

And so Tami sat down with this young woman. Patiently, she answered her questions. When Tami's vocabulary reached its limits, she opened the Bible and shared further. The girl eagerly explained her new understanding and belief to the couple and asked for prayer, and together they prayed a simple prayer to confess her sins and invite Christ into her heart. "I'm a new person! I'm so full of joy!"

"I am also so full of joy!" Tami exclaimed. "I rejoice in welcoming you into the international family!" To Tami, it was the greatest Christmas gift she could imagine.

Over Chinese New Year, there was a long vacation. MSI had arranged a retreat for all their workers, so Tami and Sharon flew to Hong Kong.

"Look how MSI has grown!" Tami exclaimed to Sharon when they arrived at the MSI retreat center. There were fifty people, including quite a few families, all working with the same vision for China as they were.

Worshiping together, singing, praying, playing, and listening to messages was a source of spiritual and emotional refreshment for Tami. "It feels so good to worship freely again!"

Sharon and Tami usually spent their Sunday "church services" as a twosome, so being with a bigger group of people was a welcome change. Both Tami and Sharon took turns sharing about their experiences since they had moved to Xichang.

Tami also shared about her recent Martian experiences in a city where all mannequins have Caucasian hair color and features. "One day I was standing, a bit too still apparently, along a busy shopping street in Xichang when a passerby mistook me for a mannequin and reached out to check the material of my skirt! Thinking she was trying to pick my pocket, I swatted her hand away. I scared her half to death when I moved!"

Everyone laughed, and Tami could not stop herself from also sharing one of her recent culinary experiences. "Drunken shrimp. Have you ever tried that? These are the freshest shrimp I've ever eaten. They certainly were not overcooked. They were not even dead. In this local specialty, the chef takes live shrimp and marinates them in a series of sauces, letting them flush out their little digestive tracts. They are served in a mixture of alcohol, chili, and other spices. The ones on the bottom of the dish are in a drunken stupor, but the ones on top, because they're not fully soaking in the alcohol mixture, tend to wake up and start moving. Once one jumped out of the dish! The key is to take one that is not moving and hope that it doesn't sober up on the way to your mouth—'cause it's rude to throw it back!" The audience roared with laughter.

Visiting Hong Kong restaurants, Tami noticed the difference from only one and a half years before when she had arrived in Hong Kong for the first time. She was now able to read menus and no longer accidentally ordered noodle soup with "various cow organs." *What progress*, she chuckled.

Drs. Leung extended warm hospitality to her. Based in Hong Kong, they served as advisers to MSI and often led short-term medical teams into China. They also arranged for Tami to speak at various churches in Hong Kong, sharing about her work and life among the Yi.

She ended her talk with, "We are only two women, soon to be three, doing this work. With two million Yi in the Great Cold Mountains, what can the three of us achieve? Yet when I question this, God has spoken to me with the words from Joshua when he faced Jericho. He only had a few men, whereas Jericho seemed unconquerable. And what did God say to him? 'Joshua, walk around the city and worship and pray!' And this is what we are doing. We can only worship and pray. The harvest is great. We need more workers. We especially need workers who are Chinese and know the language. God is calling the overseas Chinese to serve in China."

Chapter 17

THE MARTIAN
AT HOME IN CHINA

"Last month, I was a tourist. This month, I am a tourist attraction. It's great to be back in Xichang! And I am even enjoying being a Martian again!" Tami wrote in her newsletter.

Tomoko flew in with Tami and Sharon on their return from Hong Kong to Xichang. From now on, they were a team of three: three pioneer women in the gateway city waiting to move up to the Great Cold Mountains. Tomoko, a nurse from Japan, had a quiet and humble spirit. Her love for China was obvious. Tami instantly knew they would make a great team.

Having studied Chinese for the past eight years, Tomoko spoke excellent Mandarin. Unfortunately, she spoke hardly any English. *From now on I will have to speak Chinese every minute of the day, at work and at home. Call this real language immersion!* Tami said to herself.

The days at the Mister Hotel were now over. The MSI leadership had decided that the women should rent an apartment in Xichang. Their apartment building was located off a small street between the hospital and the health school, about five minutes' walk from each place. They spent the first two weeks "power shopping" for all the necessities. Some of the household words were not in Tami's vocabulary. So when Tomoko said "We need such and such," Tami would nod agreeably and follow along to find out just what it was they needed. Her Chinese vocabulary soon included the words for "curtain rod," "screw," "hot plate" and "fuse." When Tomoko and Tami were on their own, Tami had to describe or demonstrate things for which she did not know the word. It reminded her of the previous year in Chengdu when she and Naara were roommates, using pantomime to pass along such information as, "You might want to cover your toothbrush. A bug crawled over it this morning."

Shopping also included hot discussions over whether the newly purchased refrigerator should be delivered to the apartment on the back of a motorcycle or not. Fortunately, they settled for a truck.

Dr. Taylor bought a water filter in Chengdu for the threesome. Tami was impressed. "A leader who takes the time to help us shop for the basics is a real servant leader," she commented.

"Our place is starting to look like a real home. After living out of suitcases since last fall, this is just wonderful," Tami told Sharon excitedly. They also soon found out that they were living in a "real" neighborhood. They heard their neighbors going to work, washing clothes, or stir-frying dinner, and they heard neighbor children practicing musical instruments. All day long, people wheeled their rattling carts between the apartment buildings, selling things or offering services. "Buy bread! . . . Selling milk . . . Pots and pans repair!"

At one stage, Tami thought about taking a tape recorder to catch the "Sounds of Sichuan." It would feature the health school students' exercise music: *one-two-three-four* repeated roughly one million times accompanied by march tunes blared over loudspeakers at 6:45 every morning. Then there was the tune their shower water heater played and the neighbors' incessantly barking—but really quite musical—dogs; the deafening mishmash of horns, bicycle bells, and bad mufflers on the busy street; and topping everything, their musically inspired but severely tone-deaf neighbor singing karaoke at the top of his piercingly loud voice, flat and out-of-tune. One night, Tomoko and Tami seriously discussed the pros of power outages! The thought of causing a power cut crossed their minds more than once.

Living in a Chinese community also meant daily interactions not just with their neighbors but also with the merchants and service people nearby. The lady who made their bedspread with her curbside sewing machine greeted Tami every time they met, and they would chat. The "yogurt lady" would also often stop Tami for a longer chat. It was a tremendous opportunity for her to learn more about their lives, joys, and sorrows. Tami was eager to share her faith, but she knew this was not appropriate in China. Wisdom and patience for the right moment was needed.

"We are often inclined to share the gospel, either because we are overwhelmed by the numbers of people who have not heard the name of Christ or because we don't feel like we're doing enough. We need to be sure, though, that we are doing His work, not our own, and that all of our own plans and desires are crucified," she shared one evening with an MSI short-term team. "Our willingness to leave our own countries and work in this poor area can be a light that shines and draws people to Him, without having to speak too many words."

꒱

"Annie, Annie, are you okay? No response! Open the airway, check for breathing and pulse. Start CPR. One and two and three and four and five. *Breathe*. One and two and three and four and five. *Breathe*. Now it's V-fib. Shock at two hundred joules. And again. Somebody put in an IV. Epi! Tube her. More shocks. More epi. Lidocaine . . ."

Such was the sound of the resuscitation course co-organized by the Xichang Health School and MSI. On an earlier trip, Dr. Taylor and his team had brought in the man-sized mannequin for the life-support course. They all had a good laugh when they heard how custom officials mistook the mannequin for a stowaway in Dr. Taylor's luggage! Seven Singaporean doctors and nurses had arrived to teach the two-week crash (no pun intended) course on cardiopulmonary resuscitation for local health care workers. With it, Tami got a crash course on the Chinese terminology for abnormal heart rhythms, medications, and parts of the teaching mannequins and defibrillators. Just as "ventricular fibrillation" got shortened to Vfib, so the Chinese equivalent, *xin shi xian wei xing chan dong*, was shortened to *xin shi xian chan* or even to *shi zhan*.

Well, it's better than studying household items, Tami thought!

"Zhi shan!" The students who participated in the first course were senior doctors and nurses, many of whom had left clinical work for teaching and administrative work. They struggled with the vast amount of new knowledge in their handbook and during lectures. Being not-so-young, many of them were breathless and had aching muscles and joints after practicing CPR on the mannequins. The training venue was far from ideal: small, with insufficient tables, insufficient electrical sockets, no wash basin, and a noisy, hot environment.

That evening, the team leader, Dr. Tham Kum Ying from Singapore, shared, "At times, I felt utter frustration. I watched impatiently how they struggled to learn, thinking that there will be an unacceptably high failure rate at the exams. But then I watched Tami and Sharon, how they lovingly and patiently came alongside these doctors and nurses, and I knew that God was teaching me some serious lessons. How Tami and Sharon moved among them, encouraging the perspiring and tired participants, and giving tips on how to cope with the physical 'hardship' of CPR practice, will forever be imprinted in my mind. This is what I would call 'true love.'"

Another Singaporean team member added, "And their faces! When I watched Tami and Sharon, I could see so much joy and peace in serving here."

Yet another team member interjected, "And how well Tami understands the local language. It puts me, a Singaporean Chinese, to shame that *she* has to translate for *me*! She has become one of them. She is an incredible witness for God!"

At the end of the course, the inevitable banquet took place, and speeches were given. The Chinese participants spoke about their initial surprise at how real the mannequin looked and how well the defibrillators worked. The next surprise was that the mannequins and defibrillator did not fall apart after being used by more than forty doctors and nurses during the course, and their third surprise was MSI's generosity in donating the mannequin and defibrillator to the health school. The course was successful, the first of many more to come.

～ॐ～

Tami enjoyed being back on the pediatrics ward in the Xichang hospital. After rounds with the Chinese pediatricians, she often went back to see the patients on her own. The parents appreciated her willingness to spend extra time examining their children and answering their questions. The students often followed her, and this opened up opportunities for Tami to teach them how to do physical exams, how to diagnose diseases, and how to give patient education. She often had to thumb through the dictionary to try to give clear answers.

At times, the students would dig deeper.

"Dr. Tian Ni, why did you come here?"

"Because I love China." It was the answer she always gave.

"But why do you love China so much?"

And sometimes Tami dared to share further.

"Because *God* loves China."

"But how do you know that God loves China?"

"Because that is the character of God. He *is* love. He loves everyone, every culture, every nation. And He wants to have a relationship with every one of us."

One of the nurses from the pediatrics ward served Tami silkworm cocoons, a local delicacy—with the critters still inside. They had been fried in chili, so they tasted pretty good as long as she did not think about what she was eating. Afterward, she could not help thinking that the cocoons had turned into butterflies. Perhaps this was the true meaning of having "butterflies in the stomach!"

Tami knew she was really starting to become part of the community when she was invited to the wedding of a Yi friend from the pediatrics ward. His bride was Tibetan, so she was excited to be going to a Tibetan-Yi wedding ceremony!

The first day, the ceremony was held at the groom's parents' home, a traditional courtyard-style house out in the countryside. The courtyard in the center of the house was full of small tables and stools and was decorated with two severed pigs' heads (very fresh looking), a clothesline haphazardly draped with towels, and many red paper cutouts of the "double happiness," a Chinese character used as a wedding symbol. Music from a karaoke set in one corner mixed with the clinking of tiles from several intense mahjong games scattered around the courtyard. As the honored foreign guest, Tami ate inside at the head table.

After dinner, she stepped outside the room to look for the restroom. As she waited for it to become vacant, she drew stares and comments from the new arrivals who had just realized that a Martian had been invited to this wedding! As soon as she entered the bathroom and closed the door behind her, she was startled by a big *snort*. The resident of the back half of the room was a medium-sized pig, which was equally startled to see a foreigner! In the near darkness, Tami could just pick out the "toilet." It was a trench running along the front of the pigpen. Odor-wise, she had been to worse bathrooms in this country; this one was not too bad, pig and all.

The groom and his bride, wearing a beautiful red silk dress, entered the courtyard amidst the smoke and noise of firecrackers and made their way up to the porch in front of the main room. The ceremony itself was a series of blessings shouted through a microphone by the groom's sister as the happy couple bowed to their guests, their parents, and the family altar. In the past, the blessings had traditionally wished the couple an abundance of children, but this time, their sister wished them "planned conception"—very appropriate for China's "one family, one child" policy.

The ceremony on the second day was hosted by the bride's parents in Xichang. This time, the entry of the bride and groom was traditionally Tibetan, with the loud blowing of a shell horn. They were presented with two *hadans*, long white scarves, amidst the blowing of the horn, applause, and the spraying of string. Tami journaled all her observations that evening.

Her culinary adventure of that month was *mayi shang shu*—"ants climbing the tree." It was so strange that she made a "Guess what's for dinner?!" contest out of it in her Martian newsletter. Readers had to come up with the most delicious-sounding dish that met the description. The winner was a friend from Michigan who wrote suggesting that the "tree" was a shaped chocolate cake with icing, and the "ants" were bits of chocolate shavings. Tami went on to explain the real version: the "tree" was made of bean thread noodles lightly fried with garlic and chili, and the "ants" were small bits of ground pork.

But then Tami came across a dish that required pictorial proof in her culinary column! It was called *Pashachong*—roughly translated as "sand creepy crawlies." This food item broke two of her previous dietary rules: "Never eat anything that lives under a rock" and "Never eat anything with more than ten legs." In fact, this creature had twenty-two. They were served these lovely twenty-two-legged creatures at a banquet where it was rude to refuse to eat. Fortunately, they were well fried, so there was not much of a taste. Weeks later, Tami, Tomoko, and Sharon had a blast serving them to out-of-town guests and watching the guests' reactions. Record for nonstop screaming: fifty seconds. Record for running from the living room to the door: 0.8 seconds.

Looking at Tami, Tomoko commented, "I think you are now really feeling at home here, aren't you?"

Without any hesitation, Tami nodded, "Yes, I am. This is where God wants me to be."

At that moment, Sharon stormed into their apartment. "I have great news! The Public Health Bureau has given us permission to move up to Zhaojue!" The three women were so excited that they danced in the room. Then they went on their knees and praised God. At last, God had opened the doors to the mountain village. They had so much to thank Him for.

"We need to prepare well," Sharon said when they got up.

"Yep, we need to buy some medical equipment for Zhaojue hospital," Tami added. "This is best done in Chengdu."

The three sat down and took notes.

"We also have to renew our visas and medical licenses there," Tomoko commented.

So off they went on the long journey from Xichang to Chengdu. On the train, Tami happened to sit next to a young Chinese scientist. Their initially casual chat turned into a lengthy discussion of comparative religions, science, and the Bible. Tami shared her own spiritual journey and all the basics of the gospel with him as daylight turned to dusk and dusk to darkness outside the train windows.

All along the way there were special joys. In Chengdu, they stayed with friends and deepened friendships. The opportunity arose for Tami to visit her old language tutor. Tami had given her some books to read before she had left for Xichang one year ago—and so they had some precious moments together discussing spiritual insights. Tami savored those rare moments of sharing her faith.

Medical equipment procurement became yet another part of Tami's ever-broadening job description. At the shop they found that the two ventilator sets they had ordered were not in the store. The boss made a phone call, and about ten minutes later, a woman pulled up on a bicycle with a ventilation bag and mask, packaged only in a flimsy plastic bag, tucked in her bicycle basket. Tami asked them where the second one was, and the boss promptly sent the woman off to fetch it. Ten minutes later, she returned with another bag and mask in another bag in her bicycle basket. Then Tami asked for the laryngoscopes. Another phone call! This time a man showed up on a motor-cycle with both laryngoscopes in plastic bags dangling from the handlebars. Getting batteries so Tami could test the laryngoscopes took another fifteen minutes of lively discussion. Finally, they set off with what they needed.

On the long train ride back to Xichang, Tami reveled in her memories. Her thoughts drifted to the Yi. Soon she would be living in the very midst of them. She looked at the medical equipment she had stored away in her luggage. *These will show good will to the hospital staff,* she thought.

Back in Xichang, the days were filled with the excitement of packing and sorting through things they would need up in the mountain village.

"It's the time of the year again for the Torch Festival," Sharon announced to Tami and Tomoko one day. They needed no further prompting, and off they went to join the festivities. They watched the cow fights, which were similar to last year's but livelier this time because there was a female cow around to keep the bulls going. On the last night, they joined a vast parade of torchbearers and then danced around bonfires as fireworks bloomed overhead and crimson lanterns swung in the breezes along the streets. A TV camera caught Tami dancing the traditional circle dance. The tape ended up played on the TV news in Xichang, then in Chengdu, and who knew where else!

"I am so happy to be here in China," Tami exclaimed, her face glowing from the strenuous dancing. "I feel so much at home. And tomorrow our prayers and dreams will be fulfilled when we move to our mountain village. It is going to be the home that we have been waiting and praying for."

Chapter 18

MOVING TO THE MOUNTAIN VILLAGE

The road from Xichang to Zhaojue wound steeply up the mountains, occasionally passing through small Yi villages consisting of a few scattered, dilapidated huts. Chickens flapped, squawked, and fled to the sides of the loose gravel road as the loud diesel bus passed through, emitting large black clouds of smoke from the exhaust pipe. The higher the road, the more rocks were strewn on it, deposited by the frequent landslides. Potholes were ever present. At times, the driver was able to miraculously transform the bus into a seemingly agile overland vehicle. But it was difficult for the heavily laden bus. Its suspension was far too soft and had seen much better days! Four-wheel drive would have come in handy as the frequent mud landslides had left the road surface dangerously slippery.

Despite the bumpy, edge-of-your-seat travel experience, the journey was full of beautiful vistas, especially when crossing the mountain ranges. It took them about four hours to get to Zhaojue. For Dr. Broomhall and his team, forty years earlier, it had taken four days on mules and horses. Tami and her team had often traveled up the road in the past years, but this time, the trip was more meaningful. Now they were going to live in Zhaojue. The hospital had given them housing within its own compound. A bigger miracle—the Public Security Bureau had granted them permission to live there.

"Although we have taken this road many times in our preparatory visits, it is different each time," Tami wrote in her newsletter. "I have gone up by moonlight, fog, and sun, in early spring and the height of summer. Today, there were high clouds in many shades of white and gray, tumbling over each other but letting brilliant sunlight through to sculpt shadows on the mountainsides and send streamers down onto the lake's surface. On the slopes above Xichang, the rice was nearing harvest, its terraces forming golden steps edged in green marching up to red clay villages."

Tami tried to take some pictures from the moving car. There was one brief traffic jam when a herd of sheep was determined to stay in the middle of the road. Higher up, the bright yellow-gold fields of buckwheat had already been plowed under, the exposed red soil awaiting the next planting. Here were the now-familiar sights of children herding sheep just a little smaller than themselves, women loaded down with huge bundles of sticks on their backs, cows taking their time to get off the road. One woman carried two children—an infant hanging in a blanket in front of her and a slightly older child tied to her back. A few times, the driver stopped in villages to chat with people he recognized, and the local kids got some Martian viewing of Tami. It was obvious that many of them did not believe their eyes when they saw her.

The apartment was on the ground floor. It felt cold, desolate, and dirty. There was only one heater in the center, but fortunately, the beds had fluffy warm comforters. One of the pipes in the bathroom on the left side of the apartment was noisily leaking. The toilets were Chinese squat style. The ceilings were decorated with fancy carving tiles, and the living room light was tacky green and displayed a "scenic" painting in the middle with white shell shapes on the periphery. It almost looked like a disco palace. Tami wondered how she could make this place into a home. Their apartment shared a courtyard with several other tiny, simple, one-story homes. They all looked like they could tumble down in a moment. Through the bare windows of the surrounding apartments, they could see gray concrete floors and cement walls.

"The other apartments look so much worse than ours. I'm grateful for what we have," Tami said as she rolled up her sleeves and started cleaning the bathroom.

"We are the first foreigners to live in this area since Dr. Broomhall left!" The thought was awe-inspiring as the three contemplated it during their evening fellowship time. They knew they could not take this privilege lightly. They had to be sensitive to the political and cultural issues involved.

Tami was struck by the two characters that form the Chinese word for "miracle." The first character meant "God," and the second meant "trace" or "footprint."

"God still works miracles and leaves His footprints in our lives!" Tami wrote in her newsletter. "Since we moved up here, we've experienced His hand of protection as we had to travel back to Xichang several times. During the rainy season, the road is treacherous. Landslides often cover broad sections, and a bridge near Xichang keeps washing out. Twice we had to get off the bus, walk across a temporary bridge, and wait for another bus on the opposite side. Thankfully, when we were moving all our belongings and our new beds up here, the truck was able to cross a slightly more sturdy bridge."

Zhaojue was surrounded by bare, rolling mountains. Patches of occasional trees and rice terracing broke the pattern in places. The buildings in the town were mostly red brick, some with aluminum garage-door-style storefronts. Trees lined most of the streets, and pigs strolled freely along, rooting through the garbage. Mules dozed in the shade of the trees with their owners squatting or sitting nearby, chatting, smoking, or selling things. Mingled with the Yi were many Tibetans. They sat at the street side with amazing collections of animal skulls, horns, and bones spread out on blankets for sale. In the background, music, news, and entertainment programs blared out over the public loudspeakers for most of the day. At the end of the road they lived on was a tiny cinema with a curtain for a door, enabling movie dialogue to be heard for a block or more.

Zhaojue never seemed to rest. The deafening sound of horns, bicycle bells, and trucks on a busy street was ever present, day and night. Neighbors swatted their cotton quilts with bamboo sticks in the mornings, emitting a near musical *bing-boing-boing*, and in the evenings they sang heartbreaking, mind-numbing karaoke for hours on end. At night, dogs barked incessantly. The neighbors' chickens were a particular nuisance. Tami described them in her newsletter as "Task-oriented, not time-oriented, so will crow at any hour, day or night. Talented—able to imitate a caterwauling tomcat, a squeaking door, or a dying pig. Seriously! These chickens must be a mutant breed of chickens with something wrong with their vocal cords!"

Being back in the Zhaojue hospital was bittersweet. The hospital had gotten a facelift, with fresh paint, new beds, and tiled floors. Underneath, though, the problems were unchanged—the staff's lack of compassion and motivation, the poverty, prejudice, and hopelessness were still there. Kids still died of diarrhea and pneumonia. Adults came in after their cancers had passed the treatable stage. Patients left and went back to the witch doctor before antibiotics had a chance to fight their infections. But there were lots of joys, too. Because of her improved language ability, the senior doctors consulted Tami more frequently about new or difficult patients. There was in particular one new doctor who was very bright and eager to learn. Every day, Tami looked forward to their lively discussions about heart arrhythmias, antibiotic choices, ulcer therapy, or whatever was pertinent that day. They also started to spend more time together outside of the hospital.

One day, Tami sat outside the Zhaojue hospital gate, waiting for the hospital car to fuel up and take them to the village to examine TB patients. She purposefully and slowly took in the ordinary scenes around her. A toddler, bare bottom clearly visible through the generous slit in his pants, clung to his mother's parked bicycle and practiced a few tentative steps. A mother sat on the grass, laughing and playing with her infant. Two men herded an intimidating bull just past the mother and child, and a man perched on the peak of a slanted horse cart eyed Tami carefully as he trotted by. An old woman with a long cape, once elegant but now faded, sat curled up in a corner. A huge pig grunted happily through the trash on the main road. Tami closed her eyes, trying to embed these scenes into her memory.

As Tami was heading from the medical ward to the small X-ray department, two little kids spotted her. They yelled "Auntie Fei" and ran toward her. The little one, a four-year-old Yi girl who spoke excellent Mandarin, bowled into her with arms wide open for a hug. Tami squatted uncomfortably to stay at the children's eye level. Squatting for hours, like many Asians do, was still difficult for her. They sang songs and performed nursery school dances. They begged Auntie Fei to tell them stories and sing them songs. The little one was a totally uninhibited performer. Her dances were a delightful mixture of childhood clumsiness and the grace of traditional Chinese dance. The children promised to be her Yi teachers. Tami played with them for almost an hour, singing about the old lady who swallowed the fly and telling them the story of the Three Little Pigs. By then, a larger group of kids had gathered, and they performed "the eagle chases the chicks," a half-dance, half-crack-the-whip game where one child, who played the Mother Hen, tried to protect the row of "chicks" lined up behind her from the child pretending to be the eagle. What fun it was to be an auntie, Tami thought.

Soon their apartment was ringing with the excited voices of their new hospital coworkers and their children. The visitors enjoyed looking at the photos from Colorado and playing group games. Karaoke machines came into heavy use, giving all a chance to share their musical talents. If there was an opportunity, the three MSI workers would sing their theme song, "Love Never Fails."

In the kitchen, trash was sorted into two bags by category: "consumable by pigs" and "not consumable by pigs." The contents of the former bag regularly became slop for their neighbor's pigs. When they were unsure in which category an item would belong, they did careful research, namely taking it to the pigpen behind their house (downwind, thankfully) and performing a taste test. And indeed, two out of two pigs tested loved banana peels. The women thought about trying coffee grounds next. Pigs on caffeine? Well, maybe not.

The neighbor kids drifted in and out of their place like it was their second home. One weekend, the three women decided to invite the neighbor's family over for dinner.

"We should offer them a Western meal; I'm sure they would like to be exposed to something new," Tami suggested. "How about spaghetti bolognese?"

Agreed, they went back to Xichang to buy some of the ingredients. After peeling six pounds of tomatoes, the meal was prepared, and the neighbors arrived. Tami never forgot their faces when they took their first spoonful.

"Never again Western food for our Yi neighbors," Sharon declared after the neighbors had returned home.

"Oregano and tomatoes obviously do not meet their taste," Tomoko added, laughing. "They sure had problems finishing that meal!"

Not long after they had settled into Zhaojue, a medical short-term team from Singapore arrived. "The aliens have landed—and will hold a health fair," Tami announced cheerfully.

Two "bacteria" darted in and out of the screaming "teeth." The Singaporean bacteria was huge and the Taiwanese one was small, but both were ferocious in their attacks. Forefingers wriggling by their foreheads, they mercilessly charged into the crevices between the teeth. Shrieks of terror and cheers emitted from three hundred children witnessing this "brush your teeth" demonstration. These school children had just received a free dental checkup by a dentist from the U.S.

A curious mob of five hundred patients surrounded the MSI doctors and nurses who had set up next to the town center monument. The atmosphere was part clinic, part carnival, and part zoo—with all of them on the inside, as Tami commented. Red, yellow, and green posters on nutrition, along with anti-smoking cartoon messages, hung on makeshift wooden partitions. Western concepts of privacy and modesty were out of place here, and the gawking of the onlookers contributed to the festive carnival-like atmosphere.

Grabbing local staff or patients to translate, Tami, Tomoko, Sharon, and the team of visiting doctors took medical histories in a mixture of Chinese and Yi and examined patients on two beds that had been partially screened off. They felt bellies for tenderness or big livers after digging through layers of sweaters. Straining their ears to hear heart murmurs over the din of pop music from the cassette seller's stall across the street was a challenge to the team, compounded by the rumble of trucks and buses passing by. Spectators called out to their friends and relatives who were being examined by the team, and policemen chased would-be-but-unregistered patients out of their enclosure. Amidst the chaos, Tami was having a blast seeing patients, giving health advice, and writing X-ray requests and prescriptions in Chinese with occasional help from Chinese colleagues.

My study of medical terminology is paying off, she reflected thankfully.

The two sunny, bright days of the health fair were the only two days of the season that the weather was not damp, rainy, and cold, providing a wonderful reminder of how God had His hand in all this. Dr. Reggie Tsang was the team leader, and with his genuine love for kids, he attracted the crowds. An entertainment team provided a medley of animated songs, including "I've Got Peace Like a River," "Home on the Range," and of course the MSI theme song "Love Never Fails." Red and blue balloons were given to little children who were brave enough to practice their recently learned English: "Hello," "How are you?" and "My name is . . ." The team named a few particularly friendly children Annie, Cindy, David, Debbie, and Esther, and they even got them photographed in a photo shop.

One evening, while the team sat together to reflect on the day, Reggie shared with the group, "I have heard many stories from the locals about how they appreciate it that Dr. Tami, Sharon, and Tomoko have moved up here. Stories about how villagers have been touched by their love and work. Some said it was not so much the skills they brought or the new equipment, but most touching of all, their attitude. They treat the patients so kindly. Some others said, 'They work very hard; every day they go around and check on their patients.'"

Another team member added, "When I watch these three pioneer women here in this mountain village, I cannot help but conclude that *joy* and *peace* are words that true service brings."

As a team, they read the words of Isaiah 55:12: "You shall go out in joy and be led forth in peace."

Tami agreed. All the games and balloons were great fun, but the greatest joy was the wonderful opportunity to be out among the local people, touching, listening, helping in whatever way they could, and showing God's love in a tangible way.

Chapter 19

WINTER

Winter arrived in Zhaojue, and Tami started to understand why the Great Cold Mountains were called the great *cold* mountains. It was bitter cold. Worse still, the cold was a damp kind of cold, penetrating skin and bone and numbing the mind. Tami was not sure where it was colder—inside or out. Outside, it was cold by virtue of geography and elevation; inside, houses were barely heated and windows and doors always open, thus equalizing any small temperature gain the insides might have acquired.

The same open window fetish they had in Chengdu, Tami lamented.

When Tami arrived at the hospital one morning, the cold had once again cut short the ward rounds. She found the doctors, nurses, and other medical personnel huddled around the small electric heater at the nursing station, desperately trying to absorb some warmth. At this time of the year, fewer patients came to the hospital. This was not really surprising, since, if they did come, the worry was that they might catch pneumonia. There was always a cold draft blowing through the hospital.

"Good morning," Tami greeted her colleagues. "Anything new?"

"No, there were no new admissions yesterday. Not really surprising considering that many of the paths to town are blocked off by snow and ice," Dr. Zhao, her senior colleague, replied.

Tami stretched out her hands and feet, trying to attract some warmth from the small red glowing element which one could barely see glimmering at the center of the iron heater.

"How do the people living in the mountains survive in this kind of weather?" Tami said, shivering and trying to keep her voice steady.

Dr. Zhao smiled, wrapped his arms around himself, and said, "They have grown used to the harsh conditions by wearing many layers of clothing. They often do not wash themselves for weeks and months until the weather turns warmer."

The head nurse popped her head into the room, "One child with bron-chopneumonia in Room Three. I need one of the residents to check on her."

Tami followed the young resident doctor from Chengdu through the bleak corridors. As they entered the patient's room, they were overwhelmed by the stench of the toilet further along the corridor.

Perhaps that's the reason why the window doesn't even have a lock on it, Tami thought.

Groups of Yi people dressed in their blue-black costumes sat on the rickety, fragile-looking beds. Mattresses were scarce, but this child had been lucky enough to get one. Next to the bed, the child's mother was busily cooking on an open fire. The child was shivering and looked pale. As the resident examined him, a racking cough violently shook his small, frail body.

"How long has he had this cough?" the doctor asked.

"At least three months," his mother replied. "He has lost so much weight, and now he is so weak that he can barely stand up."

At the end of the examination, the young resident discussed the diagnosis and management with Tami. Both knew the child had tuberculosis and needed urgent medical treatment. It was yet another case of seeking medical attention too late.

In the apartment of the three pioneer women, one precious electric heater was strategically placed in the center of the living room. Trying to warm up in front of it was not unlike roasting on a spit. Close proximity for too long without carefully rotating resulted in charring; too much distance in being "underdone." The three women soon took on the local customs of not showering (except in extraordinary need) and wearing as many clothing articles at any one time as possible. Tami's personal record was fifteen articles just for indoor wear. And that was not counting the overcoat, scarf, hat, and gloves which were added necessities for outdoors.

჻

Before long, Christmas was approaching. "Wouldn't it be neat to do something for Christmas in the Zhaojue hospital?" Tami suggested.

"That would indeed be a historic moment. The first Christmas celebration in Zhaojue for at least forty years," Sharon commented enthusiastically.

And so the three pioneer women started planning. It ended up with a whole week's worth of celebration. They celebrated Christmas with the hospital staff and acted out the Christmas story, complete with little kids as sheep, shepherds in traditional Yi capes, and wise men in Yi-style turbans. More than a hundred people watched and listened. They had quite a combo of costumes, with Joseph in a bathrobe and Tami as one of the three wise men from the east. First, Tami put on a crown to symbolize the King of the East, but the crown got vetoed as the "kings from the east" are better translated as "Eastern scholars/PhDs." Tami ended up wearing a blue sheet as a wise man. They had great fun! And yet, the three women knew it was not all about fun. They quietly prayed that the audience would understand the best gift of all, the true meaning of Christmas.

A week later, Tami was pensive as they celebrated New Year's Eve together. She had now spent two and a half years in China. There were only six months left until her first term would come to an end. It had always been planned that she would return after the first three years to do more training in the U.S. She wanted to do a fellowship for further specialty training in infectious diseases.

Tami had already started sending off applications to several reputable U.S. teaching hospitals. "Matchmaking," they called the process in the U.S. "Matchmaker, matchmaker, make me a match!" Tami added laughingly. The matching was done by a computer that put together lists of programs and lists of applicants, and then came up with a "match" for the applicants. Applying for specialty training from ten thousand miles away was hardly the normal situation. So Tami figured that if she were to get a match at Emory University or Tulane, it would be an indication that God had opened the door for her. God had already answered her prayers for smooth e-mail connections and very positive phone interviews, so she trusted it would all go well.

She prayed Psalm 27:8 for the upcoming year: "My heart says of you, 'Seek His face!' Your face, LORD, I will seek . . . for these people, for my own life and future, for our team. I need to clearly see Your priorities, and not let my life be ruled by urgencies."

Not long after the Western New Year, the Chinese New Year, the most special time of year for the Chinese, arrived. People traveled long distances to join their families for the reunion meal on New Year's Eve. On Chinese New Year morning, they would make *tang yuan*, balls of sticky rice flour with sweet sesame seed paste inside, symbolizing enduring family unity and fellowship.

The year to come was "the Year of the Tiger." Everywhere, people greeted each other with *xin nian kuai le*. Children wore new clothes, and everyone decorated their doorposts and doors with red banners welcoming prosperity into their homes. The bright red and gold character on the banners meant blessing and happiness. Pictures of tigers were hung everywhere. Tami thought of the bright banner her family had put in front of their home in Denver when she was a child.

Tami spent New Year's Eve with three different sets of local friends, thankful to be welcomed into their families on this special day. She spent the next evening with some friends on-call in the medical ward in the hospital. They watched TV programs together and at midnight went outside to listen to the firecrackers. Firecrackers were forbidden, but still often used. As she walked home from the hospital, the continuous rumble and crackle of firecrackers surrounded her, echoing off the mountains. It sounded as if the air itself had shattered into thousands of fragments and was sliding down like a cascade of stones, as if the mountains had been turned to brittle paper and were being shaken by an angry giant.

The next day, she joined the pediatric staff on the ward for *tang yuan* and then had more at a local official's home. She did not think she could manage to eat any more, but there were still more sticky rice flour balls to come.

Even from her remote location in Zhaojue, Tami tried to follow one of her favorite football teams, the Denver Broncos. A diehard Broncos fan, she was desperate to watch the Super Bowl. After checking with all of the big hotels both in Zhaojue and in Xichang and finding that they no longer received any satellite stations from overseas, Tami gave up on the idea of watching the big game. But then God intervened.

Excitedly, she wrote home: "This morning, I tried again, just before leaving for the hospital. When I tuned the TV, I found a channel we'd never had before—a satellite station out of Canton, and it had THE GAME! Awesome! Just awesome! Denver must be going totally berserk! And I got to watch it! Even though I had prayed about this, coupled with an apology for even voicing such a stupid request, I still can hardly believe it. One of the best Super Bowls in the past decade. Needless to say, the Broncos won!"

Chapter 20

THE GREAT COLD MOUNTAINS

T he expanse of the Great Cold Mountains was vast, with peak upon peak stretching as far as the eye could see. All around, each mountain ridge led on to the next ridge, drawing a multitude of crisscrossing lines against the horizon. Several months into the winter, Tami said to Tomoko and Sharon, "I am ready for spring, real spring. No more washing vegetables in water that feels like liquid nitrogen. No more 'romantic' dinners by candlelight. No more games trying to keep a candle burning in the bathroom when taking a shower with no shower curtain! No more days on end without electricity when winter winds blow down our power lines."

Days turned to weeks and weeks ground to months until at last, spring showed signs of arriving in late April! Then slowly, the signs of the change in season came. The plum trees tentatively opened their bright pink-white blossoms. Over the next weeks, their blossoms filled the hospital compound with a sweet and lingering fragrance. Often the petals drifted into the hospital—a welcome decoration in the otherwise dark and dingy corridors. Outside the hospital, petals painted the otherwise bare mountainsides with delicate strokes of silver-white and pink.

With the longer days, the neighboring children visited Tami in her apartment in the evenings for games, songs, and stories. Tami relearned how to jump rope and taste innumerable mud "birthday cakes." The kids very patiently explained the complicated rules of their games to her and also taught her some Yi. A group of them took turns singing Yi songs for her. One little girl asked Tami to recite the lines from the Christmas play and then corrected her mistakes.

What amazing memories these kids have, Tami thought. She was glad that the Christmas message was imprinted in their minds.

With the arrival of spring, the hospital was planning a greening exercise. The director of the hospital informed the MSI workers that the community would help to plant bushes, trees, flowers—in short, anything green. "You and your organization are welcome to help in this community effort," he told them.

Tami, Sharon, and Tomoko prayed and discussed what the response of MSI should be. MSI donated eleven pine trees to the hospital. Nine of the smaller trees were named for the fruits of the Spirit; the two bigger ones were called "Grace" and "Righteousness." As the trees were being planted, Tami and her teammates watched and prayed intensely that these trees would become trees "of righteousness, a planting of the LORD, for the display of his splendor" (Isaiah 61:1–3).

⁂

The sun was up and brightly shining above the far mountain ridges. It was the perfect weather for a jog, with cool crisp air and a light breeze streaming across the valley. Tami's seven-year-old Yi buddy joined her for the jog up one of the nearby mountainsides. The girl wore an ankle-length, dark-colored Yi-style skirt. Despite this, she managed to keep up remarkably well. They walked up the hill past the village post and butcher and sauntered down a dusty path to the outskirts of town.

The next day, Tami's Yi buddy brought two other little Yi friends to join them for a hike up the same hillside and then on to a pine forest on the other side. The girls delighted themselves in the innumerable interesting plants, rocks, and bugs along the way. Tami's vocabulary for plants, rocks, and bugs expanded rapidly! On the return trip, they passed by a river. The children waded into the river looking for fish, trying to catch them with their bare hands. The water was cold but refreshing after the long trek. The children spread out on the hot riverside rocks to dry and happily chatted in their local dialect for some time.

"Auntie Fei," the children called out. "Come and watch our show!"

Laughing, Tami watched the children's own impromptu "Xichang fashion show." Along the way, they had found some old shoes which they now paraded and strutted in all sorts of ways. Anything seemed to be able to set them off giggling, and nothing could stop them.

Tami and the children wound their way back to town and then to her apartment. Her hands were full of fragrant wildflowers, her pockets full of "beautiful" rocks that the children had collected for her.

"Just one more stone, Auntie Fei, you have to see this one! And please also keep this one . . . it's so special! Promise you will keep it!"

"Auntie Fei, what makes the flowers and trees grow?" one of the Yi boys asked.

Tami explained, "A long time ago God created the earth. He then said, 'Let us make stones and plants and animals on it. And also humans.' So God created the world and everything that is in it. And until today He still cares for it and still loves it. And He loves us, too—even you kids!"

"Oh, Auntie Fei, we learned that many great good and bad spirits made the world a long time ago. They made both the good and the bad things. We cannot see them, but we know they are close by. At nighttime or in storms, we are often scared of them." As the children went on to share more about the animistic beliefs they were taught at home, Tami listened intently while praying for the right words to give in answer to their many questions.

Tami regularly hiked into the mountains to find solitude, peace, and time to pray. Looking down at the hospital from the mountainsides far above, she often prayed that these eleven pine trees planted in the hospital grounds would take root and grow into strong trees, not only in the literal sense, but more importantly, in the spiritual sense. "Lord, bind up the brokenhearted, free the captives of spiritual darkness, and comfort all who mourn here." Oh, how she longed that "love, joy, peace, patience, kindness, goodness, faithfulness, gentleness, and self-control" (Galatians 5:22–23) might rule there instead. "May people ask about the name tags on the trees that display the names of the fruits of the Spirit, thereby giving us a chance to share Your transforming power," she prayed.

She continued to pray for individual people she had met recently. She especially prayed for the Yi girls who went on the nature walks with her.

"God my Father, please open the hearts of these children to Your truth, so that they might find Jesus, the Truth incarnated."

Tami drew in a deep breath, slowly exhaling while taking in the colors of the mountains. The warm afternoon sun drew yellow-orange patches onto their sides. She traced the rugged mountain ridges where they met the deep blue sky. The colors were coming to life. Shades of green alternated with patches of brown, gray, and black, tipped with patches of white from the receding snow. Here she could feel God. Here He was so very real, so transcendent. Since she was a child, she had been able to see His exuberant signature written among the peaks and the valleys of mountains. In times of difficulties and discouragement, she found God speaking to her through His creation: "If I can make all this expansive splendor, you know that you can trust Me with all your life."

She wrestled with God about the next steps in her work. She interceded for her teammates and her colleagues in the hospital. The mountains reminded her so much of her home in Colorado, of all the peaks she had climbed together with her parents and her friends. As she was reminded of home and her friends and family there, she began to lift them before her Lord.

As she gazed out across the Great Cold Mountains, she reveled in the splendor of God's creation. She thought about mountains in the scriptures. Many prophets and apostles had climbed onto the tops of mountains to seek God. Noah built an altar to God on Mount Ararat. Abraham heard God speak on Mount Horeb. Moses received the Ten Commandments on Mount Sinai. Elijah climbed Mount Carmel to call upon the Lord. Jesus brought His disciples to a mountaintop to witness His transfiguration.

She burst into spontaneous praise and worship, quoting the words of Psalm 48:1–2: "Great is the LORD, and most worthy of praise, in the city of our God, his holy mountain. It is beautiful in its loftiness, the joy of the whole earth!"

But even as she prayed and worshiped in the mountains, Tami was reminded of the dangers of spiritual mountaintop experiences. She had seen many Christians seeking only the passionate highs of religious experience, not balanced by the ordinary daily grind of loving, persistent service to God.

True worship of God is not just on mountaintops. True worship means putting ourselves fully into all aspects of Christian servanthood, she thought.

She meditated on Romans 12:1: "Offer your bodies as living sacrifices, holy and pleasing to God—this is your spiritual act of worship." Tami smiled as she remembered the Gospel story: the very next thing Jesus did after His transfiguration on the mountaintop was to heal a sick boy. Tami looked down the valley. She knew she had to walk down to the valley again, both in the literal and spiritual sense, in order to do what God had called her to do: to heal the sick.

Chapter 21

THE MARTIAN DOCTOR

It wasn't long before the locals figured out that Tami was not just a Martian, but a Martian *doctor*. They stopped her on the street or in the market to ask her to evaluate their medical problems. So Tami would take out her stethoscope and examine the patient in full view of passersby and shopkeepers.

The China Youth Daily heard about Tami in the Yi mountain village and sent a reporter. He followed her around for five days, recording her every move and word on film and in his notes. There were times when Tami got tired of having a camera in her face when examining patients or when teaching on medical rounds, but his questions about her motivation and beliefs gave her the chance to share what was on her heart. A few weeks later, the story was published with the title of "The American Rose." It appeared in the *Sichuan Daily Newspaper* as a model for all medical professionals in the province.

One Saturday afternoon, twenty-seven patients were admitted to the hospital, all with the same symptoms. They all presented with headache, dizziness, nausea, vomiting, and abdominal pain. The cases caught the attention of the whole village, including the media. After some diligent detective work, Tami found out they had all eaten fried potatoes dipped in salt and spices. Initially, there was concern that the potatoes were the culprit, since they had been sprouting. However, it soon became clear that those who had eaten the plain potatoes were not ill, but those who had dipped their potatoes in salt and spices were.

Tami quickly escaped the news reporters and hid in her room. Her Internet connection had decided to cooperate, and after a long search, she finally found the answer. The culprit was the sodium nitrite used in salt production. It had contaminated the salt the patients had dipped their potatoes into. Apparently, the potato seller had cut corners by using cheap, industrial-grade salt rather than the government-inspected variety. This was confirmed when the spices went to Xichang for chemical analysis. Fortunately, all the patients survived their poisoning. Tami found the whole scenario so fascinating that she turned it into a quiz story and sent it to all her doctor friends around the world, giving some but not all of the clinical clues.

Cases at the hospital continued to be interesting, although often frustrating. One ten-year-old girl had TB meningitis. When Tami entered the room to do a spinal tap, she encountered a chicken and three family members sharing the room with this sick child. The little boy next door was suffering from methanol poisoning, and both his eyes were basically destroyed. Tami had little hope that he would ever see again. The patient in the same room had mixed alcoholic and hepatitis B cirrhosis with a hugely swollen abdomen. Both alcohol abuse and hepatitis B were common problems among the Yi. Not much could be done for this poor patient with end-stage liver disease. These cases reminded her to teach her Yi and Chinese colleagues that prevention was so much more important than cure. It all boiled down to this: work in and with the communities should be the most important focus.

HIV was not a big problem yet in the Great Cold Mountains, but it would surely soon become an issue, one best tackled sooner than later. But tuberculosis was on a major surge, affecting basically every village in the mountains. "I need to learn how to become more effective in the management and control of TB and HIV," Tami told Sharon. "That's the main reason I want to do the infectious diseases fellowship in the U.S."

Sharon was working in the surgical ward. One of her patients had been addicted to drugs for four years, and his left arm was to be amputated because of wound infection after all the drugs he had self-injected into his veins. Sharon tried everything she could to save his arm, coming by every single day to change the dressing.

One day when she was changing his dressing, he asked her, "Will God forgive all my sins, including drug addiction and sins against my parents?"

Sharon was moved by his conviction. They prayed together, and two miracles happened. He became free of drugs, and his arm completely healed and did not need to be amputated anymore. These miracles changed him completely. He became a new person. His mother was so overwhelmed by the changes she observed in her son that she said she wanted to believe in the same God. The son's faith transformed the family.

One day, a three-month-old girl was admitted with severe pneumonia. She had been ill for several days and was cyanotic from lack of oxygen when she arrived. Her parents were poor farmers, and they had bundled her in her father's jacket and a dirty shirt far too big for her. Tami quickly put her on an oxygen mask and prescribed antibiotics to treat her serious lung infection. Over the course of the next week the child gradually improved, but she was so weak that she barely ate. Tami showed the mother how to express breast milk and put it in a cup to feed the baby more easily, but even that was not working.

One afternoon when Tami went to check on her, the girl's father lamented, "She is not going to survive! She is not eating! I am going to take her home to die."

"The baby is improving on treatment—we just need to be patient and keep trying to feed her," Tami reassured the father. But he was not convinced and started packing the baby in a bundle.

If there is anything I learned during my rotations in pediatrics in Rochester, it's how to feed even the most stubborn baby, she thought.

She grabbed the bottle, gently took the baby out of the father's arms, and started to feed the girl. The baby took a while to learn how to suck on the bottle and kept falling asleep. Tami did not give up, and she tried every trick she had learned. Finally, the baby swallowed a couple of mouthfuls, and the mother happily shouted excitedly, *"Dui! Dui!"* ("That is correct! That is correct!").

The parents helped the baby get in a better position, and soon she had the hang of the bottle and had sucked down two ounces. Within minutes, the baby became more alert. The parents' once-anxious faces were all smiles. The simple act of feeding their child had given them more hope than any of Tami's words could ever do. Returning home that evening, Tami announced happily to Sharon and Tomoko, "I fed a baby today!"

In spring, a large medical team from Singapore, England, the Philippines, the U.S., and Malaysia arrived, under the dynamic leadership of Dr. Lawrence Soh from Singapore. Tami jokingly called the visit, "Medical Circus Visits the Mountain Village." After their experience last fall, Tami and Sharon had decided to run the health fair inside the hospital clinic this year. But instead of being less zoo-like, it ended up being an indoor zoo instead! At one point, the hospital Party Secretary seriously suggested moving the whole thing out to the street to improve crowd control.

Tami spent the first day fetching forgotten items and physically dragging patients into some semblance of a line. Whenever she was not watching, crowds of patients and their relatives poured into the internal medicine room (only twelve by eighteen feet!) trying to be seen sooner. As a result, the four doctors were squashed against the back of the room among much confusion and high noise levels. In three days, they saw over eight hundred patients, most of whom were incredibly creative in finding ways to cut in line. The MSI team held a Pap smear program for cancer screening among Yi women and an eye program for those with eye problems. The surgeons performed a series of small surgeries together with their Chinese and Yi surgical colleagues, and there were several concurrently running general medical clinics seeing everything from minor cases like cold symptoms to patients who were identified as suffering from TB.

They also all worked together to prepare colorful and eye-catching illustrations for a public health display. The next day, the health education program was held on the street. The crowds loved the displays, in particular Sharon's puppet show. It was an animated introduction to the adverse effects of smoking and taking drugs. Much of the public health education centered on TB and HIV/AIDS. A two-year-old was spellbound until her dad took her to a place where she could see behind the curtain of the puppet show. Her face fell as the magic disappeared, but the older children listened attentively even after they had peeked behind the curtain. One wizened old man took the blackened test tube from their smoking demonstration, promising to spread the word that smoking blackened the lungs and that one had to stop smoking.

After the hard work, the visiting team introduced some games. A handball game night was arranged for the hospital staff and their children. For hours, they played together with their Yi colleagues, rubbing shoulders and mud against each other.

During one of the evenings with the team, Tami shared that she had found an infectious disease training program in the U.S.

"Does this mean that your matchmaking efforts for the infectious diseases fellowship has worked out, Tami? I remember how you described it in your prayer request in one of your Martian newsletters, " Dr. Lawrence Soh asked.

"Yes, God has opened the doors. I was accepted into Emory University in Atlanta," Tami announced. "I will have to leave in less than two months so that I can join the fellowship program." Despite feeling exuberant about the acceptance into Emory, there was also bittersweetness at the thought of leaving.

"We should have a farewell party for Tami!" Sharon announced.

Others agreed, and they busily prepared for the party. The Zhaojue hospital staff all wanted to participate in the farewell for their beloved American colleague. Even the hospital chief announced that he wanted to join in. The evening was filled with fun, games, songs, and skits. Wearing a balloon twisted into the shape of a fish or swan on the head was *the* high fashion during the party, and everybody had a blast. The Yi colleagues taught the MSI team dancing, and in turn, the team showed them how to make even more grotesque balloon twists!

At the end of the evening, the Yi hospital director stood up to give a speech that he concluded with the words, "We have noted your sacrificial services, dedication, and compassion toward our poor Yi patients. You have set an example to our local doctors. We are all sad to see you leave." The doctor looked directly at Tami. "Dr. Fei, please promise to come back!"

Tami nodded. "Yes, I will come back."

Some team members and Dr. Lawrence Soh also gave thank-you speeches for Tami's three years of service in China. Lawrence said, "Tami, we have worked with you at two different health fairs. We are all so impressed that a beautiful American lady like you gave up all her comfort and career to serve here in this part of the world that hardly anybody knows. Tami, all we can say is that you are a NATO girl!" Everyone looked at him questioningly. "Yes, a NATO girl. You are a 'Now Action, Talk's Over' kind of girl!" They all laughed and clapped.

When Tami went to bed, she reflected on the past few years. Her struggles with the language, the culture shock, the emotional roller coasters, the flexibility lessons, the illnesses she had suffered, living in the Mister Hotel in Xichang, and now living in a gloomy apartment in the hospital compound of Zhaojue—it hadn't been easy. But she did not regret a minute of it. Indeed, the joy she was experiencing was inexplicable. She thought of the words she had recently read by Hudson Taylor, "An easy, non-self-denying life will never be one of power. Fruit-bearing involves cross-bearing."

She had very little time left to wrap up her work in China. Most importantly, she had to concentrate on all those patients who were diagnosed with serious illnesses during the health fair. They needed follow-up and proper care. She was encouraged to see that one Yi doctor really took an interest in caring for the patients. This was a doctor who had previously followed her, often listlessly, on the ward rounds. His change of heart was a direct answer to Tami's prayers.

There was so much to do before leaving. Many looked her up and wanted to talk to her about the deep issues in life. She and Sharon and Tomoko had just started to break ground and build up trust. The health fairs had added to the visibility of MSI and the work of the three pioneer women. It was sad to leave at this stage. Yet, she knew it was the right time to go. She needed to specialize further so she could return to China with higher qualifications and serve better.

The old bicycle that had served her so well had to be sold. No description would fit better than the following: "Bicycle to sell: most parts are new (as parts have been replaced by the week); subtle color scheme (blends in well with hundreds of other bicycles), top-secret source of friction, which makes it a great 'exercycle.' Entertaining—you won't need a bell!" She chuckled at the thought of putting up the ad.

As Tami was working on a drug list, she discovered a Chinese company called "Western Medicine Pharmacy" and came across some very interesting concoctions. They were so funny that she included them in her next Martian letters: "Cough mixture. It is prepared mainly with Wuzhow upright snakes biles. Dose: Children shall be reduced according to age. One vial twice a day."

She explored further and found a Chinese medicine called "zhengzhong liquid brain strengthener." Intrigued, she went on to read the English-language explanation: "Action and Indications: Tonifying Qi and enriching the blood. Strengthen the brain and reinforcing the intelligence. It is indicated for such symptoms as insomnia and amnasia."

"Guess, they couldn't remember how to spell *amnesia*," she chuckled.

She read on: "It is indicated for such diseases as febble-mindedness and declining memory, and overstrain complex for study. It is good for dizziness and feeling of fellness."

Fellness? Going-to-fall-over kind of feeling? she wondered. "Hmm . . . it is also for 'dysphoria and dreaminess.' Dreaminess? Is that a treatable medical condition?"

Thinking about her culinary adventures, she was tempted to add a few more choice items to her newsletter. Her latest discovery, a local "taste treat"—dog meat fondue—she decided to skip.

"I think we should call the restaurant that serves dog meat fondue 'Bark and Barf,'" Tami suggested to Sharon and Tomoko.

Tami also thought it appropriate to skip mention of live baby mice dipped in whiskey. And maybe she should also skip chicken, duck, and fish heads? Going for fish heads was a lost game anyway. Tomoko and Sharon loved fish heads so much that there was usually nothing left.

Her seafood-loving teammates also had other treats for her. Tomoko had a special Japanese treat that she had brought back during her New Year break. They were cheese strips with thin slices of fish pressed on each side. Tami teased Tomoko, saying it was a tragic waste of perfectly good cheese, which was very difficult to get in China and definitely considered a rare delicacy in the Great Cold Mountains. She also lovingly teased her about special Kobe beef. Apparently, in Kobe where Tomoko came from, they chose certain calves, fed them beer, and gave them a daily muscle massage to make their meat very tender. "It *is* excellent beef, Tomoko! Don't get me wrong there. But I'm sure some people would consider it a tragic waste of perfectly good beer!"

What could round out her series of culinary adventures? It had to be shark stomach. "Yes, shark stomach. This is one of those foods that fits the 'I just ate WHAT??' category," she wrote. "It is beige and spongy with a mild salty flavor, so I initially thought it was some sort of reconstituted seaweed."

Shopping in the Yi stalls around Zhaojue, she found some beautiful Yi lacquer-ware and hand-painted Yi ladles, bowls, and pitchers which would make beautiful gifts for her friends and family back home.

Saying farewell to Sharon and Tomoko was not easy. When she finally boarded the plane for Chengdu at the Xichang airport, there were many officials, doctors, nurses, and children to see her off. Two years ago, she had arrived in the Great Cold Mountains and everything had felt so foreign to her. Now, it was her home, and she felt so much a part of it that leaving was painful.

When she arrived in Chengdu, Tami had one final goal. She wanted to buy a handwritten Chinese calligraphy banner with her beloved text from 1 Corinthians. The night market next to the river in Chengdu was the best bet. Hundreds of banners with Chinese calligraphy were sold there. She prayed that she would find what she was looking for, and she met an old Chinese man with a very bright smile. They started talking, and it turned out that he had once been a doctor and that he was a believer. After retiring from medicine, he made his living making and selling Chinese calligraphy. Tami asked him whether he would be willing to write out the words of 1 Corinthians 13 in Chinese calligraphy. They opened the Bible together and read through the verses.

The old doctor's face shone. "Very much willing," he said. "But the text is long and will need four separate banners." They settled on a price.

The next day, Tami, with the four banners under her arm and all the belongings she had accumulated over the past three years in the plane's cargo hold, flew off to Hong Kong and then on to the United States.

Tami in 1993 at her
Medical Residency
Quarter at Beijing's
Children's Hospital

The Wilder-Smiths
with Sharon and
another friend

Original Exchange Doctors to the U.S. from China in 1990
at a picnic celebrating Tami's Emory Graduation

Dr. Leung , Dr. James Hudson Taylor III, Tami, and Dr. Matthew Koh on her arrival in China

First MSI Team of
Sharon with Tomoko
and Tami enjoying
"central foot heating"

Local Sechuan officials meeting with Dr. Taylor and Tami

Tami pictured with the "Super Welcome" Mandarin speaking medical team from Singapore

Auntie Fei (Tami) with little hikers

Tami and Sharon with the training class of Health Workers

Tami's impromptu Doctor call on the street

Tami making a Yi home call with "Barefoot doctors" (in white coats)

Tami visiting Nara and family in Mongolia

Tami in traditional
Yi dress

Tami hiking
in China mountains

The infamous
bicycle

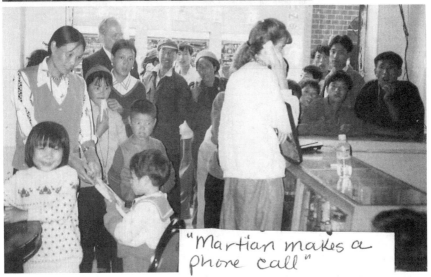

"Martian makes a
phone call"

(Tami wrote ▲)

PART
three

FINAL JOURNEY

Chapter 22

THE MARTIAN RETURNS TO THE UNITED STATES

A s the plane started its descent into Denver, it banked steeply, opening up views of the Colorado Rocky Mountains. Tami saw patches of snow in the higher locations and could not help thinking about the Great Cold Mountains she had left behind. Then the aircraft leveled off for the last part of the landing, and the skyline of Denver, twinkling in the midday sun, was welcoming her home. She could not wait to get out of the plane to embrace her parents and deeply breathe the fresh Colorado mountain air again.

"Mom! Dad!" Seeing her parents waiting for her at the baggage retrieval belt, she ran toward them. "I missed you so much." Shedding tears of joy, they hugged each other.

"I'm so thankful for all the help and support you have given me over these past three years in China. I'm so fortunate to have such great parents! Not everyone is as blessed as I am."

Her parents had printed and sent out her numerous newsletters, most notably her Martian letters, to supporters all over the world. They had sorted through mountains of mail, canceled stolen credit cards, paid bills, and managed to maintain Tami's medical license and hospital privileges on her behalf. Most importantly, they had done some miracle paperwork to get her fellowship sorted out at Emory University!

"You must have invested several thousand trees' worth of paperwork, not to mention the forest necessary for the health insurance!" Tami chuckled.

"We are happy to help in any way we can. It makes us feel part of your ministry," her parents declared.

"It feels good to be at home again!" Tami took a deep breath of the fresh air. "And isn't it great that I'm arriving in time for Tim's wedding?"

༄

Tami moved to Marshall and Sherrie Williams's home in Atlanta after a brief stay with her family and friends in Denver. The fact that these friends offered their home to her just at a time when she needed it was yet another reminder of how God was looking after her in the practical details of life.

Life back in the United States soon proved to be quite a change and challenge. "People here in the U.S. do not stare at me as if I'm a Martian, but sometimes I feel like I've returned to Mars," she wrote in her Martian letter to her friends.

> I've had to pull out all the adaptation skills and flexibility I learned overseas in order to adjust to this land of voice mail, beanie baby crazes, and paperless hospitals. I've had to learn new vocabulary, like "road rage" and "chat room," to be able to participate in daily conversations. At work, there are new drugs to learn about, and many of the old bacteria have new names since they were reclassified based on DNA. I'm slowly learning to surf the net and am getting reacquainted with car repairs and parking. Oh, for that ancient but functional bicycle that could be fixed with just a tire pump and a hammer! And by the way, if you happen to see me in the grocery store or wherever, please say "Hello, Tami" not just "Hello!" Since I heard "Hello" at least fifty times a day in China, I no longer pay any attention to it on its own.

Tami went on to explain some of the differences she had noticed between East and West:

> There were situations in China that were difficult to describe to Western friends, but there are also some things here that I'll *never* be able to explain to friends in China. Demo apartments have fake cereal on the dining room table. The supermarket's produce section has a recording of thunder that precedes the sprinkler system used to keep the veggies moist. In this automated, mass-produced society, I miss the individual faces of farmers and their kids who

sold us their produce in open markets where *real* thunder meant the end of the shopping day.

I have so many reasons to be thankful during this time of transition. Friends and churches have welcomed me back with open arms, eager to offer any help that I need and to listen to my stories from China and my struggles with readjusting here. New Chinese friends have welcomed me into their homes, feeding me great Chinese food and letting me speak Chinese, act Chinese, and stay caught up on events in China.

Tami soon found an apartment to rent in the vicinity of Emory University. While unpacking and sorting out her belongings, she carefully unwrapped the four banners with the complete "Love Chapter" in beautiful Chinese calligraphy. Her thoughts returned to the many times she had sung these words in Chinese with her friends and colleagues, to the officials in the Yi hospital and to the little Chinese and Yi children she so loved to be with. Her father was helping her with the renovation of the apartment, and he offered to put up the banners on the wall.

"Please be careful, Dad. These banners are my most prized possessions!" Together they put up the banners at a central location in her apartment. "I want them to catch the attention of every visitor," she said.

༄

"These words are so beautiful!" Dai exclaimed as she stood in front of the banners, tracing the lines of the Chinese characters. Dai had just left China to study at Emory University. And Tami had offered to share her apartment with her.

"These words are from the Bible," Tami explained.

"I don't know anyone who loves in a way as it is described on this banner," Dai continued.

"Yes, I agree. None of us have that kind of love ourselves. It is only through God's love that we may be able to love others as He does," Tami explained.

Dai was moved. "You know, in China it is all about 'I give you something, so you will give me something back.' That is our culture."

"Dai, the Bible says that God gives freely."

Dai was impressed. "I want to learn more about the meaning of these words."

Over the following months, Tami shared the gospel with her new room-mate. She taught Dai how to sing the Love Song. Together, they had fun discovering or rediscovering American culture and food. They also prepared Chinese meals and invited Chinese colleagues over. And Tami was thrilled that she was able to keep up her Chinese language skills.

One of Tami's first priorities was to rejoin the International Fellowship in Atlanta. It was part of the Intown Community Church she had attended before she left for China. This church had faithfully supported her through-out the years. During her time away, they had kept up a thriving ministry to foreign students.

"Welcome back home, Tami!" Nicole Mares gave Tami a warm welcome hug. "I'm the new missions administrator at Intown Community Church. I took over from Paula Helms when she left for China. Paula always told me how much your example and testimony had an impact on her decision to serve in China."

"I've brought a Chinese fan with calligraphy as a gift to the church," Tami said, handing the fan to Nicole. It came in an ornate purple flowered box. Nicole opened the fan carefully and studied the Chinese calligraphy.

"Thank you so much, Tami. This is such a special gift! You know, I've re-ally enjoyed reading all your Martian letters. So beautifully written, with such a great sense of humor! I always wait eagerly for the next one, and guess what? Your letters are passed on from person to person in our fellowship as we all love your anecdotes and funny descriptions—in particular your culinary adventures!"

Nicole continued, "You'll be glad to know our pastor Joe Laird has a very special heart for China. He is very much looking forward to your in-volvement in the ministry to the Chinese here in Atlanta. Your language skills and understanding of the Chinese culture will help break the ice and deepen relationships."

"Sure! There is nothing I would like to do to more." Tami thought of the materials she had developed as a youth leader. She could use them for the services of the international fellowship.

In the months to come, Tami became active in the social events commit-tee. She helped write many skits and sermons, and she always had an open home for her Chinese friends.

Tami's fellowship in infectious diseases at Emory University turned out to be everything she had hoped for. She immersed herself in patient care, research, and teaching. Endless hours were spent reading through textbooks and journal articles to get updated on recent developments and new insights in infectious diseases. Being in a large leading teaching hospital meant that fellows of the infectious disease course were exposed to many illnesses with unusual presentations and rare causes. Finding the right diagnosis was helped by the availability of an immense range of laboratory and imaging investigations, as well as books and colleagues to check with. How different from rural China, where the doctors were equally keen to get the diagnosis right, but due to a lack of resources, often just had to guess the diagnosis. Tami enjoyed preparing cases for presentations at the grand rounds.

One evening, the telephone interrupted her preparations for the grand rounds. "Hi Tami, it's Tim. Welcome back!" Brother and sister exchanged some jokes and old memories, and Tim said, "Tami, I can't wait to see you in Detroit!"

"Yes, and what an occasion. Your wedding!"

"Actually, I have something to ask you about that. Kristin and I would like you to be my best man—or maybe I should say my 'best person'—for our wedding!"

"Wow, Tim . . . what an honor. Of course I would love to. I'm so happy for you two!" The two talked and talked, about the past, the future, and anything and everything that crossed their minds.

Putting down the phone, Tami sat down for a while. Sure, she and her brother had their share of squabbles as young children, but she remembered how amazingly close they had been, especially as teenagers. She had a great brother. She pulled out the poem he had written for her several years ago for Valentine's Day:

VALENTINE POEM
To the sister that has chosen paths that glorify God,
I will always watch in amazement and admiration.

Though I specialize in being a pain,
you continually forgive me and even treat me as an equal.
I will never be an equal, just a proud observer.

Your advice and input to my endeavors opens up opportunities to me,
that I could not gain on my own.
That, I can never repay.

I hope for your continued success and
pray that God will continue to light your path.

Wishing you some Colorado Blue Sky and a

HAPPY VALENTINES DAY!

From your little brother with Love,
Tim

As Tami thought about her brother's upcoming marriage, she had a quiet laugh over the Chinese newspaper clip that had been written about her when she was living in Sichuan. Her language teacher at the school in Chengdu had taken a liking to Tami and had kept in contact even after Tami had left Chengdu. She followed Tami's travels from Chengdu to Xichang and then on to the Great Cold Mountains, and she was so impressed by Tami's service to China that she had shared the story with a national daily Chinese newspaper. Tami took out the newspaper clipping and read.

Her American name is Tami Fisk, but we affectionately call her Tian Ni. She is a "soldier of globalism," determined to devote herself to helping China's poor. She is full of joyful enthusiasm and devotion. Tian Ni now lives in a remote mountainous area not too far from Xichang. She is reluctant to leave that area, as she loves the people there so much.

When I asked her "Isn't your life there lonely?" she replied, "Sometimes I'm a little lonely, but usually I'm too busy and I have no time to think about loneliness."

I asked her: "Do you want to get married someday?"

"Sometimes I think I'd like to, because I'm already over thirty."

I wanted to know more. "So, what are your criteria for marrying?"

She answered me in the following way, "He definitely must like China, and he must be supportive of my work or come to China and work with me."

"Isn't this standard a little too high?"

"No, not too high. What I have shared is just the basics, the bare minimum."

"Why?"

"Because I've decided to work in China for a number of years. That's my ambition, my most important goal. So, if I find a husband, he should have similar goals."

"What if you can't find that kind of a husband, though?"

"It doesn't matter. I would be a little sad, but I really would have no regret, because I am devoted to God and His call for me is to be in China."

She is such a wonderful young lady, even willing to pay any cost, not begrudging her youth or her love life to realize her ideal of helping China's poor.

How funny some of the "Chinese English" expressions were! Tami put down the newspaper piece and chuckled. She was still not sure whether she should be flattered or horrified by the article!

Tami soon became close friends with the bride-to-be, Kristin. The wedding day arrived quickly. Kristin had arranged for the dresses and makeup for the bridesmaids and Tami. Tami hardly ever used makeup, but for the big day she agreed to use some. With her brown hair put up, the eyeliner brought out her sparkling blue eyes, and blush accentuated her fine facial features. The dress emphasized her tall, slender figure. Tami looked stunning. Several of the male guests commented to Tim how beautiful his sister was. When Tim told this to Tami, she simply laughed.

She basked in the happiness of her brother and his bride. She delivered her carefully prepared speech as the groom's "best person" and was overjoyed when Tim approached her afterward.

"Thanks so much for your great speech! It was truly amazing. Really meaningful words. You could have drawn the attention to your work in China, but you did not. Your focus was just on Kristin and me." He gave her a gentle hug. "It's so special that you can be here with us to celebrate!"

It was a happy day, though almost surreal. Quietly, Tami thanked God for the wedding, for her loving family, for her home, and for granting her one of the most prestigious infectious diseases fellowships. Things were looking good.

Chapter 23

CANCER

I t was definitely blood. She checked again. No doubt about it . . . her finger was tainted with blood when she touched her left ear. There was some scaly dark tissue on the lower aspect of the earlobe, at the place where, several years ago, she'd had a lesion removed. Tami was alarmed. Without any delay, she went to see a specialist.

The dermatologist examined her ear and was concerned. He immediately took a biopsy, a small tissue sample of the earlobe, and sent it for further investigations. Tami did not have to wait long. Two days later, the pathology result came back. What she had not dared to think was now written in black and white.

It was melanoma. Skin cancer.

Melanoma. Tami's heart sank. One word, but she knew it would change her life. Her brain raced. Had the cancer already spread to other parts of her body? She could not afford to lose any time. Running between ward rounds to care for her own patients, she managed to arrange for further examinations at the hospital she worked for. Within days, she had a thorough body check, CTs, MRIs, and bone scans done. Together with the specialists, she looked carefully through all the results.

There was some good news, but also some bad news. The good news was that no spread of the cancer to remote parts of her body could be found. The bad news was that they did find one enlarged lymph node in front of the ear. One could even palpate it with the fingers. Without much further delay, the decision was made to remove most of the left ear and to extend the surgery to her neck and remove all neck lymph nodes.

Only three months after she had returned from China and started her fellowship at Emory University, Tami found herself in the operating room. Waiting for the anesthetic and worried about what was awaiting her, Tami focused on God.

Lord, the past week has passed in a haze. Lord, I can barely look beyond the haze. Lord, I trust you. I surrender my anxiety to you. Quietly, she started praising and worshiping Him.

Finally the anesthetist arrived. "Are you ready, Tami?"

"Yes, I'm ready," came Tami's firm reply.

A few days later, Tami stood in front of the mirror. The bandage had just been taken off, revealing her ear and neck. The tumor and most of her ear had been removed, along with twenty-two lymph nodes from her neck. Earlier in the morning, she had been given the pathology results. One of the lymph nodes was indeed cancerous, which meant the cancer had gone beyond the limits of the small cancerous area of her earlobe. As a physician, she knew the implications all too well. Melanoma that had gone beyond the original site had a poor prognosis.

The mirror showed the gnarled little ear stump covered with scaling blood crusts, all that was left of her ear. She gripped the sink with both hands to steady herself. Would she ever be able to get used to this? She traced the long scar downwards, from the ear down to her lower neck. Stepping closer to the mirror, Tami tried to force a smile. She did not recognize herself. What was wrong with her mouth? With a thumping heart, she realized the left side of her mouth was drooping downward. This meant that parts of her left facial nerve had been damaged during surgery—a complication the surgeons had warned her about. Tears welled up in her eyes. Standing there, frozen in front of the mirror, tears trickled down her cheeks. What would the future hold?

Her thoughts went back to the many times at Christmas when her family did mystery jigsaw puzzles. She saw herself sitting with her family in front of the fire putting together all one thousand pieces. Patiently, with time, the puzzle would come together. The puzzle of her life had also been coming together so nicely. And now, it was as if her own puzzle had been tossed in the air, all the pieces irretrievably scattered!

All the treatment she would need to go through from now on. All the uncertainties about the prognosis. How long would she have to live?

"Lord," she burst out, "I do not understand. I thought the pieces of my life's puzzle were all so neatly put together by You, leading me to serve in China forever. But now! Now my plans are falling apart. My plans to return to China are falling apart. Why, Lord, why?" she cried.

All of a sudden, she was reminded of the evening with Helen Rosevaere many years ago at Wheaton College. The words of that evening echoed in her head: "Can you trust me in this difficult situation, even if I never tell you why?"

The answer was crystal clear to Tami, and she spoke out loud: "Yes, Lord. If somehow, somewhere this fits for Your purposes, I trust you in this, even if I don't understand why."

Wiping away her tears, she took her Bible. *Lord, speak to me through Your Word.*

The Bible opened at the book of Jeremiah, her eyes catching Jeremiah 29:11: "'For I know the plans I have for you,' declares the LORD, 'plans to prosper you, and not to harm you, plans to give you hope and a future.'"

She read the words again and again. The words sank into her heart. Slowly, she felt a sense of calm return to her. "Thank You, Lord, for speaking to me."

It was one of the verses in her life that she had read and studied so often, but the verse gained a whole new meaning for her now.

She went back to look at herself again in the mirror. She reached for her brush and started combing her hair over the remains of her ear as best as possible. *The loss of beauty does not matter, really. What matters is that God knows me and gives me all the hope I need.* She pulled her shoulders back. *I will keep my hair long over my ear and neck so people won't notice the damage too much.*

That evening, she sat down in front of her computer and wrote an e-mail to all her friends and supporters around the world, explaining what had happened to her. She ended the letter with the words: "I don't know what the future holds, but I do know Who holds the future."

The immediate future held injections of interferon. Interferon was given to melanoma patients to combat the cancer by boosting the immune system. For four months, Tami injected herself with interferon under the skin every second day. Tami likened it to "flu in a syringe" since it caused her fatigue, muscle aches, fever, and chills. It was like constantly having the flu, not just for a week, but for four long months. Her energy levels were low. She lost weight. Her hair thinned. But despite all this, she continued to work in the hospital seeing patients, doing research, and pursuing her training in infectious diseases. She was grateful that she could continue to do the work, even if she felt under the weather most of the time. She was looking forward to finishing the interferon course, after which she planned to gain some weight and then get reconstructive surgery for her ear.

Alas, it was not to be! After Tami completed her course of interferon, she underwent a series of repeat scans. To her shock, the scans showed new spots of disease activity. Of particular concern was one spot in a region deep inside her neck, behind the throat.

"Tami, although the tumor recurrence is only small, the location makes it impossible for us to access and remove it," the lead surgeon explained. "Frankly, this is inoperable."

The word "inoperable" cut deep. There were also palpable nodes in her neck in the area around her scar. Tami knew that things had to move quickly to prevent further spread.

Three chaotic weeks followed. "Three *very* long weeks," she wrote to her friends. The experts on melanoma had differing opinions about what the best treatment in her particular situation should be. As medical consultation after consultation followed, treatment plans often changed—sometimes daily. Surgery followed by radiation was the standard treatment. Chemotherapy was another option. Because the recurrence seemed to be localized within the original surgical area, the opinion of the doctors in Atlanta was that the toxicity of chemotherapy probably outweighed its benefits.

She frantically obtained addresses of other specialists in the U.S. and consulted them over the phone—and they agreed that chemotherapy might not be the best choice at the current stage. She explored other, less toxic options. One of those options was a melanoma vaccine followed by surgery. She found out that in Philadelphia, university oncologists were doing cutting-edge research on a new type of vaccine against melanoma which seemed to have promising results. This vaccine entailed taking out tumor cells from the patient, modifying them, and then giving them back to the patient in the hope that the immune system would be able to better recognize and fight the cancerous melanoma cells. If she were to opt for this approach, known as autologous vaccine, she would have to move to Philadelphia, sorting out her insurance and all the other lo-gistics involved in receiving treatment in another city. Despite all these challenges, she knew she would tackle all of it if it would improve her chances of healing.

All the looming decisions made her more and more anxious to move forward quickly. Examining her neck, she could feel the lumps in her neck growing from day to day. She decided to quickly arrange for the flight to Philadelphia and for an appointment with the specialist.

⸎

"Tami, you have recurrent disease, and we have not had much success with our new autologous vaccine in cases with recurrent disease," the oncologist in Philadelphia told her.

Tami swallowed, but she didn't give up. An appointment with a surgeon in Philadelphia had also been arranged for that day. The surgeon found more tiny nodules in her neck and advised that it would be impossible to remove all the lesions in surgery without some kind of pretreatment first. At the end of the day, the suggestion from the experts in Philadelphia was to undergo multidrug chemotherapy, after which the decision had to be made whether to do surgery or something else.

There was hardly any time to reflect. Tami had to book her return flight quickly and receive treatment. She felt numb. Everything around her was tumbling. She tried to focus on what had to be done next. She took strength from the words she had read in her quiet time that morning from 2 Corinthians 4:8, The Message: "We've been surrounded and battered by troubles, but we're not demoralized." The passage went on to declare that even though on the outside it often looks like things are falling apart, on the inside God is making new life.

The next day, Tami saw the surgeon in Atlanta who agreed that there were new spots—new since last week—and said it was good he had not tried to operate because more would have popped up after surgery. Despite all the frenzy in the past weeks that delayed the start of her treatment, Tami saw God's hand in all this. There was a reason for all this waiting. The doctors had confirmed what she had started to suspect: her cancer, though still localized, was aggressive and rapidly growing. This meant it should be treated aggressively and systemically. Surgery and local radiation would not be enough; she needed chemotherapy that would kill the cancer cells wherever they were in her body. This was a grim new insight, but at least she now knew what she had to face up to.

Although the prospects of chemotherapy were perturbing, Tami was relieved that finally a decision had been made. She would take "biochemo lite"—three different chemotherapeutic drugs in addition to some immune stimulants to boost her immune system. The plan was to remove any residual lumps after two rounds of treatment. She started treatment the next day.

༖

"These three weeks have been the most difficult time in my entire life," she wrote in her letter to her friends. "And dealing with all the uncertainties, the difficult decisions, and the paperwork related to insurance issues was sometimes more stressful than dealing with the disease itself."

Sunday was her rest day, a day to spend with the Lord. She shared the bad news in the evening church service. The members cared deeply for her, and the evidence of this touched her heart. During the service, members of the congregation prayed for her. Afterward, some came up to her to pray once more and offer her practical help whenever and wherever she needed it. Tami was encouraged—this personal touch meant a lot to her. She could feel God's hand upon her.

Stepping out of the church, she took a long walk by herself. She needed to spend some time on her own. She knew that despite all the support, the journey ahead would be a lonely one.

It was evening. Behind her, the last glow of the sun cast highlights of golden amber across the grass. Everything had been drenched an hour earlier by a brief thunderstorm, and now the evening felt cool and fresh, and with the fading light, almost surreal. A half-moon hung heavily overhead. As she walked, images of China filled her mind. The recent weeks had been a roller coaster. She thought of her early years in China and how she had also gone through an emotional roller coaster there. She almost smiled when she thought of her lessons in flexibility in Xichang and Zhaojue. Some aspects of what she was going through now were really quite similar, except that these last few weeks had been flexibility lessons in fast-forward. Had God been preparing her for an even bigger test? But she also knew that the recent lessons in flexibility had come close to breaking her.

Lord, she confided, *I cannot take care of my illness and its management, all the decisions, and arranging the paperwork for medical insurance as well as rearranging my call schedule and rounds in the hospital. I cannot be the doctor for my own illness. Please lead me to a doctor who will coordinate my treatment. I want to be a normal patient receiving treatment for my illness, and separately a doctor when I'm at work.*

Another thought crossed her mind. *Lord,* she continued, *help me to learn to be grateful for all things, be they small or big.*

That evening she sat down to write an e-mail to her friends.

Dear friends and supporters,

Although I would rather be in China, I am very grateful to be in the U.S. at this stage to deal with my illness. I have a good job, good health insurance, and an instant network of physicians of all specialties. As part of my infectious disease fellowship, I rotate from hospital to hospital each month, but this month, I just "happened" to be at Emory Hospital. That means I can continue working and run across the street for doctor visits in the Emory Clinic, and downstairs for X-rays and blood work whenever necessary. I also have a great extended family here who have welcomed me back with open arms and have looked after me when I was in need and have lifted me up faithfully in prayer through this difficult time. I will work relatively normal hours (sixty-five hours or so) this week. For now, I prefer to stay busy.

Tami planned a trip to Denver, but the trip had to be delayed because of low white blood counts from the chemotherapy. Calling her mother, she explained, "Mom, don't worry. The flight was delayed for a purpose. I was able to help my Chinese friends who needed me to help translate when they were in hospital. They had to go to the emergency department after a car accident. And the highlight was that I was able to celebrate China's fiftieth anniversary in Atlanta with more than one hundred members of the Chinese community. We paraded around downtown accompanied by flags, balloons, music, and the chanting of slogans like 'Long Live China,' and 'I Love China.' The best chant was 'Made in China,' but of course I couldn't join that one. I was feeling very weak, but I really enjoyed the day. What a blessing to be in Atlanta for this."

Taking chemotherapy and continuing work at Emory was not easy. Her colleagues were very understanding, and she was given a lighter rotation. Her attending physician suggested that she should interrupt her training so she could focus on the chemotherapy, but Tami did not agree. She felt that work would distract from her sense of physical ill-being. And she reasoned that if her life was to be short, it should be filled with meaningful work.

After several courses of chemotherapy, her immune system weakened and she had to stop some aspects of research on live bacteria for fear of getting dangerously infected herself. She had to choose another research project. Tami tried as much as possible not to change her clinical rotation or take time off, even if she felt quite ill. She certainly did not want to be a burden to her colleagues. So she often gritted her teeth, and with the resolve so typical of her, got through long hours in the hospital even if she felt utterly exhausted. It was important to her that her colleagues did not notice how badly she was suffering.

With each cycle of chemotherapy, she felt worse. She had lost ten pounds over the past months and was gaunt. At the end of the first round of chemotherapy, she felt awful. Waves of nausea shook her body. Bending over her bed, she vomited profusely into the bucket. She felt faint. Tears rolled down her cheeks when she realized that she had no choice; she had to phone her colleagues and excuse herself from work.

Tami sank back into her bed and cried, "Oh Lord, heal me. Please heal me."

Chapter 24

INTENSIVE CHEMOTHERAPY

Tami's e-mails, sent to her close circle of friends and supporters, were forwarded to other friends who again forwarded them to their friends and supporters. Prayer groups sprung up in Atlanta and Denver, and soon in various places around the world, in particular among her Christian Chinese friends. Her MSI colleagues in Hong Kong and China were deeply affected by the news of her illness. Dr. Taylor, Sharon, and Tomoko were particularly shaken by the news, and they fervently prayed for her. They set aside times of fasting and prayer in addition to praying for her during daily morning devotions in the MSI office.

The e-mails soon reached Singapore, home of many of the doctors and nurses who formed the short-term MSI teams in Xichang and Zhaojue that Tami had coordinated in the past. They had all grown to love and respect her. Her plight triggered many prayer meetings in Singapore.

The news reached New Zealand via the couple who had served alongside Tami during the sheep donation project in the Great Cold Mountains. Prayer meetings took place in the North and South Islands of New Zealand, spread to Australia, and then were held in MSI offices around the world in Canada, the United States, the United Kingdom, and other parts of Europe. People and prayer groups who had never met her were touched by her e-mails and prayed for her.

Tami received much encouragement through the many thoughtful e-mails and letters from all over the world. She was often surprised by which corner of the world they came from. Although she wanted to respond to the messages, she was too weak to do so. She barely had the strength to make it through another day of chemotherapy and work at Emory.

Halfway through her chemotherapy, she noticed that the nodes in her neck were not shrinking. They were not growing, but they were certainly not shrinking. She knew this was not a good sign. She now had an excellent team of doctors who managed her illness, and she was grateful for this. A whole series of repeat scans was ordered. Going through the scans and blood work was routine for her now.

✧

"Tami, your cancer is even more aggressive than we thought. We need to change your therapy from biochemo lite to the most aggressive chemotherapy." The doctor carefully explained what Tami already knew. "This chemotherapy will, however, make you very ill. You will not be able to continue work. As a result of the chemotherapy, your immune system will be depleted. You will be in the intensive care unit for many weeks. There is a high risk that you may die of an overwhelming infection."

Tami asked a few questions. All through the conversation, she kept up a steady and confident attitude. But she was able to do this only by silently praying throughout. In her heart of hearts, somehow God had been preparing her for this news during her quiet times over the past few days.

In the ensuing days, Tami watched pieces of a puzzle come together. Who would look after her during the chemotherapy? She could not go through this type of aggressive chemo without constant nursing care and support. The answer was obvious: Her mother was a nurse. And her mother had only very recently sold her own business and was now free to look after her.

Tami phoned her parents, and they immediately set everything in motion. Within a short time, the arrangements for her chemotherapy in Denver were settled. Tami packed up her research work, her laptop, and her scientific journals so she would have "some work to do in Denver." Her colleagues arranged for coverage for her rotation at Emory. So in late 1999, Tami moved home to Denver.

It is good being at home again, Tami thought.

Her parents welcomed her with great warmth and care, and she immediately felt relaxed and at ease in the familiar surroundings. Her body was already battered by all the treatments she had received. They all knew that attempting further chemotherapy would be risky, even life-threatening. The tension within her family was palpable. Would Tami survive the next weeks?

"Shall we do one of those hikes we used to do when I was small?" Tami suggested to her parents. "We need to prepare and pray for the aggressive chemotherapy ahead. And we should do this before I become too ill."

The next day, the family set out for the mountains. It was a picture-perfect day. The Colorado sky was at its brightest blue, the bright sunshine at its most welcoming. It was the height of the Aspen color season. Golden leaves shone as if lit from within, shimmering against the azure skies. A breeze gently rocked the trees, just enough to make one feel fresh. They chose an easy climb.

Tami's heart ached as it was evident that her strength was greatly reduced; she had a hard time keeping up with her parents. In the past, she would run way ahead of them and then back, encouraging them to push themselves harder up the mountains. Now she was the one to fall behind. Tami pushed herself as much as she could. Her heart was racing; her muscles felt sore. Deep inside, she made up her mind that as soon as she completed chemo, she would start training again. Should she train for a triathlon? She had always wanted to do that!

They arrived at a lake in a deep valley where three mountain ridges converged. A perfect spot to rest for a while. At the lake shore, they soaked up the sun and renewed their energy. As they sat there, surveying the lake and the dense foliage in the valley, they took the courage to address the issues they were all facing.

Her father broached the subject. "Tami, we will go through this ordeal together. We know God will uphold us."

Tami turned around and gave him a big hug. "Thanks, Dad. Thank you, Mom and Dad, for all your support and love throughout my life."

"Tami, we are all praying for your healing," her father continued.

"Dad, I know you are. I am too. I pray for healing every day. And I've no doubt in my mind that God can heal. On some days, I turn to Him in desperation. Other days, I'm in close communion with Him and have such peace knowing that He has the best plans. Maybe His plans are different from those I would wish for. But He is in control, isn't He?"

They were quiet for a while. Tami's mother was struggling against the tears welling up.

"Mom, we can cast all our anxieties on Him because He cares about us. Remember 1 Peter 5:7?" They had learned this verse by heart together many years ago. Tami put her arms around her mom. "God can do immeasurably more than all we ask or imagine, Mom. He will continue to guide us with His presence and give us sufficient strength to do His will."

Holding hands, they prayed together for a long time. They prayed that Tami would survive the chemotherapy and implored God that He would heal her. They went on to intercede for Tim and his wife in Detroit, for Dr. Taylor in Hong Kong, and for the work of MSI in China.

At the end, Tami's mother looked up confidently. "I had the impression from God that you will get through this chemotherapy, Tami. It will be difficult. But you will get through."

Tami nodded. "Somehow I believe that, too."

They walked home down the winding trail without talking much, quietly taking in the radiant colors of the late fall afternoon.

The next weeks were hard. After Tami started on the aggressive chemotherapy, she battled high fevers, diarrhea, and vomiting. She was placed in intensive care. The vicious side effects of chemo had kicked in. Her immune system was precariously depleted. Her white blood cells, all-important for preventing infection, were almost completely wiped out. She had to be cared for in an isolation room in the intensive care unit. Nobody was allowed to visit her; if there were visitors, they had to wear masks, gloves, and gowns so they could not pass on any infection to her. Tami lost all her hair. She lost more weight and had no appetite at all. Vomiting became a constant feature. To stop the vomiting, she was put on sedative drugs, and she often drifted in and out of consciousness.

"One day, I hallucinated an entire college football game. It was between the Burritos and the Coffee Carriers, both with cute little mascots. The Burritos came back from behind to win it, although I've forgotten the final score," she recounted later.

At times, she had no strength to pray or read the Bible, but she rested in the knowledge that others were praying for her. It was like her brain had gone into hibernation. Later, she wrote that probably the best part of the intense treatment in Denver was her lack of memory of it, a result of the high doses of sedatives. When she was conscious, she often felt depressed, without purpose or hope. However, when the heavens felt like brass, she remembered what a friend from China had once cautioned her: she had told her never to forget that "no matter what, you have eternal life!" This simple truth lifted and carried Tami in critical times of doubt so that she was able to say, "God renewed me spiritually with, as best as I can describe, a spirit of praise."

Between cycles of treatment, her blood counts normalized. This meant she could spend some time at home before the next cycle started. She tried to catch up on all the things she had not been able to do in the past weeks. She wrote up some research, visited, and received friends. All too soon, the next round of chemotherapy started.

"Each time is tougher and more difficult to recover from," she e-mailed her friends.

> It seems that among other things, white blood cells make you feel good, and not having them makes you feel lousy. I could write you a whole saga on vomiting—the good, the bad, and the really ugly— but I'll spare you. I will, though, share with you one item—my Mom asked me last Friday if I had vomited out of my nose like I did in the past weeks, and I very happily said no. That became my "thing to be thankful for" for that day. Today I'm extremely thankful for something else: an abstract I submitted with my research mentor that I wrote in between chemotherapy cycles, partly still in a drug haze, has been accepted! This means I will go to the big AIDS meeting in San Francisco in February next year—*if* I am still alive.

At the completion of the next treatment, she was able to be at home again. Mission Hills Church members often brought meals to help her gain weight. They decorated her room and plastered the walls with many "Get Well" wishes and prayer items. She felt upheld by her church family in Denver and by her church friends and work colleagues from Atlanta who also kept in close contact. Especially encouraging to her were the many phone calls and cards she received from her Chinese friends.

A very special visitor was Dr. Taylor with his wife Leonie. They were on a speaking tour in the United States and had set time aside to travel to Denver to visit Tami. They spent several days with Tami in her home.

"Thank you so much for coming," Tami welcomed them. "I'm so sorry you have to see me in such a bad state." Tami was thin and had lost all her hair.

"Tami, we are so pleased to be here with you during this difficult time. Aren't we brothers and sisters in Christ during the good and bad times?"

Dr. Taylor's smile was warm and genuine. "We bring you special greetings from Sharon and Tomoko. They both miss you very much. They also send special greetings from the director of the hospital, the director of the Public Health Bureau, and many doctors you worked with in the past years. They all hold you in high respect, and all of them hope that someday, you will be able to come back. Tami, you have had an incredible impact in China during your three years. Without your service and example, we could not move ahead as we are doing now. The people there trust you, and because of the trust you have established, they trust MSI and the workers we are sending in now. You cannot imagine how fundamental you are to our work, Tami."

Tami took a deep breath. "Thank you, Dr. Taylor. To be honest, I often did not feel that way. My Chinese was lacking, I had problems adapting, the work did not progress as fast as I thought it could. I often felt awkward during the meetings with the officials. I really—"

"No, Tami," Mrs. Taylor interrupted gently. "You showed them what it means to be a humble servant leader, and the Chinese officials admire you for that. They know what sacrifices you had taken professionally, financially, and personally to go to China and serve their poor. They love you. They trust you. And they respect you. It is because of your example and your pioneering spirit that the foundations of MSI are set."

Tami's thoughts briefly drifted off to China, to Sichuan and the Yi people she so loved and wanted to serve again. During lunch, the Taylors shared memories from China with Tami and her parents, who enjoyed hearing about China as the land had become so much a part of their lives too. After Tami had a short rest, the Taylors returned for more discussions.

"Tami, you have more insights into the real needs of the work in Sichuan as you have firsthand experience. Give us your thoughts on how we should plan the next year, which colleagues to team up together, and where we should place them."

For the next hours, they discussed details of the work in China. "Tami, are you not too tired to continue?" Mrs. Taylor asked after a while.

"Yes, I'm tired. But I would not want to do anything else in this moment but discuss the MSI work together. It means so much to me, and I would rather tire myself out than not do this," Tami replied.

A few hours later, she was indeed too exhausted to continue. She sighed, "You know, I would so much love to return to China. I often think of the children in our compound, the hospital staff, the directors and their needs. I wish so much that I could return and serve more."

"You sound like my great-grandfather," Dr. Taylor replied. "My great-grandfather, Hudson Taylor, said, 'If I had one thousand lives I would give each one of them afresh again for the work in China.'" He paused for a few seconds and then added, "But not for China. No! For Jesus!"

Tami was deeply stirred by these words. Missions, medical missions in particular, had always been her life goal, her main purpose. But indeed, it should never become more important than God. "Not for China. No! For Jesus!" The words rang in her heart. As they parted, Tami prayed, "Lord, I have given my life to missions. Now I offer missions to you. You are the only One I want to serve and worship with the whole of my heart. My life belongs to you."

In November 1999, her intensive chemotherapy was over. Tami had survived it. With her parents and friends, they gave thanks to God. Now it was time to repeat all the scans again to find out how well the chemotherapy had worked.

Chapter 25

VALLEYS AND PEAKS

The results of the tests were not as good as Tami had anticipated. The CAT scans showed essentially no change. There was no growth, but no significant shrinkage either. Status quo. The months of intensive chemotherapy that had taken such a toll on her body had not achieved what she had hoped for. Her energy drained out of her as the disappointment sank in. But there was no time to rest now. She had to find alternative treatment options. *Novel* treatment options.

I have to persevere, she thought. *I just have to press on.* She took out the High Road Prayer she had stored away for so many years. Lying down on her couch, she reread what she had written when she was only nineteen years old. Her eyes were caught by one passage: "Lord, I can trust that You discipline us for our good, that we might share in Your holiness. I ask You that You will provide the necessary strength for me to endure this discipline."

She put away her essay and prayed silently, *Indeed, I want to pray that You will enable me to come forth as gold and to be mature and complete, not lacking anything.*

The next weeks felt like déjà vu of the year before. Treatment plans changed by the day. Because so much research was going on to improve the outcome of the melanoma treatment, there was no real standard therapy. Experimental drugs were not part of standard treatment, and one had to take part in a clinical study to be offered a new drug. Tami found out that once again at the University of Colorado, experts were working on new experimental drugs in clinical studies. Her hopes were immediately raised. After detailed and lengthy consultations and discussions with the specialists, disappointment struck again. She was found not eligible to join the studies.

Tami searched for other treatment alternatives. The National Institute of Health in Washington offered some new experimental drug therapies. But here once more, there was disappointment in store for her: again she was told she was not eligible.

"Lord, so many flexibility lessons again. And emotional roller coasters. Help me, please," she prayed in desperation.

After further discussions, the next option suggested was radiation of the neck to shrink the nodules and lymph nodes in that region. But where should she have this treatment done? Should she do it in Denver where they had most experience? Fortunately, her cancer specialist in Denver came up with a practical solution. He suggested going to the University of Alabama in Birmingham where the specialists also had considerable experience with this treatment. As Birmingham was only two and a half hours away from Atlanta, this meant that Tami could continue work on her research project and her hospital work, commuting from Atlanta for the radiation treatment of her neck.

As soon as her insurance issues were resolved, she flew back to Atlanta. She arrived just in time for Thanksgiving Day. A group of friends invited her to celebrate Thanksgiving with them. When she was asked to share about her recent weeks, she stood up to talk. Her eyes reflected both the pain she had gone through and her faith in God.

"There are lots of reasons to be thankful. Even in times of pain, discouragement, and disappointment, God always gave me a sign of His presence." She paused. "My mind keeps coming back to the words 'not by might, not by power, but by my Spirit.' God can and will bring glory to Himself through my situation, through human or supernatural means. Please think of me when it's difficult to remember this."

Paula Helms was in town on furlough from China. They shared their experiences and memories from China together and often did not know whether to cry or laugh.

"Tami, I went through a real culture shock in our first year in China," Paula shared honestly. "It reminded me of your Martian letters. They always encouraged me to keep on going. When I felt I had nothing else left, it was your sense of humor that carried me through the difficult times."

When Tami and Paula were invited to lead a Bible study together for the Chinese fellowship, Paula encouraged Tami, "Tami, your Chinese is so much better than mine. You should lead this evening. Your testimony is so powerful."

Tami prepared carefully. Praying about what she should share, she decided that she should speak about her journey with her illness.

"Joseph was a man who was sent to prison even though he did nothing wrong. It was a terrible thing for him. What a waste of his precious life." Tami looked around the group of Chinese students and professionals. "Often things happen in our lives that we don't understand. But God has a bigger plan that we can't see." Tami swallowed. She shared her struggles against cancer. "I can only encourage you that even when we can't see God's hand, we can always trust His heart. We may not understand what's happening in our lives, but we can always trust God's love. And as we trust Him, He will use it for something great."

In the next weeks, her friends drove her back and forth to Birmingham for the radiation treatments. Others offered her overnight stays in Birmingham, should they be needed. The radiation doses were high. They led to severe mouth sores. Because of the pain associated with swallowing, Tami was reduced to living off pasta and protein shakes.

Now I can't get the food down, but at least I'm not bringing it up, she thought.

During the next four weeks, she was able to concentrate a little more on her laboratory research work. This was the work she wanted to present at the upcoming AIDS conference in San Francisco in February.

For Christmas, Tami returned to Denver to spend the vacation time with her family. Tim and Kristin flew in especially to be with her for the weekend. Her Chinese friend Dai from Atlanta came as well. They introduced the family tradition of doing mystery jigsaw puzzles to Dai. It took them most of the day to finish, but the cozy atmosphere in front of the fireplace kept them going till late.

Christmas dinner was celebrated with another Chinese couple, and it was filled with laughter and joy. While everyone savored the Christmas goodies, Tami sipped on protein shakes and blended vegetable soups. Her mouth was still very sore from all the radiation.

At times, she tried to get mashed potatoes or pasta to slide down her sore throat. Her mom creatively added variety by changing the shape of the pasta ("Shells, ribbons, or rigatoni tonight, Tami?") or by changing the flavor of ice cream or the type of frozen fruit that went into the berry-flavored protein powder. The whole family celebrated when they saw that Tami had gained three pounds by the end of Christmas!

By New Year's, the sores had healed sufficiently for Tami to graduate to real food, including fresh fruit and veggies. And so they started pulling out the leftover Christmas turkey and stuffing from the freezer for Tami to enjoy. With some more weight gained, her blood counts bounced back to almost normal much more quickly. Tami now felt strong enough to venture out into the snow that had covered the mountains around Denver.

"Dai," she said, "let's go cross-country skiing."

It was such a joy to be out in the snow and sun again. Dai, who had never skied before, fell frequently in the beginning, and they laughed and laughed. But by the end of the day, the two managed to finish quite a long loop—slowly for Tami, as she was still weak, and slowly for Dai as she was not yet confident in cross-country skiing!

At the end of the year, Tami sat down to reflect. What a year it had been! Would this next year be her last? Had this been her final Christmas? She penned the series of peaks and valleys of the year in her newsletter to her friends and supporters around the world. The memories of the high points, highlighted as balloons, were those that had kept her going during the tougher times. She finished the newsletter with the verse that God had given her early on when she had just received the diagnosis: "For I know the plans I have for you . . . plans to prosper you and not to harm you, plans to give you hope and a future" (Jeremiah 29:11).

As she drew strength from these verses, her thoughts focused on the near future. She had just heard that there was a slim possibility she might be able to join a new drug trial at the University of Colorado.

Chapter 26

A NEW DRUG TRIAL

On the very day she arrived in Denver, Tami met up with an oncologist at the University of Colorado who was involved in a groundbreaking trial related to melanoma. The trial had only just been approved. From the initial assessment, it appeared that Tami was eligible to take part. The study entailed two drugs. In an e-mail she wrote, "Both drugs look good in tubes and in mice, but since I am neither, no one really knows how they may work in me." The good news was that both drugs were given by mouth. This was a great relief after all the injections and infusions she had received over the past one and a half years. One drug was a chemotherapeutic drug similar to a standard drug given to many cancer patients around the world. The other drug was a novel development, a new kind of immune therapy. Both drugs seemed to have few serious side effects. Tami felt this was almost too good to be true.

She enrolled in the study in January 2000. The trial allowed her to stay and work in Atlanta, but initially she would have to fly to Denver every three weeks to receive medication and safety monitoring. With Emory University, she arranged to continue to do research but no clinical work, which would allow her the flexibility to travel between Denver and Atlanta. The airfare was covered by the drug company.

"Well, being a guinea pig at least has some perks," she jokingly told her friends and colleagues.

The initial months on the new drug combination were bliss compared to all her previous treatments. She tolerated the drugs very well, having hardly any side effects. Her blood counts remained stable, and she continued to put on some weight. This meant she was able to work long hours and catch up on some of the research projects that had been sidelined due to chemotherapy.

But uncertainties about the effectiveness of the treatment surfaced early. The nodules in her neck did not shrink significantly. Then again, she argued with herself, they had not been much affected by the radiation treatment either. She was still very tired, and a repeat workup showed that her thyroid gland was not producing enough hormones and was probably worsening her fatigue. Thyroid hormone replacement treatment increased her energy levels at least partly.

Another important reason for her lack of energy was identified as anemia, for which she needed iron tablets. Her work schedule was also becoming hectic again, as she not only had to finish both of her research projects within a short time period due to her mentors leaving Atlanta, but was also running a study related to tuberculosis and HIV for which she had to enroll a large number of patients within a short time.

Here I am, enrolling patients for a study while I'm enrolled in a study myself, she thought.

Tami was pulling fifteen work hours per day for several weeks in a row, and she felt really worn out. At one stage, she noticed some enlargement in the right side of her neck. This would need to be checked out during her next doctor's appointment.

During this time, Gary and Linda, her friends from Chengdu, were on home assignment in the U.S. with their four children. They were about to return to China, but they decided that Gary should visit Tami first. They held so many fond memories together from their time in China.

"Tami, you look great," Gary said awkwardly on the day he came. They were walking through the green university campus in the cool of early evening.

"Gary, don't worry; I know I don't look great. The radiotherapy has led to some scarring and discolorations in my neck, but at least I'm glad my mouth doesn't droop as much as it did right after the surgery. How is Linda?"

"Linda sends her regards. She wanted to come as well, but the kids combined with the packing made it impossible for her to come. She prays so often for you. We all are praying for you."

"Send her my love too. Tell her I often remember those chocolates we ate together that Naara brought from Mongolia. And how is your little one? Little darling Megan?"

"Megan is now four years old. She still remembers you as Auntie Tami. We will never forget how you helped us when she was so sick as a little baby in Chengdu. You literally saved her life."

"Thanks, Gary." Tami shook her head and smiled, happy memories from China playing through her mind. "Wow, what times we had together. How is the rest of the family?"

"They can't wait to get back to China." Gary again looked awkward. "I'm so sorry you can't come back with us, Tami," he said quietly.

"Yes, I would love to go back to China." They were both pensive for a while, then Tami picked up the conversation again. "You know, I'm still involved in various Chinese fellowships here. China is here in Atlanta, Gary. I continue to speak Chinese, and we often have great Chinese meals together. Recently in one of our Chinese Bible study groups, we were discussing Philip and the Ethiopian. It was exciting and encouraging to be reminded that God still works the same way today as in those days. He sends some of us to the uttermost parts of the earth, while others stay at home. Everywhere are opportunities to share the gospel. I feel that rather than sending me back to the uttermost parts of the earth, God can and will continue to use me here for the time being." She thought for a while. "And then there are my friends who work with me in the Chinese fellowship. Some of them are considering going to China because of all the stories of China I've told them."

"You're such an encouragement to all of us," Gary said. "And through your testimony, now others are going out." He took a deep breath and sighed. "Although I agree with what you're saying, I still often find myself asking why it is that *you've* got cancer. You have the best qualifications to be out there. You have the best Chinese of all of us. While we are still struggling with the language, you mastered it to a level that you could even converse with officials and work in a hospital. Why should God cut short your ministry in China?"

Tami struggled to find words. She took some time to respond. "Gary, it's not that I'm avoiding the hard questions. I've often asked myself a lot of hard questions on this theme. But I've come to realize one thing. The one question I should *not* ask is, 'Why me, God?'"

Tami looked at him with an intense gaze. "I sometimes think the better question is, 'Why *not* me?'" She paused. "As a doctor, I've seen so much illness, so much suffering and death. Why should it not also affect me? The hardest question for me at the moment is not why, but how. How do I cope with all this suffering?" Her face looked pained as her feelings poured out.

"I have become so sensitive to needles, for example. After having been poked more than hundreds of times, I just can't take it anymore. The latest complication I had was a blood clot in my arm where my IV line used to be. The clot was so big, it was pressing on a nerve to my hand, the ulnar nerve. It was really painful. The line had leaked and contributed to the nerve damage. Around the same time I had to be put on hormonal therapy for heavy menstrual bleeding. The hormones probably contributed to the clot growing further. Now I'm still bleeding, but I have to start taking a blood thinner to keep the clot from expanding. Not a nice combination. A small matter in the big picture, but it almost freaked me out."

Gary was not sure what to say.

Tami went on. "That's not all, Gary. I'm feeling a lot of frustration with the medical system. I have to chase down my own results and collect records, X-rays, and CT scans to show to the specialists in the various places I get treated in Atlanta and Denver. Having my treatment split between two cities certainly doesn't help. Every visit requires at least two and a half hours and multiple phone calls before and after."

"Tami, I think you are really courageous," Gary responded.

"Many people have told me that. But I really do not feel like I'm courageous at all. At times I feel so weak, even too exhausted and drained to minister to my own roommate or my colleagues at work. I wish I could be a greater blessing to all."

Gary cut in with quiet intensity. "Tami, you are! You are a blessing to all of us! The way you are going through this with God is a testimony that is stronger than many testimonies on the mission field!"

They walked on quietly for a while on the university campus, studying the pattern the late afternoon sun was casting through the trees onto the pavement.

After several minutes Tami continued, "Last week, I read through Isaiah 63. When I came to verse nine, God spoke to me. In that verse it says that 'in all their suffering He also suffered.' God also suffers. Jesus cried when He saw others suffer. At Gethsemane, He was in agony Himself, and He pleaded with God to spare Him from the suffering of the cross. He truly suffered. I think the more I understand how God suffers with us, the more I can be open to admit that I'm suffering. Yes, I'm suffering. Yes, I still do not understand everything. I'm still on a long quest. But God has taught me so much over the past two years, more than in all the good times together. And I'm grateful for that."

Both were quiet again for a long time. Then Tami turned around.

"Gary, do you remember the sermon you gave to our small fellowship meeting at Christmas in Chengdu? It's several years ago now, but I never forgot your words! You told us about the virgin Mary who conceived although she did not want to conceive at the time. You told us about the aged Elizabeth who wanted to conceive all her life but was not able to. If you read the story without God in it, you said, it sounds almost absurd. Only when you see the story through God's eyes is there meaning and purpose! And God turned the world's history around through those two women."

"It means a lot to me that you still remember that," Gary said, touched.

They turned toward the campus restaurant. It was obvious Gary was in deep thought. "Tami, have you ever—" He stopped. "Maybe I shouldn't ask. But have you ever had people tell you that maybe you are not healed because of a lack of faith?"

"Oh yes, one person."

"Wow, that must have really hurt," Gary said.

"No, not really. I felt pity," she replied.

"Pity?"

"Well, not actually pity for her," Tami chuckled. "I felt pity for other suffering people whom she might approach with the same painful statement. So I explained to her about the reality of suffering in the Bible, in Job's life for example, even in Jesus' life. And there are so many other examples, of course. Moses, Joseph, Daniel, just to mention a few."

They walked on, and Tami continued to share her thoughts as an evening breeze kicked up. "Yes, Jesus performed miracles during His time on earth, and He continues to do miracles now. But while Peter experienced the miracle of being able to escape prison, Stephen was not able to escape his suffering; he was stoned to death. While Lazarus was raised from the dead, others died. Some are healed, others are not, although the words 'by his stripes we are healed' apply to all of us. In heaven all of us will indeed be healed."

They watched as the sun set over the buildings of the campus.

"Do you believe that He will heal you?" Gary asked.

"I believe that God *can* heal me." Tami looked at him steadfastly. "However, my faith will not waver if He does not."

Chapter 27

MIRACLES

"I have so much to be thankful for recently!" Tami wrote to her friends about six months into the new treatment. After initial concerns about growing nodules in her neck, her most recent scans showed that the tumors in her neck actually looked smaller! One of the nodules looked as if its center was dying. This indicated not only stable disease, but actual improvement.

I'm tolerating the chemo pills very well—only a few minor headaches and a little bit of fatigue. My anemia is improving, the bleeding has stopped, and three times in a row (a true record!), my clotting time has been in the right range. I will have to be on the blood thinner for six months, but at least they don't have to poke me to check my clotting time twice a week anymore. My "main vein" was getting harder and harder to get blood out of each time.

My energy levels are so much better. I'm trying to wind up my next research article and a presentation this month, and then I'll be back working in the hospital, though in a sort of accessory position. This means if I get tired and need to rest, or when I have to go to Denver, someone else is there to cover. My department has been really great to me! Furthermore, I do not need to travel to Denver on a three-weekly basis anymore. Another reason to be thankful is that my second research project was selected to be presented as an oral presentation at the Infectious Diseases Society of America in New Orleans in a few months' time. It is unusual for a fellow to give an oral presentation at such a big meeting. Also, I've been invited to Dartmouth in October to present these data and lecture on the prevention of tuberculosis in AIDS patients. They will fly me up there and even give me an honorarium! After

losing all my hair last year, there is now a real "perk": I have now
naturally curly hair! It's long enough to cover my ear now! It's cool
and very easy to deal with—great for Atlanta in the summer. I
just wash it, brush it, and go! It's amazing to look back at the same
time last year—new lumps were popping up every few days; we
were debating all different treatment options all over the country.
This year is SO much different.

Three good months followed.

Then all of a sudden, she noticed three black nodules on the stump of
her left ear. With tears pouring down her cheeks, she phoned her parents
in Denver.

"I have three new black nodules on my ear! This can only mean one
thing: my melanoma has returned," she sobbed.

The news was truly terrible. It meant the current trial had failed, and as
per study protocol, Tami would be taken out of the study. She would need to
find a new treatment. "The more things I've been treated with, the fewer new
things I'm eligible for—a real Catch 22," she told her parents in desperation.
"There may not be any other treatment options at all, if I think about it.
Please pray. Only God can intervene!"

"Tami, this is so difficult! Difficult for all of us. We will pray for you. All of
us will pray for you. We will rally for you day and night," her parents assured her.

Slumped in her chair, Tami continued to sob. She took up her Bible
and started reading for hours and hours, through the whole book of Isaiah.
Reading the Word strengthened her. *Lord, I put my life into Your hands. My
life is Yours. I surrender my pain, my hopelessness, and my discouragement to
You. My only desire is that You will be glorified.*

As she read, Tami had the impression that God was speaking to her and
was comforting her. Feeling more at peace, she opened her laptop and sent
out an e-mail to her friends, updating them on the recent development and
asking for prayer.

The next day, she went to see her oncologist in Atlanta. The oncologist
agreed with Tami's self-diagnosis. "Indeed, these new black nodules look very
much like recurrent melanoma. You have to see the oncologists in Denver
now, as they are responsible for this new drug trial and need to assess you to
make a decision on what to do next."

Immediately, Tami flew back to Denver. Her parents picked her up at the airport and drove her to the oncology center. Carefully, the oncologist examined Tami's ear. She looked very concerned. Several other oncologists entered the consultation room and examined the ear. They called in a world-renowned melanoma specialist from Australia who happened to be visiting Denver at that time. All of them agreed that the clinical diagnosis was cancer recurrence.

"Tami, we are sorry. This does not look good. We will have to stop the trial drugs. We'll schedule you for surgery to have these nodules removed."

While waiting for several other tests and appointments with various specialists, Tami remained calm, quietly praying most of the day. Knowing that hundreds, if not thousands, around the world were praying for her gave her a sense of peace.

That evening, she looked into the mirror. Could it be true? She looked closer. Indeed, the nodules looked smaller! Thinking that it might just be her imagination, she measured them and reexamined them the next day. And the next day, and the next day. They were shrinking! On objective measurement, there was no doubt!

She was due to see the surgeon to set the date for the surgery, but there were only scaly small lesions left on her ear. The surgeon examined her, and his comment was, "I can't see any nodules on your ear!"

The oncologists and Tami tried to convince him that the lesions had been bigger and darker before, but all the while Tami felt excitement growing.

"Well, agreed, we need to be sure," the surgeon said. "So we'd better take a biopsy of this lesion. We have to be certain whether this is melanoma or not."

The biopsy was performed that very day. Tami, her parents, and all her supporters prayerfully waited for the results. Unfolding the report of the biopsy, Tami took a deep breath, then quickly skimmed through the report.

Jumping up, she exclaimed, "I have awesome news!"

Excitedly, she sat down to write an e-mail to all her prayer supporters around the world:

Subject: Awesome news!

The piece of my ear that was removed last Friday shows NO melanoma cells. A little area on my neck that had shrunk over the last several months was also removed, and it shows a few dead cells

but again NO melanoma cells! What happened?? Either three oncologists, including a world-renowned melanoma expert, and one
internist (me) are crazy and imagining things, or GOD HEALS!
I know what my answer is because I saw and felt them blue-black
things, and then watched them shrink away with no treatment.
I have been off therapy since we found these three weeks ago. I
thank God, and I thank all of you for your prayers. This is just
awesome! Hopefully, I will be able to continue in the current trial.
Negotiations with the drug company are going on right now since
I had actually been pulled out of the study.

Tami was allowed to continue the trial. There was no recurrence of
disease and therefore no reason to take her out. She continued to take the
two drugs that seemed to work so well.

A few months later, she underwent yet another series of scans to assess
the progress. Awesome news again! The scans confirmed that her disease was
showing signs of regression. Some of the nodules were continuing to shrink.
Her radiologist, viewing her latest CAT scan, congratulated her by saying
"Mazel tov!" The oncologists in Denver and Atlanta were all very pleased
with her progress.

A few months later, at a follow-up appointments in Denver, her oncologist asked, "Tami, you are thirty-five years old now. What are your plans for
the future?"

Tami's breath caught. "Future? I've only planned three-week blocks at
a time for the past two years. In fact, very often, I was planning my funeral
rather than my future."

"Tami, all the scans confirm that your melanoma is stable. You are
in remission. In fact, if this was any kind of cancer except melanoma, I
would suggest that you could stop treatment now. However, for melanoma,
we want to make sure that we kill off every last cell. You are tolerating the
drugs very well, so I suggest that you continue the same combination for
the next few years."

Years? Tami's mind raced. This was the first time since her diagnosis that
the oncologist was talking about "years."

Even so, Tami's first answer was easy. "My plans are to finish my infectious disease fellowship. Because I was so ill so often, my training was often

interrupted. I enjoy the research I have been doing for more than a year, but I need to get back to clinical work so I can complete the fellowship in time."

"What are your plans after that?"

Tami's heart jumped. The oncologists were always the ones most careful when choosing their wording. If even the oncologist was thinking beyond the fellowship, that meant that she should do so as well! Without further hesitation, she responded, "After my fellowship, I want to go back to China."

"Tami, I think that an overseas posting is indeed possible." The oncologist smiled. "You can plan for three or four months overseas at a time from next year onward. You will need to come back after each period for checkups and to reassess further management."

Tami looked at the oncologist as if through a haze. The words she had just heard were the best news she'd had in years.

"Guess what the oncologist said?" Tami exclaimed excitedly to her parents when she returned home after the appointment. "I'm officially in remission! This means that my cancer is under control, stable, or whatever you want to call it. I'm so thankful. I just can't tell you how thankful I am! It looks so good that I may even be allowed to go overseas next year!"

"Tami, that is such wonderful news! We praise God with you!" Mom said. She looked at her husband and then said carefully, "But going overseas? Tami, don't you think you're overdoing it a bit?"

"Mom! Dad! Please understand. Going back to Asia is my greatest desire. That is what I really want. If God has given me more years to live, then that is how I want to use them."

۶

Tami overflowed with thankfulness for her improved health. It felt so good, yet also so strange to plan for the long-term again.

"It is like reverse grieving," she explained to a colleague. "One day you think you're going to die, and suddenly, you realize you have to focus on living and planning for the future."

With all the strength she could muster, Tami willed herself to finish her fellowship. There was a lot of catching up to do. She was behind schedule in several areas. She immersed herself in clinical work, caring for her patients with great concern and empathy. She prepared case presentations for grand rounds and abstracts for scientific conferences, and she was involved in teaching and mentoring junior doctors. Whenever the opportunity arose, she shared her faith in God openly with patients, students, and colleagues. But she was not a person of many words. Every day, she expressed her faith by living it out practically. Her faith was a natural part of her and her care for her patients.

The Winter 2001 University of Colorado Cancer Center Newsletter carried a full-page feature on Tami. The journalist wrote, "Two years ago, Dr. Fisk was not counting on a future. She was busy battling end-stage melanoma. Enrolling in a Phase 1 clinical trial was her only hope for survival. After only a few months in the clinical trial, Dr. Fisk went into remission, nodules shrank and spontaneously disappeared, and biopsies were surprisingly negative. Now cancer has become less a part of her life than she would have imagined two years ago."

Tami knew there was much more behind what the journalist had written. She knew her healing was God's extraordinary intervention.

Then another miracle occurred. The following month, she managed not only to finish her infectious disease fellowship but to do so on time, in exactly three years. She just couldn't believe it! It was wonderful! A special bonus to her celebrations were the very positive comments and assessments her mentors and supervisors gave her.

Beyond all expectations, she had completed her advanced training. And now she could do what she had never dreamed she would do again: plan to return to Asia.

Chapter 28

BACK IN ASIA

Dear Dr. Fisk,

    I'm extremely pleased to notify you of your appointment to the faculty as an Assistant Professor of Medicine, effective July 1, 2002. This will prove to be an excellent opportunity for you to develop an outstanding academic career. I want you to develop clinical, research, and teaching academic programs in the areas of global emerging infectious diseases. Your clinical responsibilities will initially be mainly in the Division of Infectious Diseases at Emory Healthcare and the Crawford Travel Clinic . . . Approximately 50% of your time will be devoted to clinical activities in Infectious Diseases, and the balance to research.

Tami couldn't believe her eyes when she read the letter. Professor David Stephens was offering her a faculty position that involved work at Emory Healthcare and the Centers for Disease Control (CDC) in Atlanta! Holding the letter in her hand, Tami read it over and over again, praising the Lord as she did so.

"Thank you, Lord. I thank you so much, as I know that this is Your provision! Thank you for Dr. Stephens. He knows about my cancer, but he still has given me this extraordinary opportunity to be a faculty member. And what encouraging words he has for me! 'To develop an academic career'!"

Global emerging infectious diseases? What a task! Tami started dreaming. Indeed, this job was her dreams come true, her prayers answered. This job was everything she had hoped for, or rather, *dared* hope for. The most important part was that Dr. Stephens shared her vision for global health. During her fellowship, she had met him and told him about her work in China and her plans to return. He had responded that they needed people like her with a vision for global health.

"Tami, you are hardworking and dedicated to your work. You are caring, insightful, and resourceful. I like that," he had said to her.

And now she held the letter of appointment in her hand! Most amazing was that this position would give her the freedom to do research work overseas—and not only freedom. Dr. Stephens's letter implied that work overseas was even mandated. There was already some talk about a grant proposal to do research in Asia.

She looked at the salary offered in the job package. For the first time in her life, she would receive a reasonable income.

"Lord, show me how to use this money wisely. Lead me to missionaries and projects in the world that You want me to help sponsor."

A few missionary friends came immediately to mind. In addition, she wondered whether she should buy a condominium in Atlanta. Would that be a wise thing to do, knowing that she was still battling a potentially terminal disease? *I don't know how many years God has in store for me. I have to learn to plan ahead without knowing what will happen.*

After some consideration, she decided that she would go ahead and buy a two-bedroom condo in Atlanta, very close to the university. One bedroom for herself, and one bedroom to let out to a Chinese student or colleague.

She enjoyed her work in the Crawford Travel Clinic. The job suited her well. She had to give professional medical advice to travelers prior to their travels, including advice on how to minimize risks of acquiring infectious diseases overseas, such as how to prevent malaria or taking the right vaccines. She brought in much of her own experience and knowledge gained on her travels around the world. She enjoyed meeting all sorts of travelers, from the budget traveler and adventurer to businesspeople, politicians, and VIPs, and particularly, she enjoyed counseling those who went out to do mission, relief, or development work in developing countries.

A large part of the work at the clinic involved looking after travelers who returned home sick, be it with malaria, diarrheal diseases, parasites, skin problems, or exotic tropical diseases. Tami found the work fascinating, and she spent long hours at night reading up on rare tropical diseases. The clinic was also involved in a large worldwide research network of travel medicine providers called GeoSentinel. Atlanta was the site where all the data were centrally collected.

"Tami, do you want to take part in a large research project analyzing data related to diseases that returning travelers present with at travel clinics?" Professor Phyllis Kozarsky asked.

Phyllis was the director of the travel clinic, a very dynamic and interesting boss to work for. Yes, Tami was interested. The research project involved countless hours sifting through tens of thousands of electronic data and applying statistical tools to evaluate whether certain travel destinations were associated with a certain risk of travel-related diseases. Noticing Tami's knowledge and astuteness in travel medicine, Phyllis asked Tami whether she would also be willing to write chapters for the prestigious Yellow Book, the bestselling travel health book published by the Centers for Disease Control. Tami was thrilled to contribute.

Not long after she commenced her faculty position, Tami's routine work at CDC and the Travel Clinic was suddenly interrupted. Anthrax hit the news in the U.S. Letters mailed to news media offices and two U.S. Senators were discovered to contain anthrax spores.

Overnight, chaos and confusion emerged in the public sphere, and the government called on the CDC in Atlanta to coordinate the effort to prepare the nation for bioterrorism. As more and more people developed anthrax, the academic staff at the CDC was asked to track new cases, respond to media inquiries, and write interim guidelines for the CDC Web site. Tami joined in the frenzy surrounding the anthrax crisis. As the drama unfolded, all other work was suspended. This was a race against time. The general public was rapidly becoming nervous and was starting to overreact. Panic was beginning to surface. Tami spent most days and evenings at the CDC, sometimes working as late as three in the morning. And so did her colleagues and mentors. Her task was to describe the first cases of anthrax, characterize them in a way that clinicians would recognize, and diagnose new cases earlier. Together with a large group of CDC doctors, she helped write a breakthrough article on the clinical presentation of anthrax. It was published in the Emerging Infectious Diseases Journal, a prestigious medical journal.

"Although it's certainly not a desirable situation, it's exciting to be at CDC right now. Even President Bush came to CDC to thank us for all our hard work," she told her parents on the phone. "All of us are extremely exhausted. It's time for the hype over anthrax to pass away so we can focus on our other work and research projects again."

In another chat with her parents after the anthrax crisis died down, Tami mentioned that she was in the process of writing up a grant application to do research in Asia.

"Tami, do you really think that this is a good time for you to go to Asia?" her mom countered.

"I understand and value your concerns, but I don't think you have to worry. The work is not high risk, and the oncologists tell me that I'm still in remission. They grant me periods away of three to four months at a time, but only to places where I can do regular blood tests at medical centers of international standard." Tami sighed a little as she continued, but her excitement picked up again quickly. "My mountain village in China may indeed not be the right place for me at this time, although I'm still praying for that door to open again. There's a prospect of doing research at the Thailand Center for Disease Control in Bangkok. Bangkok has excellent facilities, and I have CDC colleagues there should anything happen to me. We are planning a large epidemiological study on causes of fever in Thailand. It's not China, but at least it's not too far away from China. And maybe the research will open up doors into China in the near future. I'm taking it step by step. The first step is to win the grant."

"Tami, we know you are sensible. We will support you in your decisions. We continue to pray for you every day."

Tami won the grant. And so she became the Visiting Scientist for the International Emerging Infectious Diseases Program at the Centers for Disease Control and Prevention in Thailand. Her prayers had been answered. She was back in Asia.

Chapter 29

FAREWELL FROM
THE MOUNTAIN VILLAGE

Tami moved to Bangkok, the capital of Thailand, and found a small apartment to rent not too far from her office at CDC. Her work was mainly done in Thailand, but she often had to travel back to Atlanta for scientific meetings, clinical duties, and further research projects. "Not the closest commute," she mused.

The familiar smells, the hectic traffic, the noise, the food stalls, the smiling faces, the crowds—what a joy to be back in Asia! She even embarked on studying Thai in order to bargain for food and clothes in the local markets. And not surprisingly, she fell in love with Thai food. She decided to do what she had done in China: try every exotic dish she came across! Her days were full to the brim, the way she loved it. The only reminders of her illness were the daily routine of taking her two chemo drugs and monthly blood tests at the local Thai hospital, or at Emory if she happened to be back in Atlanta. Her blood results and scans continued to be stable. Every day she took as a day given by God, and she thanked Him. With this awareness, she took her work very seriously so as to utilize every minute she was given.

As Principal Investigator of the study "Determining Causes of Febrile Illnesses in Thailand," she was responsible for training staff in Bangkok and various other provinces in Thailand. She was also responsible for evaluation and for monitoring the data collection. Often she was the last in the office, calling out to her boss when he was switching off the lights, "I'm still here!" She wanted to make sure that everything that needed to be done was done.

As busy as she was with her job in Bangkok and Atlanta, she remained determined to visit her mountain village in China.

"I've promised the hospital director to return. And I will keep this promise," she told her colleagues.

The opportunity arose during some vacation leave. Sharon turned every leaf to make it possible for Tami to return.

"Tami, we are running a village doctors' training, similar to the ones we did together years ago. Do you want to come and teach? I can arrange for the necessary official papers and visas."

"I would be so grateful, Sharon!" Tami exclaimed.

As soon as the paperwork was complete, Tami set out to fly from Bangkok to China, and then took the familiar train to Xichang, followed by the bus ride on the rocky steep road up to Zhaojue. Tami's heart pounded in excitement.

The Yi hospital director and the Chinese officials were all standing in front of the Zhaojue hospital to welcome her. Tea ceremonies and banquets followed.

"It often crossed my mind that I would not be able to return to Zhaojue," Tami shared with Sharon and Tomoko on the evening of her arrival. "I'm sure that similar thoughts crossed through Dr. Broomhall's mind. Yet, God has allowed both of us to keep our promises."

Tami spent one week in Zhaojue, running the training course for village health workers together with Tomoko and other MSI colleagues. Innumerable pictures were taken together with the Chinese officials, the hospital director, and the village health doctors.

So much affection. Tami was touched. *What a blessing it is to be back here.*

It was exciting to see how the work in Zhaojue had expanded since she had left. MSI had purchased a Youth Center that offered training in vocational and computer skills to the Yi youth from the surrounding villages. New workers had joined. A doctor from the UK had arrived who had a vision for community development. MSI was about to sign the contract to build a new apartment block for the workers.

No more gloomy small apartment within the hospital grounds, she mused, *but it's somehow sad that we don't have that apartment anymore. However, I'm sure the better housing will make it easier for the new staff.*

During morning devotions for the staff, Tami shared her past experiences with her colleagues. "God will continue His work through you. The seed was sown by Dr. Broomhall forty years ago. Sharon, Tomoko, and myself had the privilege to water the seed. But you will see it grow to a big tree. Many years ago, when I felt discouraged, a Chinese colleague shared the vision of Nehemiah's wall. We all play a part as stones in the rebuilding of the wall. Everyone has his or her time."

Before she left the village, Tami chose to climb the mountain again. She did it by herself, praying and reflecting. Would God lead her back to Zhaojue again? She felt exhausted from climbing and knew that she could not go any farther. Reluctantly, she turned around.

"Will you come back again, Tami?" Tomoko asked Tami as she was leaving.

"I hope so," Tami answered.

But she spoke without much conviction. She sensed that her time in the mountain village was over. She had been the pioneering doctor; now it was time for others to continue the work. Her heart would always remain with the Yi people, she knew that. But somehow God was telling her that He was now using her elsewhere. She bade farewell to Zhaojue and returned to Bangkok with a sense of peace in her heart.

Chapter 30

PRODUCTIVE YEARS

Tami had not been back in Bangkok long when SARS struck Asia. In early 2003, cases of the "mysterious disease," as it was called, initially appeared first in Guangdong Province in Southern China and then in Vietnam. Tami followed the developments with great interest and concern. Dr. Carlo Urbani, an Italian physician who was working for the World Health Organization (WHO), was called to investigate the problem in the French Hospital in Hanoi, Vietnam. He examined the patients in Vietnam who had come down with the disease. He was really the first to realize that something very serious and very contagious was going on, and he sent out a warning to WHO. In response to his warning, the first worldwide alert was sent, and the term "Severe Acute Respiratory Syndrome" (SARS) was coined.

"Tami, did you hear the latest news?" Dr. Scott Dowell, her boss in Bangkok, asked her.

"What news?" she replied.

"Dr. Urbani was admitted to a hospital in Bangkok. He developed a high fever on the plane when flying from Hanoi to Bangkok to chair a scientific meeting. He was immediately taken to a Bangkok hospital and isolated. It's most likely SARS. Tami, we need to go there and take some specimens from his nose and throat, and also take some blood samples to test what is going on."

"I'll do it!" Tami responded without hesitation.

Gowned from top to bottom, with goggles, gloves, and mask, Tami entered the isolation room. Dr. Urbani was in very serious condition. He was in respiratory distress and needed oxygen. She asked him gently whether he would agree to have samples taken. He nodded. Carefully, she took the samples. Little did she know then that these samples would help identify the SARS coronavirus, and that the strain later would be named the Urbani strain of the SARS coronavirus group.

Tami and Dr. Dowell continued to visit Dr. Urbani in the hospital. His condition deteriorated day by day. After eighteen days in intensive care, he succumbed to SARS. His death shook Tami and Dr. Dowell as well as the CDC team based in Bangkok that had taken part in his care. The news quickly spread through the world. Dr. Urbani was the first UN official to die of this new disease. The world mourned him as a hero. Tami mourned him as a person.

SARS first appeared in China, then spread to Hong Kong and Vietnam before exploding simultaneously in Singapore and Toronto. Soon it reached Taiwan, leaving behind havoc. As with anthrax only half a year earlier, the entire CDC staff was involved in all aspects of the epidemic that caused so much international anxiety. Staff was deployed at short notice to go to outbreak situations.

"Dr. Tami Fisk," came the news one day, "we are thinking of sending you to Taiwan to help with the outbreak there. Your knowledge of Chinese is an asset."

"Sure, I can go."

"No," a colleague interrupted. "Tami should not go; she is on chemotherapeutic drugs and her immune system is still slightly suppressed. It would be dangerous."

Tami argued, "I'm part of the emerging infectious diseases team, so it's my duty to go wherever I'm needed. It's dangerous for all of us. I'm really willing and ready to go. And you are right. I think my knowledge of Chinese will come in handy."

Her parents were shocked when they heard that Tami was planning to go to Taiwan to investigate the SARS outbreak.

"I will take all the necessary precautions," she told them. "It's different now then it was at the beginning of the epidemic when nobody knew the pathogen or how it was spread. Now we know how it is spread and can take precautions accordingly. I will be fine!"

Tami's stint in Taiwan fascinated her. She had to communicate with the officials of the Ministry of Health in Taiwan, train infection control officials and hospital authorities, and help in the effort to determine the epidemiology of the outbreak in Taiwan. Her Chinese often broke the ice and helped develop good relationships with the officials.

"It feels like I'm again a step closer to China," she told her parents.

SARS also affected MSI. The leadership struggled with the question of whether they should evacuate all their workers from China. Tami provided professional advice, and MSI decided not to evacuate their long-term workers, as the burden to serve at such a time of need was too great. But the decision was made to cancel all short-term teams coming into China.

MSI donated masks and offered training in infection control in various places. At MSI headquarters in Hong Kong, the daily routine was interrupted. Most of the work was done from home to avoid unnecessary risk of contact in the heavily populated city. If a visit to the MSI office was necessary, the workers used masks to protect themselves. The death due to SARS of a Christian worker from another organization shook the MSI team.

A Christian Hong Kong doctor who volunteered to look after SARS patients was infected. Churches in Hong Kong rallied to pray for her. There was an unprecedented unity among churches in this time of crisis, as Christians all over the world prayed for her, for other medical workers, for their city, and for the world. Yet this Christian doctor also died of SARS.

Tami heard many similar stories. In Singapore, many Christians were early victims of the outbreak. She heard of a Singaporean pastor who visited and prayed for a church member in the hospital, not knowing at the time that the patient was suffering from SARS. He contracted the disease and died. Another two Christian doctors in Singapore died of SARS.

Tami was devastated at first, but as she pondered, she arrived at the same question she had put to herself earlier: "Why not? Why should Christians be spared from diseases? Why should Christians be spared from SARS?"

As quickly and unexpectedly as SARS appeared, so it also abated. The newly discovered SARS coronavirus had proven to be sufficiently transmissible to cause a very large epidemic if left unchecked, but not so contagious as to be uncontrollable with good, basic public health measures. By the end of summer 2003, the worldwide epidemic was under control, and no new cases were reported.

Was the SARS epidemic a glimpse of the plagues to come, as foretold in the Bible? Tami wondered.

Tami returned to her routine work in Thailand and Atlanta. In October, she was invited to participate in a workshop meeting at the World Health Organization in Geneva, Switzerland. The purpose of the meeting was to explore future clinical trials for SARS in the event that it should reoccur.

Tami was grateful to be able to participate in this meeting with its long list of eminent international experts.

⌒

"Why don't you relax more? After all, you are still on low-dose chemotherapy," several friends and colleagues asked.

"Because I want to contribute with whatever talent, training, and time God has given me," Tami answered.

And contribute she did. Tami was invited to write a chapter for an updated version of the renowned medical textbook, *Principles and Practice of Infectious Diseases* by the editors Mandell, Douglas, and Bennett. After she completed her work in the office, she would work on writing the chapter for this textbook. And there were the chapters to do for the CDC Yellow Book, and those study reports and abstracts, not to forget the scientific data that she was writing together with her CDC colleagues on SARS in Taiwan. She was also collaborating on a paper on the risk of transmission of SARS on airplanes—a paper which ended up being accepted by a high-impact scientific journal. And the paper for the GeoSentinel study also needed attention.

Despite all her busyness, she thought of ways to surprise her parents. Her parents had announced a tour to New Zealand and Singapore. When they called her from New Zealand, the connection was pretty poor.

"Tomorrow we'll fly into Singapore," they shouted, but their words were barely understandable.

Tami shouted mischievously into the phone, "Tomorrow the connection will definitely be better!"

Indeed, the next day the connection was better. Knowing that her parents would be visiting Singapore to see Tim and Kristin, who had moved to the island city for work, Tami flew in from Bangkok and was in their apartment when her parents arrived. "What an amazing surprise, Tami, making this an impromptu family reunion!"

Tami enjoyed seeing their happy faces. Definitely another hit! Several fun days followed in this modern city-state. They enjoyed the ease of shopping. They visited the Night Safari. But what Tami cherished most was that she was able to introduce her parents to the many friends she had in Singapore.

The Singaporean medical team arranged for tea at Raffles Hotel for them. Tami enjoyed introducing everyone to her parents: Dr. Lawrence Soh, who had led so many medical teams to Zhaojue; Dr. Leong, who served on the MSI board; and dozens of others. This was a good time for her to openly thank them for all their support and friendships.

"I know I've told you before, but I want to do it again. I want to give you my heartfelt thanks for all your support over these years, both during my time in China and during my illness in the U.S. I have fond memories of our times spent together in the mountain village. I always enjoyed the teams from Singapore. Do you remember how we danced the Yi dances together in the hospital courtyard? And how you helped clean my hospital apartment? You easily fit into the culture, understood the language—well, some of you did, no thanks to all that heavy Sichuan dialect!" she chuckled. "And you were so creative with the puppet shows and playing zoo in the middle of Zhaojue town." They all laughed as they reminisced about their experiences.

Tami also visited the doctor couple she had befriended in Chengdu, whose helper she'd had the privilege to lead to the Lord. Annelies and Einar had meanwhile moved to Singapore. They spent hours together sharing their experiences and discussing scientific developments in Asia.

"Tami, a book should be written about your life," Annelies brought up.

"Hmmm . . ." was Tami's hesitant response. "Interesting you'd say so. Dr. Taylor said the same. He thought it would be an encouragement for others to serve in China. In that case, maybe a booklet or so would do. But I can't really see anything special in my life that would make it worth writing a book." And they left it at that.

When Tami returned to Thailand, she was contacted by a CDC colleague, Dr. Michael Kosoy.

"Hi, Tami. I'm from the Division of Vector-Borne Infectious Diseases from CDC Fort Collins. I've heard so much about your valuable study on febrile illnesses in Thailand. I wonder whether we could work together on a rare bacterium called *Bartonella?*"

"Sure!" Tami answered. "I'm interested. I'm collecting blood samples from a very large number of Thai patients, so we could easily add testing for Bartonella."

"Well, our group in Fort Collins has already got some interesting results from previous studies. Our data show that diverse Bartonella species exist in rodents from Southern China and Thailand. We also demonstrated antibodies to rat-borne Bartonella in a small set of samples sent from a Thai hospital."

"This is really exciting! I will send you samples from my study, and let's see—maybe we can discover some new Bartonella species!"

Only a couple of months had passed when Dr. Kosoy called again.

"Tami, you will like this! We've observed a high prevalence of Bartonella antibodies in the samples you sent to us from your Thai patients. Most interestingly, we found the highest titers not against the known Bartonella pathogens, but against the species that we described in Asian rodents."

"Awesome!" Tami was excited. "We need to explore this further!"

"Well, Tami, here's the problem. The laboratory of CDC Atlanta has criticized us for doing serologies only. They claim they are not reliable and that we may draw the wrong conclusions."

"We have to change our approach then, to culturing the bacteria or at least to getting some other molecular evidence for their existence," Tami concluded. "We'll need freshly frozen human blood—that's tricky." Her mind raced. She would need to rewrite the whole study protocol and resubmit for ethics approval. It wouldn't be easy to change an approved serology-oriented project that not only included many study subjects from different parts in Thailand, but also different laboratories in Thailand and in the U.S. It also meant changing the original agreement with the Thai Ministry of Public Health. Tami scratched her head.

"It will involve a lot of paperwork, new meetings with the officials, new submissions to the ethics board and my supervisors." She thought for a while. "I will try. It is worthwhile for the sake of the project. Maybe we are on to something new! We just need to persevere."

The next months were fully dedicated to the paper war associated with the change in protocol and then implementing the change at the different field sites. But it did pay off. In the end, they did discover a new Bartonella species!

"Great news!" Tami exclaimed when the results were made official.

"Tami, this was only possible because of your research and persistence! I want to name this novel Bartonella species after you," Dr. Kosoy responded.

"No way!" came Tami's firm response. "But I will help you write a paper to be submitted to the next infectious diseases meeting in Miami."

Chapter 31

EXCRUCIATING PAIN

At the end of October 2003, Tami's fast-paced but fulfilling life fell apart. Without warning, sudden shocks of pain shot through her face. The pain was like a knife piercing her forehead and cheek, sometimes lasting only seconds, sometimes lasting many minutes. The intense flashes came in bouts, causing immediate severe nausea and vomiting. She could not imagine worse pain. She had to be admitted to the hospital, where she was given strong painkillers and medications to stop her vomiting. Morphine was needed.

Her mother flew in from Denver to be at her bedside, as did her friend Suzie from the old days at Wheaton College. Tami experienced rapid weight loss, and her vomiting was at times so violent that it caused painful muscle spasms in her neck. Tami's mom and Suzie tried to comfort her as best as they could. They massaged Tami's sore neck and shoulder muscles and tried to find the best foods to feed her. But the pain was almost impossible to control. She had no choice but to cancel her trip to the scientific meeting in Miami where she had hoped to present the data on the recently discovered Bartonella organism. It was a hard decision.

Tami felt embarrassed when her colleagues visited her in the hospital, afraid of what she would say under the influence of so many drugs. She was relieved, though, when Nicole Mares from Intown Fellowship came to visit her. Seeing her friend in such despair, Nicole spent many a night with Tami.

"Why do I have to endure such terrible pain?" Tami pressed Nicole.

Nicole whispered, "I don't know . . ."

They were both quiet, and Tami suddenly winced as yet another wave of pain hit her.

"I'm praying for you, Tami," Nicole muttered while giving support to Tami, who had to bend over to vomit.

Over the following weeks, Tami was in and out of hospital. On some days, there were fewer attacks, and she was able to return to work. Many days were spent in misery, racked by pain. The pain was unpredictable. It seemed as if every drug given to help cope with it somehow resulted in adverse effects, for which another counteractive drug had to be given. At one stage, Tami counted up to thirty kinds of different drugs being administered.

Investigations to find out what was causing her facial pain followed. The results brought bad news. After three years of remission, the cancer had recurred.

ॐ

"It is metastatic melanoma."

Tami listened in a distant haze as the oncologist spoke these words. What she had feared had now arrived. Although there was no cancer visible in the MRI of her head to explain the pain in her face, it was clear from the X-rays that there was now one new nodule in her lung, as well as some other metastases under her armpit. Despite her poor condition, Tami agreed to undergo surgery to remove the lumps under the armpit. But immediately after the surgery, three new lumps popped up under her skin. Ominously, the tumor in her neck was also growing rapidly.

As the doctors stood around her bed discussing options for further treatment, Tami's mind went almost blank.

"Tami, the cancer is spreading. The pain in your face is possibly due to tumor irritation of the trigeminal nerve. We suggest a combination of aggressive chemotherapy and a major operation whereby we remove all the tumor in the neck."

Tami could barely listen. Another flash of pain shot into her face, and she sank deep into the bed, her face distorted by the pain.

"Hospice . . ." she whispered. "Hospice is the solution, not aggressive treatment."

That night, she floated in and out of consciousness. In her drug-induced haze, even prayer was difficult, and reading the Bible was impossible. Words came to her mind from the book of Philippians, the book she had learned by heart so many years ago. The words drifted into her consciousness: "To me, to live is Christ and to die is gain. If I am to go on living in the body, this will mean fruitful labor for me. Yet what shall I choose? I do not know! I am torn between the two: I desire to depart and be with Christ, which is better by far."

It was one of the darkest nights in Tami's life. Another pain cut through her forehead, and the thought crossed her mind as to whether this was the same pain Jesus felt in his forehead when the thorns of the crown were forced into his flesh.

"Jesus, what pain you bore . . ."

She was not able to continue. Another wave of pain and vomiting shook her body. She cried, "I feel like I want to die. To be with You is my desire."

Her thoughts floated away and then returned to focus. "But then, there is still so much to do. Lord, I don't know how to choose. I'm indeed torn between the two: dying in hospice or deciding on further chemotherapy."

She dozed off. Not long after, she suddenly awoke. Her mind was clearer than it had been for weeks. All of a sudden, she just knew. She knew she should choose to live. God had spoken to her. It was not yet her time to die.

"I'm ready for further treatment," she announced the next morning.

She arranged for her flight back to Denver. The oncologists there stopped the two drugs that had worked for so many years, as they were now clearly failing. She was started again on aggressive chemotherapy. While discussions with her oncologists were still ongoing, she happened to meet a pain specialist who had dual training in dentistry and medicine. He had developed a special interest in the kind of pain that Tami was suffering.

"Tami, we should try an injection technique directly into your face at the area where the trigeminal nerve comes through the bone," he said.

Hearing this, Tami was a little apprehensive. But after reassurance by the specialist, she agreed. He took a ten-centimeter needle and filled the syringe with anesthetics. The cruel, cold, long needle looked frightening. First, he injected it into the upper jaw. Then he maneuvered the needle between the teeth into the maxillary sinus and then slowly approached the trigeminal nerve at its exit from the skull. There was sudden excruciating pain just as he hit the nerve, but within seconds the sensation changed to one of numbness. All of a sudden she felt no more pain!

"Wow, what a difference! Pain-free at last; I can't believe it!" Tami exclaimed.

"Tami, in my experience, the pain relief will last about six months, and then the effect will wear off and we will need to do the procedure again."

"Your procedure was not fun by any means, but I will do it anytime again to be without pain!"

After five months of intense pain, Tami was pain-free again. Soon she started regaining weight and strength. Then something even more incredible happened. By the eleventh day of the new chemotherapy pills, the lumps under her skin had shrunk to less than half their original size. The treating oncologist was stunned and canceled the surgery to remove them. The MRI scans of the neck mass also showed less prominence.

Was God intervening again? Was He giving her more time to live? To Tami, it was nothing less than yet another miracle. Full of gratefulness, Tami sat down to write to her supporters: "I know it sounds unimaginable. After months of misery, I'm back at work in Atlanta! I'm so thankful to God and for the many people all over the world who have lifted up my family and me in prayer."

Still, Tami knew that although the cancer lumps had significantly regressed, the cancer was still in her body. Despite this, and despite the fact that she was still on oral chemotherapy, she decided she should return to her research work in Thailand. Knowing the gravity of her illness, none of her supervisors or colleagues put any pressure on her to continue work. In fact, most advised her to take it easy or take some time off for vacation. It was Tami herself who desperately wanted to return to work.

For the next six months, she continued in her usual busy lifestyle, commuting between Asia and the United States. She continued to work on Bartonella and the discovery of other little-described pathogens that can cause febrile illnesses in Asia. The project was progressing well, although there were some frustrating delays with the shipment of specimens to the U.S.

The disease and the chemotherapy were taking a toll on her. Her energy levels were declining. She had to push herself hard to concentrate on the work, and she found herself needing more time to accomplish things. She had always valued efficiency, and the obvious lapse frustrated her immensely.

However, some good things were happening too. She enjoyed the deepening friendships with her Thai colleagues in Bangkok. Her Thai colleagues, all of them Buddhists, had been friendly to her, but there had remained a certain polite distance. Maybe it was because they didn't know how to handle her illness, or maybe it was just part of the cultural divide? Over time and increasing engagement, slowly the ice seemed to be melting. Tami noticed that, in particular, two female colleagues were much more open to talking about the deeper values and meanings in life.

When they discussed the issue of sin together, Tami explained, "We all think that we are good people and have sinned little compared to others. But this is not so. As you and I work in the field of HIV research and care, I want to draw the parallel to HIV. HIV virus in the blood makes the patient HIV positive, regardless of whether there are a few HIV viruses or many! And how can we ever get rid of HIV in the blood? We can't! It is the same for sin. We cannot get rid of the sin in our lives. Only through the clean blood of Jesus can we be forgiven." And she went on to explain the message of salvation.

Later, when she was back in the States, she spent some special vacationing time with Tim and Kristin in North Carolina. But Tami was increasingly feeling weaker, and she noticed nausea and a loss of appetite. She knew she had to go for more tests.

She flew to Denver to have another total body scan performed. Waiting for the results of the CAT scan, she felt some sense of foreboding. The oncologist examined the scans carefully. His face looked concerned.

"Tami, it is hard to tell you this," he said when he had finished. "The CAT scan has picked up the spread of melanoma to your liver. The liver has been affected in several areas. There is really nothing we can offer now. There is one experimental chemotherapy we could try, but we are not optimistic."

Being a doctor, Tami didn't need explanation. This was end-stage melanoma without hope of a cure.

Tami thought for a while. She looked at the oncologist. "I don't want to give up; I want to try everything. If the chemotherapy reduces the tumor growth, then we'll continue with the chemo. If there's further growth of the liver metastases despite chemotherapy, then we'll stop all treatment, and I will accept the inevitable."

That evening, she returned to her desk to e-mail her supporters. She signed off, "I'm not sure what God's plan is for my next few months—I just want Him to be glorified."

Chapter 32

HEAVEN IS BETTER BY FAR

Tami underwent one cycle of chemotherapy in Denver. Nausea and vomiting characterized the next weeks. While watching her hair fall out in bundles, Tami wondered what the scans would show at the end of the cycle.

Lord, give me the strength to accept whatever the results . . .

At the end of the cycle, a repeat scan was performed. The scan showed dramatic growth of the liver metastases. There were also metastases to the lung.

The chemotherapy had failed. Tami instantly grasped the implications. Holding the scans in her hands, she examined them with a physician's eye and commented with a sober voice, "This looks bad, real bad." She swallowed. "I have seen patients die of liver metastases. It's a terrible death."

The oncologist sat down with Tami and her parents. "Tami, we will now discontinue the chemotherapy. From now on, our aim is to make your life as comfortable as possible. There may be weeks or months to go. I will arrange for a visit to the hospice so you can become familiar with the place. You will also be able to meet the hospice chaplain. Periodically, we will need to give you blood transfusions to keep up your blood counts to combat the fatigue. You may also need oxygen at some point." He explained to her parents, "Tami's hematocrit is likely to be very low—that's a parameter that indicates the number of blood cells in her body, and it would normally be around 40–45. Blood transfusions will help us keep it higher."

Tami saw her parents struggling against tears. She quietly walked over to them and gave them a hug. "God will give us strength and peace throughout."

In the car on the way home, there was silence.

Some time passed.

"Dad?"

"Yes, Tami."

"Dad, do you still believe in the miracle of me being healed?"

"Tami, it's difficult to give that up."

"Dad, yes, it's difficult. I don't rule out that God will do another miracle. He has given me several years in remission—years I would otherwise not have had. To me these years were a miracle. But somehow, now, I sense He has another plan. I think He is taking me to Him."

She paused, and her thoughts wandered off. "Not my will, but Thy will," she whispered. "Those were Jesus' words, and I feel the same way."

In the distance, she could see the mountain ranges of Denver. *I've always had the ambition to climb every high mountain in every state in America,* she thought to herself. *Well, I have managed to climb quite a few—now I have one last mountain to climb: the Mount of Olives, like Jesus did.*

To her parents, she said, with a more steady voice, "His will is always the best. And the reality is that being with Christ in heaven is better by far. That is the hope I have. I want to prepare for heaven." She spoke now with determination, as if she had made up her mind. Her parents were quiet, letting her say what she needed to say.

After a short pause she continued, "And I need to say farewell to my friends and the fellowship in Atlanta."

"I'll come with you to Atlanta," her mother said.

"Yes," her father added. "We are here for you. We will do whatever you want us to do." All three cried.

Painstakingly, over the next week, Tami chose every word for the e-mail that was to be sent around the world.

Hi everyone,

This is a very difficult e-mail to write, and I'm sure it will also be difficult for you to read and process. My follow-up scans show further growth in my liver and spread to my lung. The oncologist says that there are no treatments left to offer me that might have any benefit, and anything would only result in side effects. I have stopped chemotherapy now. Since I'm off chemo now, my nausea is now minimal and my appetite is better. Around-the-clock Tylenol and Ibuprofen have helped not only the horrible soaking night sweats but also the muscle aches. My energy level is low, though a transfusion yesterday for a hematocrit of nineteen is helping. I take short walks most days and even made it out to a movie the other day. God has continued to give me an inner peace that is beyond my comprehension. Yes, there are times of tears, but I'm accepting of what's ahead and looking forward to a new body in heaven.

Love,

Tami

"The most important thing to me is that people do not lose their faith because God did not heal me. My ultimate desire is that God be glorified through my illness and my death." Tami looked serious as she spoke to her parents. "Mom, we have to return to Atlanta now before I get too weak."

So with her mom in tow, Tami set off to spend one week in Atlanta. She spent most of the time sitting in the living room receiving friends while her mother stayed in the kitchen preparing cups of tea and snacks for the many visitors. For each visitor, Tami had prepared a piece of paper with a carefully selected verse from the Bible. She wanted to encourage each one of them and draw them to Christ. She prayed for the right selection for each of the verses. For her Chinese friends, she prepared the texts all in handwritten Chinese.

The hardest thing was to prepare her farewell speech to the church. After much prayer, she chose several passages from the first chapter of Philippians. She was too weak to stand up, so they helped her into a chair. She took the Bible and read, "But that with all boldness, as always, so now also Christ will be magnified in my body, whether by life or by death. For to me, to live is Christ, and to die is gain."

While she spoke, everyone in the congregation cried. Tami noticed her mother standing at the back of the church, sobbing away. In that moment, Tami decided she would do everything in her power to ease her mother's sorrow.

When they packed some items from her apartment in Atlanta to take home to Denver, Tami had one last look at her beloved Chinese banners with the words from 1 Corinthians 13. "Mom, after I die, I want these banners to go to a person or a family who will serve in China."

She thought for a while. "I think I know who. Paula Helms and her husband have always been so faithful in their support of me, and in their ministry to the Chinese here in Atlanta. And now they are serving in China." She made up her mind. "Yes, it gives me much joy knowing that the banners will go to them."

Originally, it had been planned that Tami would join the MSI winter retreat that was to be held in North Thailand in February 2005. Since this was now not to be, Dr. Taylor asked her to prepare a videotaped message for the MSI workers. They expected more than eighty workers for the retreat. Back in her home, Tami wrote down every word of her speech and learned it by heart. She practiced her message in Chinese and in English. When she was ready, her mother helped her put on a wig and some makeup.

Tami spoke into the video camera.

"It's great to be part of the winter retreat, though I wish I could greet you in person. I would like to say a special hello to my teammates, Sharon, Tomoko, and Swee Mun, and also to Hui Kheng, Becky, Matthew, and Dr. Taylor. I look back with great joy at my time with MSI in Chengdu, Xichang, and Zhaojue. Those early years were not always easy, but it was amazing to see God opening doors for His work to begin. What He taught me then about His faithfulness, flexibility, and waiting on Him has really carried me through the intervening years.

"I have followed with great thankfulness God's work through you since then. The Lord of the harvest has called more workers for His fields. Projects that were just beginning have blossomed and born fruit, and mere dreams have become reality, thus reaching more and more Yi people and Chinese for Christ and nurturing them in Him, all to the glory of God.

"My heart's deepest desire has always been to return long-term to my beloved China, but as you know, I have battled melanoma since shortly after returning to the U.S. in '98. In these years, God has been gracious and has miraculously healed several relapses along the way, giving me periods of good health and opportunities to return to work in Asia again, in Thailand, and to briefly revisit China. God has also brought China to me in Atlanta, blessing me with friendship with many mainland-Chinese visiting scholars, and opportunities to share Christ with them, study scripture with them, and join them in praise and worship.

"Now as I face my last weeks on earth, God has again graciously opened door after door for me to encourage fellow believers and share boldly with those who for the first time are finally ready to hear about the God who gives me incredible peace. Though I begin to outwardly waste away, inwardly I am being renewed day by day. I look forward to being in the presence of our beautiful Lord and Savior, Jesus Christ.

"Let me encourage you with a verse that has sustained me at critical points during my time in China and since. First Corinthians 15:58 says, 'Therefore, my dear fellow workers, stand firm. Let nothing move you. Always give yourselves fully to the work of the Lord, because you know that your labor in the Lord is not in vain.'

I want to conclude by reminding you that for us as Christians, good-bye is the wrong word, so I say to you *zai jian*, Chinese for 'see you again.' My love and prayers are with you all."

༄

"Hi, Tami, this is Jim Taylor from Hong Kong," Dr. Taylor said over the phone one day.

"Hi, Dr. Taylor. Thank you so much for calling. How are you?"

"I'm well, although in the past months the doctors have ordered me to stay at home for the treatment." Dr. Taylor had been diagnosed with liver cancer.

"Tami, the reason I'm calling is to thank you for your video message. There was no dry eye during the retreat. Everyone was encouraged to press on in the work for the Lord in China. You remain a blessing to China even now." Dr. Taylor's voice wavered.

He continued, "The resilience you have demonstrated these past years has been a tremendous encouragement to all of us. And now you are facing a new challenge in the same beautiful spirit of Christ. Yours has been and always will be a kingdom focus. Tami, how shall we pray for you?"

Tami thought for a while. "Pray for comfort for my family. Praise the Lord for the peace He has given me. Pray that I may remain alert for a long time. And most importantly, pray that God will be glorified."

And immediately Dr. Taylor started praying, a long-distance prayer from halfway across the globe. "Tami, I would like to close our phone call with Paul's wonderful words in 2 Corinthians 4:16–18: 'Therefore we do not lose heart . . . for our light and momentary troubles are achieving for us an eternal glory that *far* outweighs them all. So we fix our eyes not on what is seen, but on what is unseen. For what is seen is temporary, but what is unseen is eternal.'"

It wasn't long after that Tami's mom took her to watch a movie. On the way, they saw an advertisement for *The Lion, the Witch, and the Wardrobe*, one of the Chronicles of Narnia by C.S. Lewis that was scheduled to be released that spring. Passing by, Tami just whispered, "That is hard." She said nothing else. She knew she would not live long enough to watch it.

Then Tami pulled her shoulders up, and with her old determination, she said. "Mom, I'd like to read C.S. Lewis's books again. He has so much to say about heaven."

Many friends visited her during her last months. They flew in from various parts of the United States. They stayed for several hours or sometimes days, and Tami's parents served them while Tami was propped up on the couch in the living room. They looked at photo albums together or just shared old memories. Tami always had a verse from the Bible on hand. Having spent a lifetime learning Bible passages by heart, she found that the passages seemed to flow more and more easily.

The couch in her parents' living room became Tami's workplace. Her mother would try to make her as comfortable as possible, and her father would bring her the laptop computer which would be steadied by pillows on her enlarging and tender abdomen. She sent e-mails to her friends and supporters around the world. In particular, she corresponded in depth with those friends who had yet to find Christ.

In one of her e-mails she wrote, "Philippians 1:12: 'Now I want you to know, brothers, that what has happened to me has really served to advance the gospel.' I just wanted to thank you for your prayers and share with you how God has been using this time in my life. Non-Christian friends who have had rock-hard hearts in the past are now, for the first time, open to hear about the God who gives me peace."

One of them was a friend from her medical school years. He was a non-practicing Jew, but he had followed her time in China with great interest. "I'm saddened and angered by your illness. I'm angered because I guess I do not understand God's plan," he e-mailed her.

Tami responded, "Go ahead and yell at God and let Him know that you are angry." And she followed this up by sending him the gospel message and recommending that he read or get the tapes of Lee Stroebel's books A Case for Faith and A Case for Christ, as well as some other books. Within twenty-four hours, he wrote to her that he had ordered the tapes! To Tami, this was an indescribable joy. Further correspondence and questioning about the faith ensued over the following days and weeks.

In one of the e-mails to him, she wrote her testimony.

Sorry for the slow reply. I wanted to send a thoughtful reply but have been a bit swamped with visitors and running low on energy—a hematocrit of eighteen is part of that. I will get my second of two blood transfusions for the week tomorrow.

I'm glad you listened to *Case for Faith*. You asked about faith and suffering. Yes, thankfully, I have believed in God, with all the blessing that entails, most of my life, but it was not always a "strong faith." In the good times, it is very easy for me, a self-sufficient (or prideful), fallible human being, to take God for granted and rely on my own resources. Then, when things are difficult, whether during tough times in China or during the low points of this illness, I'm reminded that all I am and have comes from God and that my own strength is limited. God's strength and comfort have no limits! I think a quote from one of my favorite authors, C.S. Lewis, says it well: "God whispers to us in our pleasures, speaks in our conscience, but shouts in our pains: it is His megaphone to rouse a deaf world." I did not do enough journaling during this illness, but there have been a series of milestones and lessons from God along the way, often with a Bible passage to go with them.

I'll list some:

- Early on, it was "Do not fear, I am the Lord" who won't let the "flames" or "waves" consume me (Isaiah 43).
- Knowing that God always wants the best for me and He alone holds my future (Jeremiah 29:11).
- Seeing God glorify Himself in me by a "spontaneous" (read: miraculous) disappearance of four new ear lesions in autumn 2000.
- Learning to be content disease-free or not (Philippians 4).
- Choosing life rather than death in the midst of horrible pain and nausea last spring (Philippians 1).
- Learning that God gives a peace beyond human understanding (Philippians 4).

I agree that it is friends and family who need prayer as much as I do. Though times are tough to some extent now for me, at the end I get a new body in a place of joy. They get a "gap." I'm thankful that my parents and some friends can enjoy the same peace that I do now and in the hard times to come.

Chapter 33

GRASPING HEAVEN

During the final weeks of her life, Tami's suffering was sometimes unbearable. She frequently needed gentle massages to ease her back and neck muscles. She never complained. She just told her parents and those who cared for her what was hurting so they knew where to be gentle or where she needed more soothing.

Every day, her mother watched Tami as she kept going despite the many physical setbacks, the vomiting, the pain, and the extreme fatigue. One day, when her mother watched Tami vomit her food yet not complain, she blurted, "Tami, how do you manage to persevere?"

"Mom, I remember," Tami replied tenderly. "It was you who helped me memorize the thirteenth chapter of 1 Corinthians when I was a child." And she recited, "Love always hopes, love always perseveres."

Some time later, she told her mom, "I've had to think a lot about love in these last weeks. I still do not grasp it all, but I'm discovering more and more of His love. I'd like to share my thoughts with you." Tami took a deep breath. "Some people will question why a God of love could have inflicted me with metastatic melanoma, and say that my current suffering has nothing to do with love. But it is entirely the opposite! It is all about love."

Tami had to turn on her side as her back started to ache. "Love trusts. I love Him, and therefore I trust Him who knows why I have to die so young. Furthermore, love has no fear. As I'm approaching death, I can honestly say that I have no more fear. At times I did have fear, but the more I understand about His love, the less I fear. I have often reflected on the verse, 'There will be hope, faith, and love. But love is the greatest of them all.' Why is love the greatest of all? Because love is what will remain in heaven. Heaven is all about love. While my body is falling apart, I know that love will never fail."

She turned again.

"Do you remember my assignment in high school on C.S. Lewis's Space Trilogy? The people on Malacandra did not fear death, and they knew that their bodies would be changed. Instead of imagining death as an end, they viewed it as 'the beginning of all things.' I believe the same. Heaven is the beginning of it all. Not only the beginning, but also the fulfillment of true love."

Often Tami had to be taken to the hospital for blood tests and transfusions. When waiting for the procedures, she looked around to see whether other patients needed her help or an encouraging smile or word. Sometimes she was too weak to get into the waiting room, so the oncology nurse who was so fond of Tami suggested a solution: her parents would drive Tami as close as possible to the entrance, and the nurse would come out to meet Tami in the car and take blood there. Jokingly, Tami thanked the nurse, "Thanks so much for the drive-by blood draw!"

One day her vomiting was so severe that she had to be admitted to the hospice for rehydration. She spent two nights there.

"The hospice is great," she told her friends, "and so is the chaplain. The rooms look more like home. The doctor gave me excellent advice on how to cope better with my pain. They offered me many other services. Can you imagine, they even offered to do my nails! I have never had my nails done in my life, so I'm not starting it now." She chuckled.

The hospice chaplain visited her to talk about dying. "Tami, do you have any regrets?"

Tami thought for a while. "No, I have no regrets," she replied, but then she looked toward her worn-out Chinese Bible on the table next to her. "I spent so much time studying Chinese . . ."

She sighed, and for a while, she looked sad and forlorn. Then she looked back at the chaplain, and with a spark in her eye, she added, "Oh well, Chinese is after all the eternal language. It takes eternity to learn it. I will have eternity now to get really good at it!"

Day by day, Tami became weaker. She had little appetite. Her mother tried to make her food as tasty as possible. "Mom, I think a Chinese chicken soup may be best at this point," Tami confided. So her mother asked her Chinese friends to bring some soup. For the next weeks, her Chinese friends came frequently to their house to deliver Chinese meals. Tami would relish in conversing in Chinese with them.

Tami's mother took the main responsibility for nursing her during the day, and her father stayed up with her until the early morning hours, often sleeping in the room next to her bedroom. Tami's nights were often restless. Sorrow seemed more poignant during the night, shortness of breath more severe, pain more acute. Sometimes she woke up totally drenched in sweat. Turning in bed, it was difficult to find a pain-free position. Her tummy was getting larger because more and more fluid was building up in her abdomen. The growing abdomen pressed on her diaphragm, making breathing more difficult. But she did not want to wake her father who was sleeping next door.

On such nights she thought of the new body she would have soon, the heavenly body. She thought of the pictures of heaven that she remembered so vividly from reading the Space Trilogy. Heaven would be better by far. She would be active again, running, dancing, climbing mountains . . . On one night she dozed off, only to wake a few hours later. She penned a few words. She planned to leave behind a poem for her family and friends. *It will need some more thought. I will work on it again tomorrow night.* She opened the Bible and spent the next hours reading and praying.

The next morning her father asked her, "Tami, did you get any sleep?"

"Thanks, I got a couple of hours, Dad."

Her father pointed at the Bible lying open on her bed. Tami smiled and added, "Yes, during the night I also had some wonderful hours with the Lord."

Next to her bed were books that focused on the topic of heaven. They were heavily marked, with many statements highlighted. Tami had also made handwritten lists of people she prayed for. These lists were long, with all the names in small print, ordered in columns and scheduled for every single day. She folded the list and kept it in her Bible. The list looked worn.

"Dad?"

"Yes, Tami?"

"Mom's birthday is approaching. I want to give her a special gift. Over the past years, Mom has nursed me, fed me, massaged my body—I can think of only one appropriate gift for her now: a spa treatment!"

"That's a good idea. I will buy the voucher for you."

"No, Dad, I want to do it myself. It's my gift to her."

Tami's father drove her to the spa salon and parked in front of it so she wouldn't need to walk far. With his help and support, she managed to get to the shop and select the spa treatment she thought would be best for her mother.

On her mom's birthday, she presented the gift with a twinkle in her eye: "Mom, you have given me so many massages. Now you deserve one, too."

Tami was becoming very emaciated. With every body part hurting, it was too painful for anyone to touch or hug her. One day, standing next to her mom, who was quite a bit shorter than her daughter, Tami suddenly slumped onto her mother and gave her the most affectionate hug. "Mom, I love you soooo much."

Holding each other for a long time, they both sobbed out loud. "The hardest thing of all is that I'm leaving you two alone and that I cannot care for you in your old age," Tami cried.

Others needed special farewells. "I think I should see Nicole again to say good-bye," Tami said one day. Nicole Mares had so faithfully stood by her side during those terrible nights of excruciating facial pain, but she had meanwhile left the U.S. to serve as a missionary overseas. Knowing that Nicole could not afford to visit her now because of her limited budget, Tami decided to sponsor her trip to Denver.

"I don't know what to say." Entering the room and seeing her friend in such a bad state, tears welled up in Nicole's eyes.

"Thanks for taking the trip to see me, Nicole." They embraced as much as Tami was able to bear, and they spent hours catching up with each other.

"When my aunt died of cancer, I somehow felt angry with God, Tami. But when I see you, I sense no anger. I can see God. I came to encourage you, but it appears that you are encouraging me instead! You are so full of peace."

"Nicole, I fought against the disease for many years; I didn't want to give in. I can only resonate with Paul from the Bible. I have fought the good fight, I have finished the race, I have kept the faith."

"Tami, you will receive the crown of glory that will never fade away. I know it. You will wear the most beautiful crown!"

"We all have to keep the finish line in our eyes, Nicole. Some of us arrive sooner than others. But all of us will have to face this reality one day. We are after all not citizens of this earth. Eternity is in our hearts."

"Tami, I feel almost jealous of you," Nicole commented.

Tami glanced down her emaciated body. "Jealous?"

"Yes, jealous of the intimacy you have with God. You are literally living in God's presence."

In the last few weeks of her life, Tami spent most of her time preparing for her memorial services. She corresponded with Dr. Taylor about the service in Hong Kong, with her pastor in Atlanta about the service at the International Fellowship, and with her pastor in Denver about the service at her home church. She jotted down quotes by her favorite authors, went through several songbooks and selected the pieces she thought were most appropriate, and wrote and rewrote the order of the service, the selection of Bible passages, and the persons to read the passages. She had piles of notes spread around the couch.

When Tim flew down to Denver to spend some time with her, she showed him some of the notes. "Tim, I like this quote best. It is from *The Last Battle* by C.S. Lewis, and it says, 'I have come home at last! This is my real country! I belong here. This is the land I have been looking for all my life, though I never knew it till now.'"

Tami looked serious. "This is exactly how I feel about heaven." Then her eyes sparkled. "Did you know that it was a unicorn that said these words? He said them when arriving in Aslan's country which, as you know, alludes to heaven. I guess I'm turning into some kind of a unicorn." She laughed briefly.

"Now, what do you think about these words that I found in Max Lucado's book, *The Applause of Heaven?*"

Tami leaned forward to pick up one of her notes, and then she read it out aloud:

> "What type of joy is this? What is this cheerfulness that dares to wink at adversity? What is this bird that sings when it is still dark? What is the source of this peace that defies pain? I call it sacred delight. It is sacred because it is not of this life. What is sacred is God's. And this joy is God's. It is delight because delight can both satisfy and surprise. Delight is Mary watching God sleep in a feed trough. Delight is the look on Andrew's face at the lunch pail that never came up empty. Delight is a leper seeing a finger where there had been only a nub . . . a paraplegic doing somersaults. Sacred delight is what you'd always dreamed but never expected. It is too-good-to-be-true coming true."

Both paused as they reflected on the words.

"Tim, did Dad tell you that in the past weeks whenever I found the time I watched Tolkien's *The Lord of the Rings?*" Tami asked.

"You always did love to read Tolkien," Tim remarked.

"I'm glad the film follows the book pretty closely," Tami continued. "You know, I often identify with Frodo. Poor Frodo only gets enough direction for the next lap of the journey. Gandalf only gives the occasional explanation. But as the journey goes on, Frodo understands more and more."

Tami had to rest a while to catch her breath.

"I found one quote and wanted to check with you whether it's appropriate for the first page of the memorial service. Listen, this is it: 'Gandalf! I thought you were dead! But then I thought I was dead myself. Is everything sad going to come untrue?' Tim, what do you think? Can I use it?"

Tim thought for a while and then said, "Some may not understand it, but those who know you and your sense of humor in your faith will understand it. Use it."

Tami's work was not finished. She wanted to find something for the memorial service that would draw attention to the plight of China. She finally found a song called "A Heart for China." With her English-Chinese dictionary next to her bed, she diligently translated the text into Chinese. However, she remained uncertain about some intricacies of the translation. When her Chinese friends passed by the next day to deliver some food, Tami asked for their help with the translation. As soon as she was satisfied with the final wording, she contacted the choir of the Chinese Bible study at Emory and asked whether they would be willing to sing this song for her memorial service.

"Tami, how can you prepare your own memorial service with so much detail?" one friend asked her, astonished.

"Does not the bride prepare for her wedding day in great detail?" Tami responded. "Of all these elaborate wedding plans, no part receives more attention and care than the preparation of the bride herself. Jesus said, 'I am going there to prepare a place for you,' and I am preparing myself for the place Jesus has Himself prepared for me. Besides," she added carefully, "my memorial is my last chance to be a witness for the Lord."

As she became weaker, she was not able to e-mail all her friends anymore. When a friend e-mailed to say that she just could not understand how Tami was able to face death, Tami felt that giving an answer was important. So she took all her strength, sat up on her couch, and typed on her laptop: "Why don't I fear death? Why am I at peace with things? The bottom line is that

I have an inner peace so complete I can't even understand it, and a joy that gives me strength for each day. This is absolutely not from within me or via meditation or whatever. Such limitless peace and joy in such circumstances can come only from God."

About two weeks prior to her death, Tami explained to her father all the financial matters she had settled. She then showed him a folder on her computer entitled "Last Things."

"Please, could you or Tim open this particular folder after I have died?"

Shortly after, Tami employed her doctor's training to prepare her parents for the end. "I do not know how I will die. But I thought I should let you know what could medically happen. Most likely I will go into complete liver failure that will lead to coma. A worse scenario would be that I will hemorrhage to death due to my damaged clotting system as a result of liver failure. I'm very thankful that although my body is falling apart, my mind has remained alert, and I have savored so many beautiful moments in these last weeks. This may not last much longer."

Days later, Tami's mom caught her lifting dumbbells with her thin, emaciated arms. "Tami, what are you doing?" she asked, amazed.

Tami answered quietly, "I'm exercising my arms so you won't need to lift me so much."

When Dr. Taylor phoned Tami, he said, "I would like to visit you, but I'm grounded in Hong Kong due to my health problems. MSI will fund Sharon and Tomoko to travel from China to visit you."

"Thank you, Dr. Taylor. That is very thoughtful of you. But I don't want to incur any expenses that could be better used for the work in China."

"Tami, this is MSI's gift to you."

Just days before Sharon and Tomoko arrived, Tami said to her parents, "I don't know whether I'm able to last until they come." She tried to space out the pain medication as much as she could tolerate in order to extend her liver's lifespan until her teammates would arrive. Her laboratory parameters were rapidly deteriorating, and she needed transfusions with ever-shorter intervals.

When Dr. Taylor called again, she told him, "Well, I think I will make it till Sharon and Tomoko arrive, but not long after that."

Sharon and Tomoko arrived on Friday. Tami, Sharon, and Tomoko, the three pioneer women of Zhaojue, had a very special time together. Tami was very weak and could only spend a couple hours at a time with them. Both being nurses, Sharon and Tomoko tried to make her as comfortable as possible. They propped her up with several pillows and administered oxygen when she needed it. Tami insisted on conversing in Chinese. Sharon and Tomoko shared how the work had progressed in Zhaojue since Tami left.

"Tami, the little girl who so often joined you in your walks through the mountains has been accepted to study in Xichang," Sharon said.

"The work of the Youth Center in Zhaojue is progressing well," Tomoko added.

"Dr. Zhu, the chair of the Communist Party, sends you her warmest regards. She wants to let you know how much she admires you. She says that everyone in Zhaojue will always remember you."

Tami's eyes shone. "God gave Dr. Broomhall three years among the Yi people. He wanted to serve longer, but God cut his stay short. Yet, decades later, his work continues. I served in China for three years. I wanted to serve for many more, but God cut my stay short, too. Yet, I know that God will continue His work through you and the many people from all over the world who have joined MSI."

With tears running down their cheeks, they sang together for the last time: lifting their voices in their Chinese Love Song from the book of Corinthians.

Sharon and Tomoko stayed for two days. They left on Sunday night after Tami had prayed with them for their future work.

After their going, Tami deteriorated by the hour. On Monday she rested a lot and was unable to take in any food. Mary Macaluso, her dear family friend over many years, stayed with her, massaging her swollen legs. Led by the Spirit, Mary started singing spiritual songs. With her raspy voice, as breathless as she was, Tami joined in. "Salvation belongs to our Lord, who sits upon the throne, and unto the Lamb. Praise and glory, wisdom and thanks, honor and power and strength, be to our God, forever and ever. Amen."

On Tuesday morning, another long-time friend of Tami's stayed a couple of hours with her. She remarked, "Tami, you have such a sweet and quiet spirit. You look more and more like Jesus." She helped put on the stockings and massaged Tami's legs. Tami shared the video with her that showed her farewell message to MSI.

That Tuesday afternoon, her doctor called to tell her that the laboratory results were very bad. Tami announced, "It's time for me to go to the hospice. I think it's also time to call Tim to come."

As they arranged for the move, Tami sat down with her laptop one final time.

This is likely my last e-mail to you directly. My parents will, I'm sure, provide future updates. My strength and breathing are slipping, so it is difficult for me to spend much time on the computer. Thank all of you for continuing to pray and to send such loving and encouraging e-mails and cards. My love and prayers will be with you, even if I can't keep up phone calls and correspondence.
Much love,
Tami

As weak as she was, she still wanted to walk to the car for the trip to the hospice all by herself. Step by step, she fought her way to the car, determined to make it on her own. When she arrived, she glanced back at her home.

"I am ready," she said. "I am ready to be with the Lord."

At the hospice, she was too weak to walk and had to be taken to her room in a wheelchair. She could barely talk. Yet, she insisted on one last phone call, a call to her previous high school teacher who was also a publisher.

Short of breath and very hoarse, Tami was barely understandable. "Please, with all the talk about a book about me, and if one is ever written, please do not make me a super-saint. Because I'm not."

The hospice nurses positioned her as comfortably as possible. She was in great pain, and they started a drip to ease her discomfort. When Tim arrived the next morning, he sat next to her and held her hand. Brother and sister were able to have a last time together. Later in the afternoon, she slipped into a coma. Father, mother, and brother took turns sitting at her bedside.

In the early morning hours, Tami passed on peacefully.

Epilogue

TAMI'S LEGACY CONTINUES

BY DR. MATTHEW KOH, PRESIDENT, MSI PROFESSIONAL SERVICES

W riting this epilogue for Tami Fisk is a special honor. Originally, Dr. James Hudson Taylor III had planned to write the epilogue. But with his failing health, it was not to be. In the final days before his home call, Dr. Taylor reminded me, "Make sure that Tami's biography gets published!" Were he here to write, you would feel the deep love this spiritual giant held for Tami.

Tami's tale runs in the grain of many stories, including mine. I helped process her application to MSI; I organized her orientation. While she served on the frontline in West China, I helped in Hong Kong as MSI Medical Director. Together we planned medical care for the rural poor and prepared medical teams for service. She was such a good friend, always full of fun, energy, and vision.

Tami's story is formative in the history of MSI. It will be repeated on the lips of many in Zhaojue, within MSI, and perhaps also in our history books. Tami left a legacy in her *spirit,* her *service,* and her *song.*

TAMI'S SPIRIT

"For I know the plans I have for you," declares the LORD, "plans to prosper you and not to harm you, plans to give you hope and a future." (Jeremiah 29:11)

Tami made careful plans and then committed those plans to the Lord. We in MSI had great hopes she would continue to serve in China. *After all, we thought, her career has such a bright outlook!*

Even during the years she battled melanoma, she showed such a positive spirit that sometimes we were sure she would return to China in full strength. Then her cancer recurrence cast doubt on God and His plans to give her a "hope and a future." Tami, however, revealed her spirit when she chose that very Jeremiah verse as the grounding text for her funeral. It was her shout.

"God does have a perfect plan for my 'shalom'! What a glorious hope! What a future!"

TAMI'S SERVICE

Therefore, my dear brothers, stand firm. Let nothing move you. Always give yourselves fully to the work of the Lord, because you know that your labor in the Lord is not in vain. (1 Corinthians 15:58)

From these words, Tami created a video two weeks before she went home. She was physically very weak from her cancer, but she persevered to produce this short video. First in Chinese, then in English, she urged us to "stand firm" as she testified to the grace of God and of her hope of being with the Lord. You can see the tape she sent to friends and Chinese officials at www.tamifisk.com.

The ethos of Tami's service remains. Her principles and values were woven into the texture of MSI. Tami participated in formulating these value statements:

- Inland Focus
- Government Approved
- Professional Integrity
- Professional Service Focus
- Team Approach
- Long-Term Approach
- Lifestyle, Low-Key

Even after her departure, these values are here to stay.

TAMI'S SONG

"Sing a new song to the Lord, for He has done wonderful deeds. He has won a mighty victory by his power and holiness." (Psalm 98:1)

Tami loved to sing. And she loved to write poems. In Tami's "Last Things" folder, her family found the poem she wrote only days before her death, "Today I Am Healed."

This poem has been written into a song and translated into Chinese as well as into the Yi language. Tami's second-year memorial services were celebrated in Xichang and Zhaojue in April 2007. Her life story was told over in each of these areas and also in the schools and hospitals where she had served. And again her poem was sung.

Over and over, in the hospitals and government offices of the Great Cold Mountains, they sang "Today I Am Healed." Tami's poem was also printed on a memorial bookmark.

Tami has been God's poem in MSI's services in China and in the lives of people she touched. Her poetry lives on in us, reminding us of the legacy she left not only in China, but also for the generation of men and women to serve in China in the future. In us her song still sings, echoing her legacy.

TAMI'S LEGACY

Tami served in China only three short years. That was the same duration as Dr. A.J. Broomhall's work among the same Yi (Nosu) people back in the late 1940s. Maybe three years is short to some of us. But as Jesus puts it in John 12, it is the seed that falls to the ground and dies that produces many seeds. It is not the duration Tami served physically in China that counts. Whether present in the body or absent, her life's witness in the Great Cold Mountains and among the Yi, just like the Broomhalls', continues to produce seeds. Seeds in forms we cannot comprehend, in the lives of those she personally influenced, and also in those who followed after her.   In those early pioneering years, none of us would have imagined the wide doors opened for us to serve as Christian professionals in the Spirit of Christ in inland China. Tami helped to break the ground and set the foundations for the work to grow.

By 2009, MSI had been granted favor to serve in over twelve cities of various sizes in inland China. Each year, three to five hundred short-term workers are also involved in supporting and amplifying the work led by over seventy long-term colleagues seeking to live incarnationally in inland China. Indeed, God has plans to give us a future and a hope beyond what we can think or imagine. Over the years, from the pioneering trio of Tami, Sharon, and Tomoko, the team has grown to be like a tree, a large team of workers engaged in medical, education, development, and youth work in China.

Tami's life and words stretch all our finiteness beyond the present into the historical past and to the end of time. She gives us courage to persevere with the assurance of "home" at last, our real country: We belong there, where our Triune God is waiting for us. Meanwhile, we are meant to live on and continue the work Tami started.

May I end with words of A.J. Broomhall in 1953: "My prayer is that it will arouse lethargic Christians in the homelands, and drive them to pray, and to volunteer to go where the way is still open and the need is great."

A Tami Memorial Fund has been set up to encourage medical professionals to serve in the footsteps of Tami Fisk in China. Details of applications can be found at www.tamifisk.com.

Travel Scholarship Fund in Tami Fisk's memory is with the Christian Medical and Dental Association. **To donate,** e-mail Jamey.campbell@cmda.org <campbell@cmda.org>. For info, consult www.cmda.org <http://www.cmda.org> . Click "Missions," drop-down "Scholarships."

Emory School of Medicine's **Tami Fisk Global Health Fund,** http://www.medicine.emory.edu/divisions/id/awards/tami.cfm

A LIFE FULL OF GRACE

BY DR. REGINALD TSANG, COFOUNDER, MSI PROFESSIONAL SERVICES

Tami Fisk was among the first health professionals to go full-time into the interior of China when Medical Services International was born. Her young life was a touching one, and full of the grace of her dear Lord. She worked with two nurses, Tomoko from Japan and Sharon from Taiwan, in the Great Cold Mountains of Sichuan.

This was the land of the Yi, with their famous torch ceremonies and tall mountains. The Yi people wore distinctive long capes that were protection against the freezing winters. There was no internal heating, and most people in winter would sit around a fire for much of the time, unless they were outdoors. When they were outdoors, the sun was extremely bright, and for a fair-skinned person like Tami, it was always a threat.

Indeed, the ultraviolet exposure at high altitude finally hastened Tami's malignant melanoma, a skin cancer to which she ultimately succumbed. Her life was a shining witness of dedication and love for the Lord. She had been trained as an internal medicine/pediatric specialist in the United States, but during a medical elective in China, she developed her love for the Chinese people. So when the opportunity arose for her to contribute to China, she grasped it. She was one of the first eager to step into the breach.

I love this story from her life: one day, she was standing on a street corner in Zhaojue, the historic capital of the Yi. She was standing rather still and composed. Soon, a Yi woman came up to her to tug on her clothes and inspect what she was wearing. The local woman thought that she was a mannequin, since there were no white people in that town, and probably she had never had seen a real live white person. When Tami moved, the Yi woman almost had a heart attack!

Tami was no mannequin. She was a real-life servant of the Lord, serving the Lord incarnationally among a distant people in the way her Lord wanted her to do. With her quiet, unassuming ways, it was easy to underestimate her. But when she moved, or sprang into action, she was full of the salt and light we are called to be. Her life story is one that has impacted hundreds, if not thousands, and our lives have been greatly enriched by knowing her. We are secure in the knowledge that she is with her dear Lord now, welcomed by Him as the "good and faithful servant" that she has been.

A CELEBRATION OF TAMI FISK'S LIFE

As shared by Dr. James Hudson Taylor III during Tami's memorial service in Hong Kong on March 31, 2005

We have gathered to celebrate God's grace in the life and service of our colleague, Dr. Tamara Fisk. May I share with you a glimpse of the Tami I knew?

Tami was *a Christian professional* who served with integrity. She had trained long and well—Summa Cum Laude. She strove for excellence in profession and service, always improving herself—i.e., going back to Emory. She gave all she had to medical research of AIDS and SARS and their cures; even going to Thailand, China and Taiwan while battling melanoma herself.

Tami was *a great team player.* I watched her work with an international team made up of herself, Sharon, and Tomoko, not to speak of all those short-term teams from Singapore!

Tami served with *a humble servant spirit.* She was always caring of others and their needs. She lived a simple lifestyle in the rugged mountains of Western China. She identified with the people she lived among and served.

Tami had *a great sense of humor.* She was a strong competitor in sports or games at home. She loved the outdoors, mountain climbing, and skiing.

Tami had *a heart for China* and the Chinese people. Like Hudson Taylor, she committed her life to their service. She learned the language to understand, to identify, and to serve. She longed to share with Chinese friends the wonder of new life in Christ.

Tami had *a supreme commitment to Jesus Christ*. As a scientist, she believed in the God of creation and obeyed His will. She loved God's Word and trusted His promises. Prayer was a vital part of Tami's everyday life. Her passion was to share with others the joy of new life in Jesus. She held firmly to our glorious hope—knowing "it is not death to die." Not death, not "good-bye," but *zai jian, auf wiedersehn*. Her faith in Jesus was the secret of Tami's courage, strength, joy, and peace.

Finally, a word about Tami's poem that has moved us all so deeply.

It was written in the midst of discomfort and pain, shortly before her home call. She wrote, "Today, I have been healed."

I see here a two-fold aspect of time: present and future. In the present she had been healed from questioning and complaint, anger, self-pity, distraction, and despair. We also say she was healed in anticipation of her home call: 2 Corinthians 4:16–5:5, 1 Corinthians 15:51, 53.

I see here Tami's secret.

Victory—through our Lord Jesus Christ, 1 Corinthians 15:57; Jeremiah 29:11.

Hope—she saw beyond. Tami loved 1 Corinthians 13 (long before MSI!)

Think of stepping on shore and finding it heaven!
Of taking hold of a hand and finding it God's hand!
Of breathing in new air and finding it celestial air!
Of feeling invigorated and finding it immortality!
Of passing from storm and tempest to an unknown calm!
Of waking up and finding it home!

Tami with a few of Thailand "Bartronella Tamiae" research team

Fisk Family in NC in November, 2004, upon hearing news of Tami's liver metastasis

Wheaton roommates, Kathy and Suzie, visiting Tami in 2005

Atlanta friends, IFC at Intown and Emory University

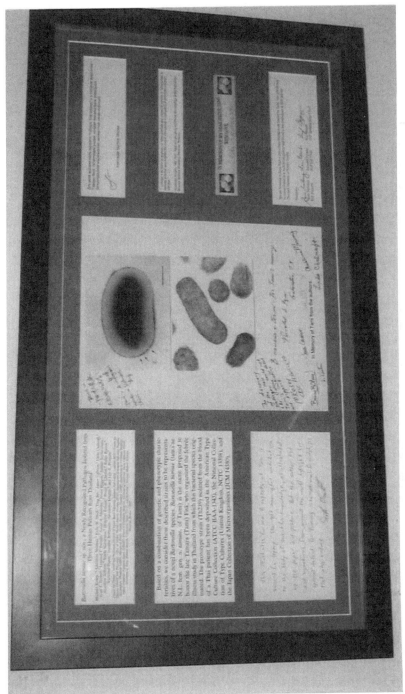

"Bartonella Tamiae" author tributes created by Dr. Scott Dowell

APPENDICES

A CELEBRATION OF LIFE: TAMI'S MEMORIAL SERVICES

Three memorial services were held for Tami: in Denver, in Atlanta, and at the MSI office in Hong Kong. She wanted them to be called "A Celebration of Life." Tami's mother chose the floral arrangements using Tami's favorite flowers, tiger lilies and snapdragons. All the flowers at the memorials had bright cheerful colors put together as she would have liked.

Tami prepared the contents of the program and bulletin in every detail. She requested that all the scripture readings be read in English and Chinese.

On the front page, her reflections were written for people to meditate upon while listening to the song "I'll Be Waiting for You."

TAMI'S REFLECTIONS

Tami's Life Verse:

"For I know the plans I have for you," declares the LORD, "plans to prosper you [give you Shalom/peace], and not to harm you, plans to give you hope and a future." (Jeremiah 29:11)

What type of joy is this? What is this cheerfulness that dares to wink at adversity? What is this bird that sings when it is still dark? What is the source of this peace that defies pain?

I call it sacred delight. It is sacred because it is not of this life. What is sacred is God's. And this joy is God's. It is delight because delight can both satisfy and surprise.

Delight is Mary watching God sleep in a feed trough. Delight is the look on Andrew's face at the lunch pail that never came up empty. Delight is a leper seeing a finger where there had been only a nub . . . a [mother] hosting a party with food made for a funeral . . . a paraplegic doing somersaults.

Sacred delight [is] what you'd always dreamed but never expected. It is too-good-to-be-true coming true." (*The Applause of Heaven*, Max Lucado)

"Gandalf! I thought you were dead! But then I thought I was dead myself.

Is everything sad going to come untrue?" (Sam in *The Lord of the Rings: The Return of the King,* J.R.R.Tolkien)

"I have come home at last! This is my real country! I belong here. This is the land I have been looking for all my life, though I never knew it till now." (Jewel the Unicorn on arriving in Aslan's country, heaven, in The Chronicles of Narnia, **The Last Battle,** C.S. Lewis)

"Most people, if they had really learned to look into their own hearts, would know that they do want, and want acutely, something that cannot be had in this world. There are all sorts of things in this world that offer to give it to you, but they never quite keep their promise . . . If I find in myself a desire which no experience in this world can satisfy, the most probable explanation is that I was made for another world." (*Mere Christianity,* C.S. Lewis)

"You'll see faces waiting for you. You'll hear your name spoken by those who love you. And . . . the One who would rather die than live without you will remove his pierced hands form his heavenly robe . . . and applaud." (On our arrival in heaven, from *The Applause of Heaven,* Max Lucado)

THE BIBLE READINGS
The following are the Bible readings Tami thoughtfully selected for us:

For God so loved the world that he gave his one and only Son, that whoever believes in him shall not perish but have eternal life. For God did not send his Son into the world to condemn the world, but to save the world through him. (John 3:16–17)

If there is no resurrection of the dead, then not even Christ has been raised. And if Christ has not been raised, our preaching is useless and so is your faith. But Christ has indeed been raised from the dead, the firstfruits of those who have fallen asleep. (1 Corinthians 15:13–14, 20)

Praise our God, O peoples, let the sound of his praise be heard;
he has preserved our lives and kept our feet from slipping.
For you, O God, tested us; you refined us like silver.
You brought us into prison and laid burdens on our backs.
You let men ride over our heads; we went through fire and water,
but you brought us to a place of abundance. (Psalm 66:8–12)
But God will redeem my life from the grave; he will surely take me to himself.
(Psalm 49:15)

May the God of hope fill you with all joy and peace as you trust in him, so that you may overflow with hope by the power of the Holy Spirit. (Romans 15:13)

THE MUSIC

Below are the songs Tami requested we sing in her memory.

I'll Be Waiting for You
(Lyrics by David Meece and Dwight Liles)

Do Not Fear (Isaiah 43)

When you pass through waters, I will be with you.
And the waves will not overcome you.
Do not fear, for I have redeemed you.
I have called you by name: you are mine.

Chorus
For I am the Lord your God.
I am the Holy One from Israel, your Savior.

When you walk through the fire, you'll not be burned.
And the flames will not consume you.
Do not fear, for I have redeemed you.
I have called you by name: you are mine.

He Will Rejoice Over You (Zephaniah 3:17)
(Paraphrase by Scott Wesley Brown)

The Lord, our God, is with you
He is mighty to save
The Lord will take great delight in you
He will quiet you with his love.

Chorus
He will rejoice over you, He will rejoice over you.
If you could only hear His voice,
You would hear the Lord rejoice,
Rejoicing over you with singing.

A Heart for China (Sung in Chinese)

As waters from many distant mountains join and flow into the same stream,
So we, though separated by continents, join our hearts in one heart for China.
Our hearts beat with the same feelings,
And with one heart we work together, enthusiastic for the gospel.
God loves China and loves us deeply too;
From near and far he has gathered our flock together.
Every moment of every day, without ceasing,
The gospel flame burns in our hearts.
With urgent steps we start out on a journey,
With moonlight as our cape and starlight gleaming on our heads.
In every home dark with hopelessness, we want to light a new lamp,
And carry Peace to each of China's peoples.
We have a sincere heart for China,
So we love China's peoples, love all our Chinese brothers and sisters, and love everyone on earth.

Appendix II

TRIBUTES TO TAMI

"Unless a kernel of wheat falls to the ground and dies, it remains only a single seed. But if it dies, it produces many seeds" (John 12: 24)

"Every time I saw Tami in the last couple of years, she radiated the peace and joy of Jesus more and more. The last time I saw her, she had an inner beauty that shone from her face in spite of the pain she was suffering. If anyone wants proof that God exists and that His presence can sustain us, they have only to look at Tami's example, both in how she lived and in the way she died."—SUZIE GOERING, WHEATON COLLEGE ROOMMATE

"She always talked openly about her illness and remarked repeatedly that God had given her incredible peace to face the future no matter what . . . A few days before her death, she started to sing "Salvation belongs to our God." What a joy-filled, Spirit-filled time together."—MARY MACALUSO, FAMILY FRIEND AND FORMER BOARD MEMBER OF DENVER SEMINARY

"Your brilliance, dedication, and selflessness have impressed me for years and years. You did not take the well-traveled path with all of its comforts and privileges. You took a path where your talents have had an incredible, immeasurable impact. The sacrifices you have made cannot be understood by most. Yet the rewards are not understandable to most either. You have made a difference all over the globe."
—JAMIE CHEADLE, APPLEWOOD YOUTH GROUP FRIEND

"Tami has never ceased to amaze me. She has done such great things in her brief thirty-nine years. Determination and courage, and above all, faith . . . Of all her accomplishments, and there are many, her faith is what most inspires me."
—KRIS EULE, WHEAT RIDGE HIGH SCHOOL CLASSMATE

"I remember how she helped me settle into life in Xichang back in 1997. In the evening, she took me to this little store, a stone's throw from where we were staying at the Xichang health school. She used crocodile clips to help make Internet connections, because we had no phone line at home. She would patiently adjust the clips to get the connection right for sending and receiving e-mails."
—SWEE MUN NG, MSI COLLEAGUE FROM SINGAPORE

"I used to look up to Tami as one of the smartest students that I knew . . . I pray that as long as I am able to continue the practice of medicine that I can serve my patients with the same compassion as Tami."—DR. MICHAEL PETERS, WHEATON COLLEGE PRE-MED CLASSMATE

"She was a very beautiful person both inside and out with a sparkle of humor that put everyone at ease . . . Tami's calm, sweet spirit, continuing in faith in her Lord and Savior even three days before her death, is a wonderful, even miraculous model for all. I'm so glad I was able to let her know how much I admired her and how great her contribution to so many lives has been. It has been a great privilege to know Tami and her beautiful, loving Christian family."—DEBBIE COOK, FAMILY FRIEND AND MEMBER OF MISSION HILLS CHURCH

"I want to thank Tami for her help while I was ill in Chengdu—a testimony which can probably be repeated by many people who knew Tami in Chengdu and were blessed by her sacrificial availability for medical matters at a time when she was studying Chinese."—RACHEL MEAKIN, WORKER IN CHENGDU, FROM THE UK

"The scene of Tami and Sharon encouraging the perspiring, breathless, and tired senior doctors and nurses during CPR practice remains imprinted in my mind till now, one decade later."—DR. THAM KUM YING, LEADER OF THE MSI RESUSCITA-TION SHORT-TERM TEAM TO XICHANG, FROM SINGAPORE

"We had the privilege of knowing Tami through our mutual association with the Centers for Disease Control, the World Health Organization, and Intown Community Church. She was an example to all of us of how a Christian should live, giving of herself to help others in a variety of ways in the U.S. and abroad, and of how a Christian should die, facing death with courage and hope, still ministering to others until the end of her earthly life. We will miss our dear sister."—BRAD AND RENEE KAY, GENEVA, SWITZERLAND

"Heaven becomes more dear as a loved one moves on ahead of us. I can imagine Tami's face glowing as she worships the One she served so faithfully."—DR. BOB WENNINGER, SURGEON, MUKINGE HOSPITAL, ZAMBIA

"My friendship with Tami began in a small student room in the university of China where we both studied Chinese language and literature. We shared many good times and less good times. We both visited museums and were involved in sports activities. In the summer we went to festivals and took part in archery, and we would watch horse racing and wrestling matches. During those times, I gained a lovely, caring, intelligent, and committed friend."—NAARA, CHINESE LANGUAGE STUDY ROOMMATE FROM MONGOLIA

"I am the director of a school in Ulaan Bataar, Mongolia, and God has used Tami's life and example to convict many of our students to live a life that really matters. When we think of Tami, we won't remember so much the sickness, we will remember the way she lived. When we think of Tami, we will think of Jesus."—MIKE AND CAROL BETH SPRENGER, SERVING IN MONGOLIA, FROM THE U.S.

"Her courage is unmatched, her bold faith etched on the myriad of lives she touched, and her sweet love for the Savior always apparent like an unfurled flag . . . bright-colored and open for all to see."—JERRIN AND ELDON TOLL, FROM THE INTERNATIONAL FELLOWSHIP AT INTOWN COMMUNITY CHURCH, ATLANTA, U.S.

"When I moved into Tami's old room in the MSI office in Zhaojue, something of the love and joy that always flowed from her heart lingered to greet me. Besides the poster with a big Chinese character for 'love' together with little characters spelling out the 1 Corinthians 13 love passage, there was the neighbor's daughter. She and her little friends often asked me about 'Fei Ayi.' Did I know her? How is she? When is she coming back? Can you tell her we miss her?"— WANDA KUNZI, MSI COLLEAGUE IN XICHANG AND ZHAOJUE, FROM THE U.S.

"We are to have the understanding and awareness that we are stewards of all He has given us—our possessions, our talent, our time. We are to shine like stars for Him in the way we use these. I can think of no better example of this than a young medical doctor—only in her thirties—called Tami Fisk."—KENNETH MORRISON, MSI OFFICE, WHEN PREACHING IN HONG KONG

"Her research project was completed last month. The good news is that we found a new Bartonella species and we named it "Bartonella tamiae." The next thing is that we plan to write a scientific paper with Tami's name as author. You will be proud of the great achievements that Tami did for public health in Thailand."—DR. SAITHIP SUTTHIRATTANA, "BARTONELLA TAMIAE" THAI TEAM LEADER

"Unlike others, Tami didn't advertise herself or ask to be introduced in the Sunday School class I taught. She just slipped in quietly and shared *if* asked."—DR. CRAIG BLOMBERG, AUTHOR, PROFESSOR AT DENVER SEMINARY

"You have been an inspiration to us who have followed your various ups and downs during these last years. You have fought a good fight, persevered, and lived to the fullest in so many ways. In the process, your light has shone brightly, and many have been drawn to the light as result."—JOE KLINGENSMITH, ROCHESTER, NY, COMMUNITY CHURCH

"I met Tami soon after coming to the States. She helped me through a very difficult time . . . comforting and encouraging me. Tami loved life, loved people, was energetic, and always helped other people."—CHINESE ROOMMATE IN ATLANTA, GA

"Tami spent quite some time on my back porch where new Fellows met for training sessions. We were always impressed by her courage and efforts to assist others, even when her own health was such a challenge."—DR. BARBARA MARSTON, COORDINATOR, HIV CARE & SUPPORT ACTIVITIES, GLOBAL AIDS PROGRAM, CDC KENYA

"Tami was the best in all respects. Her time on earth was a beautiful wonder . . . love surrounded her and was returned."—DR. JACK SHULMAN, EMORY MEDICAL SCHOOL MENTOR, DEAN AND ATTENDING

"She was a faculty member who was approachable. It was my desire that she be my faculty mentor in my upcoming ID Fellowship, but God had different plans. Her brokenness during this battle revealed her as someone depending step by step on a loving God. In our world where self-reliance is the practice, she was refreshing and inspiring . . . as she walked through the difficult times, she was always ready to lift someone else's burden."—COLLEEN KRAFT, MD, COLLEAGUE AT EMORY UNIVERSITY INFECTIOUS DISEASES FELLOWSHIP

"Tami was given an insatiable desire to serve others in a way that is honoring to Christ. She lived in our home at the beginning of her ID Fellowship, and became like family. She and a Chinese friend spent an afternoon teaching us to make Chinese dumplings."—MARSHALL WILLIAMS, INTOWN CHURCH, ATLANTA

"We met Tami at the International Fellowship at Intown, and we were astonished by her speaking of the Chinese language. She and Paula conducted a Bible study in our home. That Bible study changed my wife's life and led my wife to learn about Jesus Christ. When we made up our mind to follow Jesus Christ, we believe the Lord put the seeds in our heart years ago, but Tami watered and fertilized the seeds in our heart."—DR. GAO FENG, EMORY MEDICAL CENTER, ATLANTA, GA

"Tami had a rare and genuine love for life as a missionary, when so many try of their own efforts to force themselves to be joyful. Her joy was the Lord's."—FRAN BLOMBERG, MISSION HILLS CHURCH, MISSIONS DIRECTOR AT THE TIME TAMI SERVED IN CHINA

"We celebrate Tami's life in the Lord. 'I will gladly spend and be spent for you' (2 Corinthians 12:15). Tami became a sacramental personality; wherever she went Christ helped Himself to her life!"—DR. LAWRENCE SOH, SINGAPORE

TAMI'S POEM

TODAY I AM HEALED

Today I am healed.
Perhaps not the way you had hoped for, prayed for, waited for
But I'm in a glorious new body, free of pain, full of new strength
Free to run and dance in a place where God himself wipes my tears away
Immersed in a love, joy, and peace that we have a mere taste of during our time on earth
In the presence of my God and Savior, Jesus Christ, who loves me more than His own life
Know that today I am healed.
—Tami

今天—我已得到醫治了！

或許非如你原先所想望、祈求、等待的。

然而，現今我已有一榮耀的、新的身體，沒有痛楚、且充滿活力；

在一個神擦乾我眼淚的地方，自由地奔馳與起舞。

沐浴在祂的慈愛、喜樂及平安中—在世時我們只是稍稍一嚐！

在我神和救主，就是那愛我比自己性命更甚的耶穌基督面前

我深願您知道：

今天—我已得到醫治了！

Today I Am Healed

Lyrics by Dr. Tami Fisk, Music by Tony Wong, Copyright (c) 2007

FIRST CORINTHIANS 13, NEW INTERNATIONAL VERSION

If I speak in the tongues of men and of angels, but have not love, I am only a resounding gong or a clanging cymbal.

If I have the gift of prophecy and can fathom all mysteries and all knowledge, and if I have a faith that can move mountains, but have not love, I am nothing.

If I gave all I possess to the poor and surrender my body to the flames, but have not love, I gain nothing.

Love is patient, love is kind. It does not envy, it does not boast, it is not proud. It is not rude, it is not self-seeking, it is not easily angered, it keeps no record of wrongs.

Love does not delight in evil but rejoices with the truth. It always protects, always trusts, always hopes, always perseveres.

Love never fails.

But where there are prophecies, they will cease; where there are tongues, they will be stilled; where there is knowledge, it will pass away. For we know in part and we prophesy in part, but when perfection comes, the imperfect disappears. When I was a child, I talked like a child, I thought like a child, I reasoned like a child. When I became a man, I put childish ways behind me. Now we see but a poor reflection as in a mirror; then we shall see face to face. Now I know in part; then I shall know fully, even as I am fully known.

And now these three remain: faith, hope, and love.

But the greatest of these is love.

A SHORT HISTORY OF MSI PROFESSIONAL SERVICES (1989–2009)

WWW.MSIPS.ORG

1989–1991   ●   J. Broomhall's visits to Zhaojue

1994   ●   First MSI visit with Yenching Alumni Association consultants to Sichuan (Chengdu, Yaan) and Yunnan (Kunming, Xundian) Agreement signed with Sichuan Province Public Health Bureau and Huaxi Medical University
  ●   MSI-HK registered
  ●   Medical trips to Chengdu, Yaan, Mingshan in Sichuan

1995   ●   Medical and livestock exploratory trips to different sites Regular Medical Service trips to Yaan, Liangshan
  ●   MSI-US registered
  ●   First long-term team in Chengdu (language study)

1996   ●   Community Health Survey in Zhaojue to identify needs
  ●   Agreement signed with Yunnan Public Health Bureau Placement of first medical team in Zhaojue Placement of first English teacher in Xichang

1997   ●   Community Health Course in India Memorandum of Understanding signed with Sichuan Continuing Education College of Medical Sciences Medical Program Director appointed MSI-Philippines established

1998   ●   MSI-Singapore registered
                 MSI-Canada established
                 Medical Service started in Gulin, Luzhou
                 Agreement signed with Gulin Public Health Bureau and
                 Animal Husbandry Bureau

1999   ●   Medical Service started in Fengdu, Chongqing
               ●   Zhaojue Youth Center launched
               ●   MSI-Australia established
               ●   MSI Representative Office registered in Chengdu, Sichuan
               ●   Sichuan Chief Representative & Deputy appointed

2000   ●   Hospital Management Survey in Chengdu
               ●   Zhaojue and Xichang Hostels built
               ●   Community Health Program implemented in Zhaojue
               ●   Operation Eyesight started in Huili, Liangshan
               ●   Medical Services started in Ebian, Leshan
               ●   Medical Services started in Huili, Liangshan
               ●   MSI-Malaysia established
               ●   MSI Representative Office established in Kunming, Yunnan

2001   ●   MSI-Korea established
               ●   Zhaojue Youth Centre, Community Health, and Livestock
                  Program Directors appointed
               ●   Yunnan Chief Representative appointed
               ●   Memorandum of Understanding signed with Yunnan
                  International Non-Government Organization Society
               ●   MSI-Canada registered
               ●   Memorandum of Understanding signed with Heqing County
                  Hospital
               ●   Memorandum of Understanding signed with Fengdu Peoples'
                  Hospital

2003   ●   New Medical Program Director appointed

2004   ●   Zhaojue Mufu Medical Training Centre established
               ●   MSI Tenth Anniversary
               ●   Signing of Memorandum of Understanding with First Affiliated
                  Hospital of Kunming Medical College to run clinical dental
                  sessions

2005
- Placement of long-term workers in Meigu, Liangshan
- Inauguration of MSI-Korea

2006
- Placement of long-term workers in Luzhou and Yaan regions

2007
- MSI-Singapore celebrates tenth anniversary
- Tami Fisk Memorial Services in Xichang and Zhaojue; James Hudson Taylor III honored as Honorary Citizen of Zhaojue County (April)
- Placement of long-term workers in Dali, Yunnan
- Memorandum of Understanding on setting up a training centre on the Rehabilitation of Autistic Children

2008
- Mianyang office established for earthquake relief and rebuilding after Wenchuan 5.12 earthquake
- Memorandum of Understanding signed with Beichuan County Public Health Bureau and Mianyang Regional Foreign Affair Bureau for Earthquake relief/rebuilding
- Placement of English teacher in Beichuan Middle School
- Regular teams of therapists, counselors, healthcare workers to earthquake zone

2009
- Placement of first long-term team in Xundian, Yunnan
- Home call of James Hudson Taylor III on 20 March 2009
- Memorial Services for James Hudson Taylor III in Hong Kong, Taiwan, Chengdu, Xichang, Toronto, Singapore, San Francisco, and Los Angeles
- Agreement signed with Sichuan University on resident doctors' academic exchange with overseas centers
- Placement of first long-term worker in Jianshui, Yunnan

TAMI'S CURRICULUM VITAE

DR. TAMARA (TAMI) L. FISK (1965–2005)

Born July 11, 1965, in Denver, Colorado, United States

EDUCATION

1986	BS (Chemistry), Wheaton College, Illinois
1990	MD, Emory University School of Medicine, Atlanta, Georgia

RESIDENCY

1990–1994	University of Rochester Hospitals, Internal Medicine and Pediatrics

OVERSEAS ELECTIVES

June–August 1985:	Mukinge Hospital, Zambia (Africa Evangelical Fellowship's rural hospital)
April–June 1989:	Mukinge Hospital, Zambia
November 1991:	Medical elective, Bogota, Colombia
August–November 1993:	Medical elective, People's Republic of China (Beijing and Kunming)

PRACTICE EXPERIENCE

1994	Family Health Care, Montana
1994	Southwestern Medical Clinic, Berrien Center, Michigan
1994	Lakewood Family Clinic, Lakewood, Colorado
1995	Highlands Ranch Health Center, Highlands Ranch, Colorado
1995	Emergency Room, Swedish Hospital, Englewood, Colorado

IN CHINA WITH MSI, JULY 1995–JUNE 1998

1995–96	Chinese language studies in Chengdu
1996–97	Xichang (commuting to mountain village of Zhaojue)
1997–98	Zhaojue

FELLOWSHIP

1998–2001	Infectious Diseases Fellowship; Emory University/Centers for Diseases Control, Atlanta

RESEARCH

1986	Wheaton College, Illinois (enzyme kinetics)
1986	Malaria Branch, Centers for Disease Control, Atlanta (malaria) Mukinge Hospital, Zambia (anemia in children with malaria)
1990, 2001–02	Centers for Disease Control, Atlanta (Anthrax)
2001–03	Emory University, Atlanta (Salmonella and latent TB infections in HIV-positive patients)
2002–03	SARS in Taiwan; SARS transmission on airplanes
2002–04	Centers for Disease Control, Travel Clinic, GeoSentinel database analysis
2002–04	Thailand Emerging Infectious Diseases Program, Centers for Disease Control

TAMI'S SCIENTIFIC PUBLICATIONS

1. Millet P, Fisk TL, Collins WE, Broderson JR, Nguyen-Dinh P. Cultivation of exoerythrocytic stages of Plasmodium cynomolgi, P. knowlesi, P. coatneyi, and P. inui in Macaca mulatta hepatocytes. Am J Trop Med Hyg 1988; 39:529–34.

2. Millet P, Collins WE, Fisk TL, Nguyen-Dinh P. In vitro cultivation of exo-erythrocytic stages of the human malaria parasite Plasmodium malariae. Am J Trop Med Hyg 1988; 38:470–3.

3. Fisk TL, Millet P, Collins WE, Nguyen-Dinh P. In vitro activity of antimalarial compounds on the exoerythrocytic stages of Plasmodium cynomolgi and P. knowlesi. Am J Trop Med Hyg 1989; 40:235–9.

4. Jernigan JA, Stephens DS, Ashford DA, Fisk TL et al. Bioterrorism-related inhalational anthrax: the first 10 cases reported in the United States. Emerg Infect Dis 2001; 7:933–44.

5. Fisk TL, Hon HM, Lennox JL, Fordham von Reyn C, Horsburgh CR, Jr. Detection of latent tuberculosis among HIV-infected patients after initiation of highly active antiretroviral therapy. Aids 2003; 17:1102–4.

6. Olsen SJ, Chang HL, Cheung TY, Tang A, Fisk TL et al. Transmission of the severe acute respiratory syndrome on aircraft. N Engl J Med 2003; 349:2416–22.

7. Twu SJ, Chen TJ, Chen CJ, Olsen S, Lee, Fisk TL et al. Control measures for severe acute respiratory syndrome (SARS) in Taiwan. Emerg Infect Dis 2003; 9:718–20

8. Albrich WC, Kraft C, Fisk TL, Albrecht H. A mechanic with a bad valve: blood-culture-negative endocarditis. Lancet Infect Dis 2004; 4:777–84.

9. Fisk TL, Lundberg BE, Guest JL, et al. Invasive infection with multidrug-resistant Salmonella enterica serotype typhimurium definitive type 104 among HIV-infected adults. Clin Infect Dis 2005; 40:1016–21.

10. Freedman DO, Weld LH, Kozarsky PE, Fisk TL et al. Spectrum of disease and relation to place of exposure among ill returned travelers. N Engl J Med 2006; 354:119–30.

11. Cohen AL, Dowell SF, Nisalak A, Mammen MP, Jr., Petkanchanapong W, Fisk TL. Rapid diagnostic tests for dengue and leptospirosis: antibody detection is insensitive at presentation. Trop Med Int Health 2007; 12:47–51.

HONORS AND AWARDS

1. Graduated Valedictorian from Wheat Ridge High School
2. Graduated *Summa Cum Laude* from Emory and Wheaton
3. American Medical Women's Association Award for woman graduating first in her medical school class
4. Sandoz Award for "superior academic achievement and contribution to health care"
5. Emory Medical Scholarship (one-half tuition based on academic standing, communication ability, and leadership skills)
6. Alpha Omega Alpha (Medical Honors Society), elected April 1989
7. Medical Student Research Fellowships: 1987, 1988
8. Emory International Health Fellowship, 1989
9. Asked to consider Medicine Chief Residency, 1992
10. University of Rochester International Medicine Fellowship, 1993
11. James H. Nakano Citation, 2006: Award from the Centers for Disease Control for the outstanding publication by GeoSentinel, published in the New England Journal 2006.
12. Newly discovered bacteria named for Tami because of her instrumental role in its discovery: *Bartonella tamiae*. The publication that introduced this name appeared in the Journal of Clinical Microbiology in February 2008.

Appendix VII:

THE AUTHORS

D r. Einar Wilder-Smith is tenured Professor and Senior Consultant at the National University Hospital, Singapore. As a neurologist, he specializes in diseases of the peripheral nervous system. He is Visiting Professor at the Medical University in Chengdu, Sichuan. He also serves as Consultant to the Leprosy Mission, with a particular research interest in the early detection of leprosy in India. He has published more than one hundred scientific publications and is the author of a textbook on ultrasonography in peripheral neurology. A British physician, he has worked in countries such as China, Singapore, Papua New Guinea, Nepal, Switzerland, and New Zealand.

Dr. Annelies Wilder-Smith is a public health physician and travel medicine specialist. As Associate Professor at the National University of Singapore, she teaches the global health sub-specialization track for the Master in Public Health. As Director of the Travelers' Screening and Vaccination Clinic, she is involved in the counseling of travelers and missionaries. She is co-editor for the WHO publication *International Travel and Health*. She is Editorial Consultant to *The Lancet*. Annelies has published more than ninety scientific papers and has edited and authored several books related to travel medicine. In addition to her academic work, she is involved in development work in India and China. She is also adviser for a rural HIV prevention project in South China. Together with her husband, she has lived and served in many countries, with more than eighteen years spent in the Asia-Pacific region.

Annelies and Einar met Tami when they lived in Chengdu, West China. Tami helped them to settle in Chengdu, and a deep friendship ensued. After Tami returned to the U.S., they continued to meet at different places around the world. God intertwined their lives. Annelies followed a career similar to Tami's, in emerging infectious diseases and travel medicine.

It does not need many words to explain that Tami had a great impact on their lives.

Appendix VIII:
ACKNOWLEDGMENTS
AND BIBLIOGRAPHY

Above all, we acknowledge Tami. She was a talented writer. Her extensive diaries, letters, essays, "High Road Prayer," assignment on C.S. Lewis's Space Trilogy, and foremost her famous Martian letters, formed the substance of this biography. Where possible, we used complete passages verbatim in order to best reflect her writing talent, personality, and sense of humor. She was an extraordinary person. Her testimony had a great impact on our lives. By writing her story, we have been greatly influenced.

We also would like to acknowledge Tami's parents. The love of this family is not exaggerated in this book. It is real. We experienced it. We spent two intense weeks with them in Denver. They shared everything about Tami, their joys, their pain, the intensity of their love, and their love for God. We were often so moved that we cried together. Their hospitality was warm. They took our children to fun places to give us time to work on the manuscript. If you ever meet Tami's parents, you will understand why Tami was such an extraordinary person.

During our stay in Colorado, we had the privilege of spending one evening together with Philip Yancey and his wife. He gave us invaluable insights and advice on how to write this book. Thank you so much!

We would like to acknowledge the MSI Bulletin letters, from which we obtained insights into the stories about the sheep donation and Dr. Taylor's visit to China in the 1980s.

The information on Helen Rosevaere's life experiences was partly obtained from Tami and partly from a Web site: http://www.e-n.org.uk/3132-Digging-ditches.htm

We obtained information on Dr. A.J. Broomhall and Joan Wales from the following books: *Medical Missionaries in the China Inland Mission* by Dr. Patrick Fung and *Point Me to the Skies* by Ronald Clemens.

Tami was an avid reader. The following books were particularly important to Tami in her final days, and we would like to recommend them to you:

- C.S. Lewis, *The Last Battle*
- C.S. Lewis, The Space Trilogy: *Out of the Silent Planet, Perelandra, That Hideous Strength*

- Lee Strobel, *A Case for Christ*
- Max Lucado, *The Applause of Heaven*

We would like to thank several persons for their patience in answering our phone calls and e-mails to collect more information about Tami: Tim Fisk, Suzie Goering, Paula Helms, Debbie Cook, Roberta Dismukes, Phyllis Kozarsky, Nicole Mares, Jane Christiansen, Scott Dowell, Mike Kosoy, and many others.

We would like to thank Matthew Koh, Jamie Taylor, Ang Hui Kheng, Lawrence Soh, and Ramon Rocha for their continued support throughout this writing project. Many thanks also to the MSI office in Hong Kong for coordinating the project.

Lastly, this book would not have been possible without Dr. Taylor. He commissioned this book. He followed it through with countless Skype conversations and e-mails. We will never forget the many prayers that we prayed together over Skype. During his final days of illness in early 2009, he made further instructions for this book to be published.

Soli Deo Gloria. Our thanks and praises go to God, for whom Tami lived.